THE WORLD'S
GREATEST SALESMAN

THE WORLD'S GREATEST SALESMAN

AN IBM CARETAKER'S PERSPECTIVE: LOOKING BACK

Peter E. Greulich

An Imprint of MBI Concepts Corporation

© 2011 by MBI Concepts Corporation, Austin 78746
All rights reserved. Published 2011.
Printed in the United States of America

16 15 14 13 12 11   1 2 3 4 5

ISBN-13: 978-0-9833734-0-7   (paperback)
ISBN-10: 0-9833734-0-X   (paperback)

Library of Congress Control Number: 2011903889
Greulich, Peter Eugene, 1953-
The World's Greatest Salesman, An IBM Caretaker's Perspective:
Looking Back / Peter E. Greulich
      p. cm.
1. Management. 2. International Business Machines Corporation—
History. 3. International Business Machines—Management. 4.
Corporate turnarounds—United States—Case Studies. 5. Watson,
Thomas John, 1874-1956. I. Title

To

Thos. J. Watson Sr.

The Founder of

The IBM

and

The IBM Basic Beliefs

—

Respect for the Individual

Service to the Customer

Excellence Must Be a Way of Life

Managers Must Lead Effectively

Obligations to Stockholders

Fair Deal for the Supplier

IBM Should be a Good Corporate Citizen

Contents

PREFACE

Whether it was the Stone Age, the Agricultural Age, the Industrial Age or the Information Age, there has always been a single constant flowing through the communities that benefitted from these major cultural and societal changes. Men and women—the pioneers of each age—embraced the shift and pulled their communities, their organizations and their countries with them.

Machines will only bring success if manned by the right kind of men.

We are once again entering a "New Age." Advancing technologies are empowering individuals to achieve ever greater heights of creativity and self-fulfillment. Activities that, just a few years ago, would have taken significant monetary investment and dozens or hundreds of people can be realized by one person with determination, drive and hard work. New creations, at one time only within the realm of corporations, are now within the grasp of individuals.

Consider the new technologies that made this book possible:

- Understanding copyright law, once the domain of attorneys, is now available online and easily understood through Columbia University.

- Researching, documenting and certifying a copyright, once locked away in buildings in Washington, D.C., is now easily accessible online.

- Older works, such as the 1930 and 1934 versions of *Men-Minutes-Money* (the basis for this book), are competitively priced, purchased and shipped to arrive the next day.

- Transferring a book into a word processor, once a manual, tedious, expensive and error-prone process, can be accomplished with a $100 all-in-one home office printer/copier/scanner and its included software.

- Establishing a corporation and associated bank accounts is all online.

- A marketing website, once the playthings of technologists, can be built with drag-and-drop software with online commercial transactions.

- Printing a book, once requiring initial startup funding, inventory tracking and warehouse space is streamlined with On-Demand Printing. E-books are eliminating shipping costs.

Such technologies await pioneers to combine and exploit them. Such technologies free us from the confines of thinking as those in the hierarchy above us think; doing what those above us do; acting and behaving as they act. If we disagree; if we are not listened to; if our ideas are not valued; if we get frustrated with the lack of corporate vision and commensurate rewards; we can and should launch our own undertakings. We can become, as Tom Watson wanted every person to be, a thinking man or woman. We can realize the benefits of our own thinking.

This doesn't mean the end of organizations. A road traveled alone is still a lonely path. Self-education in a home office is good; but a supportive environment with cooperation is better and far more powerful. But those individuals who embrace this new potential, those corporations that position themselves as a whole greater than the sum of its parts, those countries that enact laws encouraging an environment of personal self-growth and risk taking—these will be the individuals remembered, the companies celebrated and the countries growing as we push toward the twenty-second century.

Organizations, to exploit this New Age, must adapt and design their policies to empower and encourage men and women to channel their energies towards a common good; capture the individual's desires and dreams into a common set of goals—whether that is in the field of education, business or government.

Such organizations will lead the way into this "New Age"—just as Thos. J. Watson Sr. led the way with The IBM into his "Man Age"—setting the foundation for a century of growth from 1914 to 2011.

Pete

ACKNOWLEDGEMENTS

In my preface I write about new technologies bringing achievements, once only within the realm of corporations, within the reach of individuals. Such individuals, though, will discover a road traveled alone is a difficult path. Success is more easily attained when the individual is accompanied by a team that provides inspiration, enthusiasm, counsel and confidence.

Jim and Tracy Willi were not just legal advisors but the first team members sought outside of my personal and IBM families. Legal advice was sought—enthusiasm was provided.

David Kassin Fried was the editor. Editors are in a profession where they are required, at times, to call someone else's baby ugly. He was appreciated for his truthful answers to my constant question, "What can be improved?" He delivered the answers with great tact. Any success I achieve with this book will be greater because of his involvement. Facts were asked for—counsel was given.

Elizabeth O'Connor, Angela Fried and my wife, Mo Greulich, are owed a debt of gratitude. I was the kid in high school forever getting an A+ for creative insight and a C– in grammar—so frustrating and limiting. Constant advice was required—and confidence was the by-product.

Thomas Graham Belden and Marva Robins Belden in *The Lengthening Shadow* and Kevin Maney in *The Maverick and His Machine*, performed diligent research on Thos. J. Watson Sr. Their background information made his depression-era leadership all the more compelling. Hopefully, I have added an IBMer's heart, soul and spirit to their flesh and blood portraits.

Humans are complex beings not easily captured in print. Thomas J. Watson Sr. was a complex personality with many reputations but a person of unfailing character, balanced honesty and forthrightness. We will need more Chief Executive Officers like him in the twenty-first century. This team helped me capture his leadership through the Great Depression.

AN IBM CARETAKER'S INTRODUCTION

There is a term today used to describe the men and women who call IBM home: IBMer.

I have never uncovered any stories or internal IBM mythology about the exact origin of the term; it probably grew out of daily usage. For most of my career, when asked whom I worked for, I never replied, "I work for IBM," or, "I am an IBM employee," but rather, "I am an IBMer."

To me, "IBMer" is an abbreviation—short for IBM Caretaker. IBMer captures the heart and soul of the person. It has no social standing associated with it, no position of stature, no power ranking within the corporation, no underlying hierarchy supporting it, no social class or pay grade; rather it defines a person's heart, a person's commitment, dedication and loyalty.

Most of all, the term defines the person using it as being in a win-win relationship with a company—a company that, in the past, saw itself as a family. For decades, we attended gatherings called "Family Days." We closed down sales offices when one of our own died and cried together at the loss. We consoled each other.

The closest we came to describing our relationship were single words like loyalty,

We have a great family spirit regardless of nationality, religion or creed.

dedication, trust and confidence. If there was one word, though, that defined IBMer, it was respect. It was the type of respect shown between members of a family.

It was a set of emotions, feelings and camaraderie that was indefinable. The IBM relationship between caretakers felt more in the realm of poetry than prose.

Learning the Watsons' Belief System

Experience makes a man valuable in setting an example for others.

I was hired in October of 1980, into IBM's sales branch office—probably one of the last vestiges of the truest, deepest of blue, IBM organizations. I learned about IBM philosophy and beliefs through the experience of others. I went to lunch with "old timers"—the men and women with thirty to forty years of IBM service. I heard their stories over early morning breakfasts, mid-day lunches or in the wee hours of the morning restoring a customer's hardware and applications to serviceability.

We were there, in the wee hours, because in our hearts we were a service organization. Service defined us, drove us and dictated to us who we were as a company. We strove for excellence within our individual organizations.

The Watsons' belief system lived, flourished and was personified in these men and women I found surrounding me. I lived in the midst of their belief system and benefited from it for thirty years. I drove myself to live up to the spotless reputations, spirits and expectations of those I respected working around me.

The Watsons intended for that spirit to extend beyond just the individual IBMer. They wanted it to touch spouses, sons and daughters; to reach deep into individual communities; to be the touchstone against which any Chief Executive Officer would be measured.

But as IBM grows through acquisition, some of the Watsons' history, their beliefs, their background and their spirit has been muted, forgotten or lost by those new to IBM or progressing through its executive ranks. Today there are two companies: There is "IBM"— what it is—and "The IBM"—what it was.

Who was Thos. J. Watson Sr.?

This question, coming from an IBMer in 2009, was the one that put pen to paper, placed fingers on a keyboard and sparked the creation of this book.

It had never dawned on me that I should explain who Tom Watson was to an audience of IBMers. But the gentleman stood before me, in all sincerity, trying to understand whom he had just seen and what he had heard.

The video he had seen was an aspiring actor playing the part of Tom Watson, recreating some word-for-word conversations Watson had with his employees. They were words to his executives, secretaries, office workers, factory foremen and sales managers.

But most of the words on this video were reserved for his beloved salesmen. They were words of inspiration, encouragement and strength. They were Depression-era words of undefeatable audacity at a time when so many companies just like his were failing all around.

These were words our salesmen, after the financial crisis in September 2008, desperately needed to hear.

We presented the videos in February 2009 at IBM Tivoli's yearly sales training for the America's team. At the time, financial institutions were reducing spending, demanding definitive proof of return on their software investments or going bankrupt. These financial institutions had always been the backbone of IBM software sales, so we needed our sales force to be creative, intuitive and not afraid of making mistakes.

Hundreds of Tivoli's top software salesmen and saleswomen were in the audience from the United States, Canada and Latin America. The IBMer who posed the question had recently joined the team through IBM's acquisition of Micromuse. This was just one of more than thirty acquisitions in my division alone. The audience—and IBM—were full of new sales representatives just like him.

"Work your way out even if you have to do a lot of experimenting."

After him, a second young man stepped up and said, "My dad always talked about IBM. He retired several years ago. He said it was the greatest corporation on the face of the earth." He hesitated for a second, then continued, "Thanks for doing this today. I think I understand now what he had and his passion for that company."

"Had" and "that company" rang in my ears.

The man smiled shyly and motioned at the collection of posters hanging on the wall, recreations of those images used by Tom Watson in the 1930s, and asked, "May I have one of those posters on the wall? I think it would mean a lot to my dad."

Could I deny such a request?

Starting to THINK

Every business needs more people who THINK.

Returning to Austin, I received e-mails from first-line managers saying, "I need my team to see this video. Can you send it to me?" In the same collection of e-mails, there were equivalent notes from salesmen in the field saying, "I need my manager to see this video." I chuckled, but realized that I had accomplished something that day—I had inspired everyone to think. Or as Tom Watson would have said, THINK.

I also realized that my IBM was no longer connected to its past, its history and its traditions. I pondered all the traditions lost over the years—like the Watsons' "IBM Family Days." They are now just the memories of an old man.

There were holes, giant vacuums of empty space in IBM's past. I started to wonder what else we are losing that will become, to a new generation, just irrelevant ruminations of old men or bygone beliefs of out-of-touch dinosaurs. What if "Watson" becomes synonymous with the Watson of *Jeopardy!*—a supercomputer without heart, soul or conscience? What if the Watsons, one of the most amazing business families in American history, are someday seen for nothing more than founding a computer and technology company?

We would not allow the Kennedy family to be remembered as just "legislators." The Kennedys were a political and social force. Similarly, the Watsons were more than businessmen. They were to American business what the Kennedys were to American politics.

Who would stand for the Watsons?

4

So the journey started. I wanted to understand, articulate and capture The IBM, as Watson referred to it, on paper. And as I saw it, it was a journey to understand one man, the founder of The IBM.

Unfortunately, Thos. J. Watson Sr. died in 1956, three years after I was born. I never met him. I could have never met him, discussed business philosophy with him or heard him speak in the Headquarters "home office." I did, however, know him, as well as his son and successor, from my thirty years of living, breathing and experiencing their spirit, their drive, their determination, their strength of character and their enthusiasm imbedded in those IBMers around me. I felt I could write a book, but something was missing.

Of the books I had read on his life, few were written by an IBMer. All people, including myself, bring some perspective to their writings; they are affected by who pays them, their history, their goals, their position in society, their knowledge and understanding of a culture— or worse, their lack thereof. And the perceptions in these books were those of a "work for hire."

Then I discovered Tom Watson's series of books entitled *Men-Minutes-Money*—a collection of almost 900 pages, some 300,000 words of his speeches and writings, most of which span the Great Depression. These speeches, editorials and publications were delivered to an eclectic set of audiences all over the world, including the United States, France, Germany, Czechoslovakia (Czech Republic), Austria, England and more.

The IBM spirit, The IBM heart and The IBM language are the same in all tongues and in all countries.

During this time, he spoke as if he could almost, through pure force of will, carry The IBM through the Depression.

It was him—his beliefs, thoughts, determination and drive—captured word-for-word for more than eighteen years, and with it were 300 individual drawings with captions, each illustrating in its own way Watson's unique brand of optimism.

I had found what I needed.

Adding the IBM Caretaker Perspective

This book is narrated from the perspective of an IBM Caretaker. I introduce each chapter with my own IBM Caretaker thoughts and insights. Sometimes these introductions provide a historical context. Sometimes they provide a precursory look at the chapter. Hopefully they will support you in working through the material and inspire you to THINK.

Maybe, by combining this IBM Caretaker's perspective with Tom Watson's words and spirit, we can define the word IBMer anew for a new generation. It will require the combined efforts of a great many,

Strength of character is the one basic trait, which will be found in people who achieve greatness.

dedicated to a great cause to renew that energy and vision of The IBM's founder. But as Tom Watson was known to say over and over again, "The IBM did not grow and survive from any great genius." It grew from the great thoughts, the great efforts, the great perseverance and the great cooperation of a great many working together to construct a whole that was bigger, better and more dynamic than just the sum of its parts.

Thos. J. Watson Sr. would not want to be remembered as "the leader" who led this charge forward but rather as the "spark plug" that ignited something in the men and women of the time. That something found its way into each of us as IBM Caretakers—as IBMers. I hope it is never corrupted by anger, frustration or hatred. I hope it is never suppressed by apathy. That is not our character; and as you will learn from this book, it is not our heritage.

How to Read This Book

In sales we say, "Right or wrong, my customer's perception is my reality." And for all of his strengths, Tom Watson wasn't the most dynamic of speakers. So one of the challenges for me in compiling this book was to take Watson's words—sometimes a bit dry and archaic—and present them in a way that's compelling to a twenty-first century audience. With your perception in mind, therefore, I have made some modifications:

First, I have taken those places where Watson referred to "the IBM" and made it "The IBM." The first time I read *Men-Minutes-Money*, "the" in front of IBM jumped off every page every time I saw it. I could almost hear the emphasis he would place on the word. This is what Tom Watson Sr. wanted to build—The IBM. He intended it to be a company set apart, a company of distinction, a company of excitement and enthusiasm, a company of character and a company representing the best of a philosophy where sentences always started with "we" and ended with "us."

Second, Tom Watson Sr. earned his legacy as "The World's Greatest Salesman." His charisma and charm were legendary. He could talk up a storm and as we say in the United States, "charm the birds out of the trees." As such, every time he spoke to an audience he displayed supreme knowledge of the immediate topic of concern and interest. He did this to capture attention. He built rapport from the outset. As an example, when he spoke before the Binghamton Chamber of Commerce, he exerted the greatest of effort and time to discuss the history of Binghamton. He took interest in his audience so they would take interest in him and his words.

Salesman can still learn something from this, but although interesting and educational, I have deleted such material to get to the core purpose of this book—expose the heart, soul and belief system that Tom Watson brought to The IBM.

Third, I have preserved the original images from Watson's *Men-Minutes-Money*, removing some that are dated and moving some images within the work. I have updated some captions—still using his words but pulling from elsewhere in the book's text. I believe these updates will shorten your journey to understanding Tom Watson Sr. and the company he built. My hope, in honor to Watson, is that this book will cause everyone to stop and THINK—and THINK as individuals.

We want you to cultivate and develop the spirit of democracy— democracy in business.

One change I didn't make was in what some may perceive as a gender bias. The word "men" will appear so often that women may feel excluded from his comments and observations.

To this I would say, "Please don't." It is a function of the times. Tom Watson, after the Depression, would move The IBM forward to be one of the most progressive and considerate businesses in the world in the hiring and promotion of women. He would establish a women's sales school alongside the men's. Then, when meeting management resistance in hiring the first women graduates, he fired the entire competing class of newly trained men, leaving only women to be placed and hired.[1]

This was certainly not fair to the men he fired, but he made a point about his philosophy of "democracy in business"—it included women. When the time came to make that fundamental organizational and cultural change, he did it with flair and determination, and he made sure that it happened not eventually, but right then.

The sales organization keeps our factory people's pay envelopes full.

These words, however, are from the early 1930s. At the time, when he looked out over his sales force at his engineers, his shop foremen and his executives, all he saw were men. So I beg your indulgence in this matter, as you join me on this journey to understand the heart, soul and inspiration behind the great man who founded this great company and great culture.

We will start following Watson on October 30, 1929—the day after the Stock Market Crash known as Black Tuesday—and we will conclude four years later in 1933, three days before Christmas, as he stands before a gathering of IBM employees and declares that, "We have seen industry rise from virtual prostration and start forward again." Don't expect utterances of anger, frustration or hatred; this man of character would shine throughout in the darkest and most desperate of times.

With a few exceptions, this book preserves the chronological order of Tom Watson's recorded words. By and large, his speeches in a given time period would carry over a certain theme—character, or motivation, or determination—making the building of these chapters a relatively straightforward process. Although I have chronologically moved a few speeches to fit, strengthen or build logical chapters, on the whole, if you start at the beginning of the book and work through to the end, you will journey through the Great Depression as seen through the eyes of Tom Watson.

Or pick a chapter, the subject matter of which you find appealing, and read it. THINK on it. Take your time. Jump around. Put it down. Come back to it.

If you THINK, you will be doing Tom Watson Sr. justice.

If you THINK as an individual, you will be doing yourself justice.

A certain group of people in the

United States tried an experiment.

They tried the experiment of making a

fortune without working,

of making a fortune through

the stock exchange.

They extended the experiment

until it exploded

and all went down to earth.

"Aspects of World Trade"

Thomas J. Watson Sr.

July 31, 1930

THE GREAT DEPRESSION BEGINS

Life's hard times had taught humility and the meaning of friendship to Tom Watson. As a salesman, he would load up a cash register in his horse-drawn wagon and set off in the early morning to find customers. He called it "walking and talking," and he was failing at it. As he struggled, his manager came down and evaluated him roughly from head to toe. This got his attention. Then the manager said, "Let's go out. We will either succeed or fail together."

Maybe a hard rough exterior covered this manager's caring and concerned heart. Maybe he had learned this as a motivational technique—to get a man's attention first and then show him that "we" are in this together. Maybe he was just a man who instinctively knew men. Whatever it was, this man exemplified to Tom Watson a core set of values that would lay the foundation for his future success.

Nothing Tom Watson had ever experienced in his lifetime, however, could have prepared him to carry The IBM through the Great Depression.

On Black Tuesday, the Stock Market plunged 13%. Ugly crowds full of fear, uncertainty and doubt milled about the streets surrounding Wall Street. This wasn't the

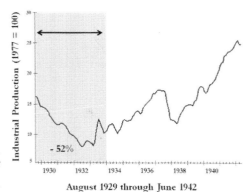

August 1929 through June 1942

Figure 1. Timeframe of Thos. J. Watson Sr.'s Speeches

Source: Frank G. Steindl, Regents Professor of Economics Emeritus at Oklahoma State University, "What Ended the Great Depression?"

first or the last plunge, but it was the beginning of an almost four-year drop in industrial production.

The market would continue its decline to lose almost 90% of its value. Companies hundreds of times larger than The IBM, with deeper financial pockets, with better connected executives, with better diversification, with longer and more prestigious histories and with access to funds that The IBM could only dream about were failing all around him.

At the Great Depression's trough, one in four people were unemployed. Unlike today, these were single income households; there were no credit cards to carry the family through the month and the loss of that lone income was the supreme financial disaster. The loss of that next paycheck meant immediate hunger, standing in food lines, homelessness and possible starvation. Men committed suicide rather than face their own failure.

Tom Watson felt that pain, and it was a great burden for him as a concerned Chief Executive Officer. He felt the constant need to employ more men.

The Spirit of The IBM

The day after Black Tuesday, Tom Watson stood in front of a class of eager, enthusiastic and possibly apprehensive young men ready to start their careers with The IBM. This day he chose to talk about spirit—the spirit of The IBM. In this, the most dispiriting of economic times, he would ask them to *"pull together as one man"* to build and keep that spirit alive.

A few short months later, he spoke before the 1929 One Hundred Percent Club. By now, the true economic impact of the stock market crash was reality. The song that epitomized the glory of the roaring twenties, "Blue Skies," was a cruel joke. There were no blue skies. There were only dark and stormy skies.

The swells of this economic storm were so large they looked as if they would have crushed any ship in their path. The storm's path was so wide and so deep there was only one conceivable course—straight ahead.

Tom Watson steered that course.

Pull together as one man.
Keep this class spirit alive.

As The IBM entered the economic storm of the century, he spoke to his team about enthusiasm, spirit, heart and an IBM language that was universal and undefeatable. He spoke of his personal responsibility to keep men employed.

His sales force would have to sell during a time when buyers were scarce. He looked to them to keep The IBM factory men employed. To achieve success, these salesmen would have to grasp hold and exploit every opportunity in front of them.

For his salesmen, it would take some "walking and talking."

It would take everything he discussed to survive this storm: spirit, democracy in business, cooperation, personal innovation, personality and ongoing self-improvement through self-study. He found a theme in education that would continue for the rest of his life; education was not just the study of the past but must include a vision of the future.

This chapter ends with Watson's closing remarks to his 1929 One Hundred Percent Club sales team. In "The Forthcoming Year," he instructed all the men who made their quotas and achieved success to head back into the field and assist the other men who were not so fortunate. For The IBM to prosper and grow the next four years—rather than just survive—it would take every IBMer helping every other IBMer.

For the first time, an inspirational maxim of Tom Watson's billowed off the tent walls to his top performers. This maxim in his closing speech at the 1929 One Hundred Percent Club must have sent chills down the backs of these men— both the young and the experienced. It resounded loudly to those desiring long careers in The IBM or those worried about their jobs and futures.

A MAN IS KNOWN BY
THE COMPANY HE KEEPS
A COMPANY IS KNOWN
BY THE MEN IT KEEPS

"A man is known by the company he keeps. A company is known by the men it keeps."

He would state, "A man is known by the company he keeps. A company is known by the men it keeps."

He was setting a standard for every businessman.

He wanted to keep each and every one of them.

He would fight to make that happen.

A man is known by the company he keeps.
A company is known by the men it keeps.

Building Careers

IBM Sales School Number 54

Endicott, N.Y.

October 30, 1929

It is really a special pleasure and a privilege for me to meet with a group of young men who are just beginning their careers with The IBM. If you review the talks you have heard in this school, you will realize that everyone has the same spirit—the spirit of The IBM. I hope that each of you has absorbed that spirit and that it is now a part of you, because without The IBM spirit you cannot possibly get anywhere in this organization.

Every man must follow the plans laid down by the architect.

That is exactly the way a business is built. It is the only way that you can build a business and have a solid organization back of you. Every man must follow the plans and specifications laid down by the architect and the engineer.

Always keep in mind the fact that if you see a chance for improvement, you must take it up with the men above you. Explain it to them, and, if it is a good idea, they will use it. They will change a policy for the entire organization, not for just one man. Any policy in our business that is not good for every man is not a good policy for the business, and we will not adopt it.

We want you to cultivate and develop the spirit of democracy—democracy in business.

The great success of our country has been built on a foundation of democracy. Democracy has been developed and is exemplified here to a greater extent than in any other country in the world.

The businesses today that follow along the lines of democracy are moving faster and making greater progress than the ones in which some men still say, "Well I have had better educational advantages than that man," or, "I have had better home surroundings than he has had; I am in a little different class and I am not going to associate with him."

14

There is no place for such men or such thoughts in The IBM organization. You all look alike to us.

As I look at you this morning, I know that this class is made up of men who used to be repair men in our business, men who used to be stenographers in our business, men who are college graduates and have just come into our business.

I cannot pick you out as individuals, because as I look into your faces, you all look alike to me.

If you can only all feel alike about this proposition, you are going to be real assets to this business and to yourselves as individuals. So cultivate the spirit of democracy—it means real cooperation. Always be willing to spend all day helping another man, even though it makes it necessary to do your own work at night. That is the spirit that exists at the Home Office.

I want you men to decide that you are all going to pull together as one man—that when you have graduated and are out in the field, you are going to keep this class spirit alive as the other classes have. Keep in touch with one another. You will bear a little closer relation to each other than to the other men in the organization.

Keep thinking about the things that you have been taught here, and follow through with all of the instructions that have been given you.

I always like to get this thought to a young man just starting out: Do not ever try to do your work the Armstrong way or the LaMotte way, or the Watson way, or any other way, because when you do, you limit your own personality, and then ninety percent of your strength is gone.

You must continue to study, in all the different ways that we teach—through reading, discussing, listening, observing and thinking.

Do not neglect any one of these five ways of studying, because, if you do, you will not acquire the proper kind of knowledge and information.

Keep this class spirit alive.
Keep in touch with one another.

Not every man who comes into this business makes a success. But when you trace the reasons for the failures you find that they are not because there is anything wrong with the business, or with the products, or the company's policies.

It is usually because they did not follow through; did not do things like the rest of the people do them, and did not take advantage of their opportunities.

We want you to cultivate and develop
the spirit of democracy—democracy in business.

—

IBM's European Visitors

Closing Banquet Toastmaster
One Hundred Percent Club

New York, N.Y.
January 15, 1930

I am sure all of you realize, as I have realized for a long time—having had the opportunity of visiting the different countries—that The IBM Spirit, The IBM Heart and The IBM Language are the same in all tongues and in all countries.

That is the beautiful thing about our international work. I had the pleasure last summer of visiting nine countries, of calling upon our agents, of holding conventions and of meeting their families.

I felt just as much at home as I feel with you in this country because I found The IBM Spirit wherever I went among IBM people.

The IBM Spirit, The IBM Heart and The IBM Language
are the same in all tongues and in all countries.

16

Contributions of Hundred Percenters

Opening Address
One Hundred Percent Club

New York, N.Y.
January 15-17, 1930

In opening my remarks this morning, I must repeat what I always say to you gentlemen upon an occasion of this kind. It is a great pleasure and a great privilege for me to have the opportunity to meet with you.

I listened with a great deal of interest to Mr. Nichol's talk, in which he gave me credit for your being here. We all like credit, but I do not like to accept credit that is not due me.

My mind went back to the first convention I held after I came into this business, fifteen years ago last May. We had very few men. We had very little enthusiasm. What we did have gave us a great start, and the other men fell in line. Enthusiasm is the basis of all great things.

Enthusiasm is the basis of all great things.

To you who are here as One Hundred Percenters, I want to say that you deserve more credit than it is possible for me to give you in the few minutes I have this morning. You have made not only a great contribution to the success of this company and to its employees, but also a great contribution to the stockholders—the real owners of the business.

You have also made a great contribution to your country as a whole, because our business is playing a very important part in the scheme of everything that is vital to the running of this country, and, in fact, of most of the world, for today, as all of you know, IBM products are being sold and used in seventy different countries.

That is due to the magnificent leadership of the men in the field.

As I look over this gathering of IBM One Hundred Percenters, I cannot help but feel just a little guilty. I feel we have not done so much for you as we have for the men who are not here this morning. Most of our efforts and energy is expended upon the lower-record men, not upon those whose records are high.

The reason why I appreciate you high-record men is that you have gone ahead. You are the leaders and we want to pass on to the men with low records the ideas we get from you, so that we can help them come to these conventions.

Enthusiasm is the basis of all great things.

—

The New Education

Closing Banquet Toastmaster
One Hundred Percent Club

New York, N.Y.
January 15, 1930

In the old days, education was a walk backward into the past, a review of other people's minds.

Modern education does all of that. In addition, it goes into the future through educational and research work, and that is why we are broadening and expanding in every way—industrially, culturally and spiritually, because we are not satisfied simply with a review of the past. We take that and add to it our vision of the future.

We are not satisfied simply with a review of the past—we add to it our vision of the future.

The Forthcoming Year

Closing Banquet Address
One Hundred Percent Club

New York, N.Y.
January 15, 1930

In closing, I wish to thank you for the vision you have given me in the past three days, of business prospects during the coming year. That is a subject that is very much discussed, particularly in New York, at this time. It is a subject that is brought to my attention very often. I am asked to give my opinion in regard to the business of 1930, our business in particular and the business of the country in general. Any opinion that I give is always based on information received from you gentlemen, either through correspondence or in meetings of this nature.

When I am asked in regard to business for 1930, my answer is going to be based on what we heard from you gentlemen last Monday. That was to the effect that our business would show in 1930 a substantial increase over the business of 1929.

I have no doubt as to the result, because you have always made good on all your statements. The organization as a whole

You are going to help the other men who are not so fortunate.

has always measured up to your predictions. Consequently, I have a very confident feeling in regard to the business of IBM during 1930. That means a great deal to a large number of people.

I know that when you go back to your territories you are going to help the other men who are not so fortunate as to be here tonight. I know that when we meet next year we shall require a very much larger room in which to hold our meetings. I believe—in fact, I am sure—that you will more than double the One Hundred Percent Club for 1930, as a result of taking back into the field the inspiration you have received here during the past few days.

In The IBM, there are no old men and there never are going to be any old men. The IBM motto is that no one ever allows his heart to get over forty years of age. Keep that in mind, gentlemen—we should hold our hearts at forty.

You have heard the saying that, "A man is known by the company he keeps." We have added to that our IBM motto that "A company is known by the men it keeps."

A MAN IS KNOWN BY
THE COMPANY HE KEEPS
A COMPANY IS KNOWN
BY THE MEN IT KEEPS

You are going to contribute thoughts, ideas and ideals to all the people with whom you come in contact.

When the curtain falls on this convention and you go back into your fields, you are going to take much of value to every corner of the world. You are going to contribute thoughts, ideas and ideals to all the people with whom you come in contact. The good that we have received here will endure forever.

As we send you back into your various territories, we send with you our company and its reputation. We are very happy to have you represent us. There are very few of the people with whom you come in contact who will ever see our factories, our executives or our home offices. Therefore, they judge our company and our ideals by you.

The greatest satisfaction and pleasure that I have in this business is in sending you out to all corners of the world, taking with you The IBM Company, because I know that you are going to represent it in the way that we want it represented. That, gentlemen, I appreciate more than anything else in connection with our institution.

They judge our company and our ideals by you.

ADVICE TO IBMERS

When Watson took over The Computing-Tabulating-Recording Company (C-T-R) on May 1, 1914, he was in Canada on company business; but because he failed to report for work at the home office on Broad Street in New York City, he was docked three days' pay—an inauspicious beginning for a career that would set the foundation for one of the world's greatest corporations.[2]

C-T-R, which would be rebranded as International Business Machines in 1924, was from the start a company on weak footing. He faced immediate decisions concerning its very survival. Some were so urgent that bankruptcy loomed on the near horizon with any misstep. He struggled constantly to obtain financing for growth.

As he took the helm of C-T-R, Watson was faced with keeping the existing C-T-R management or starting over from scratch. His board of directors advised him to clean house and get rid of everyone as "a new broom sweeps clean." Watson loved maxims to motivate, instruct and encourage his employees, but this was one maxim he apparently did not like. He, as the new broom, decided to keep his management team. Ultimately he would speak often and with pride of that decision.

During the next eighteen years he failed only once—during the Recession of 1921—to show an increase in net profits over the previous year. Speaking of his performance in 1921, Watson said, "I am ashamed of it." But he was ashamed not for missing the increase in net profits, but because the executive team didn't "hang on to our courage and our belief in IBM and in IBM men." He humbly said he received an "education" that year—one he would later exercise in the darkest hours of the Great Depression. Even through the first two years of the Depression, as GNP kept dropping and unemployment kept rising, IBM's profits would continue to grow.

I am very happy to speak to you through the Speak-o-Phone.

Tom Watson kept his hands constantly on The IBM's rudder. He implemented continuous course corrections through communication vehicles that were state of the art for the 1930s. His speeches were captured and then sometimes published as editorials in *Business Machines*, the corporate newsletter. This method provided his executive view across The IBM in a consistent and irrefutable manner.

He relished these roles of lead educator and top advisor to all IBMers: young or old, new hire or Quarter Century man, salesman or executive. He was open, forward thinking and displayed a passion for seeking out the middle ground that would establish a win-win relationship between employer and employee.

In an interview with *Forbes*, he stated, "The day of the section boss in business has passed." His mission was to make every IBM executive an assistant to his men. He wanted every employee to be convinced in his heart that he was working for the best corporation in the world. This was his management philosophy, and in this collection of speeches and essays, he lays that foundation.

For his executives, he established one of the business community's first executive schools. Executives needed to learn that they were teachers, role models and assistants to their men. The power they were given brought with it great responsibilities.

Following a meeting with his executives, he broadcasted to all of The IBM in *Business Machines* that if any man was working and enthusiastic, such a man would make mistakes. It was a part of the learning process.

A thoughtful man, however, was to be forgiven.

THINK

What every business needs is more people who THINK.

These were timeless words of wisdom applicable in any business or agency and under any economic conditions. In especially tough economic times, such as the Depression, fear can stifle creative thought and action. Fear of making a mistake and losing employment constricts thinking. In "We Forgive Thoughtful Mistakes," Watson removes the stigma associated with failure. He wanted concepts brought forward to either help the business grow or eliminate processes that prevented growth.

In "Have Faith in the Future," he demonstrates his honesty, forthrightness and heart as he instructs a new class of salesman that "it is much more important for you to get into the right kind of business than it is for us to get one man who is going to be the right type for The IBM." After all, The IBM would survive one bad decision; an individual's bad career choice could be disastrous.

He counseled men how to look for an employer. He believed he was leading the best corporation, the best organization and the best employer in the world, so he didn't fear any competition for the hearts,

THE BEST SUPERVISION IS
SELF SUPERVISION

Do not wait for your supervisor to tell you to do something.

minds or good will of excellent men. He challenged his own men to seek out other employment so that they would understand what they had in The IBM—an understanding rooted in their hearts not their heads. He believed true loyalty lived in the heart. The path to creating a company that would go on forever was through a man's heart—not his head or pocketbook.

This chapter closes with "Advice to Young Men Entering Business." Some corporate leaders might mistake this advice as just good business, but it is more than that. It is his heart on display. He was talking to these men for their "own good as individuals." He wanted them to have long careers in good health with The IBM.

To him, the overall good of the corporation was intimately intertwined with the good will of every individual.

They were inseparable.

I have talked to you for your own good
and not merely in the interests of The IBM.

We Forgive Thoughtful Mistakes

Meeting of Executives Published in
Business Machines – *The Company Newsletter*

February 21, 1930

If a man thinks about his work—if he puts real thought into everything he does—he should be and will be forgiven for the mistakes he makes.

I do not believe in criticizing a man simply for making a mistake. If he shows that he has given the proper amount of thought to a matter, and he shows that he has tried to do the right thing—I am ready to forgive thoughtful mistakes.

The things that hold back a business are the thoughtless mistakes—mistakes that are made because people have gone about their work without the proper amount of advance thought.

The only man who does not make a mistake is the man who does nothing.

When a man does a thing wrong he should go over the proposition from the very beginning and ask himself whether he really and properly thought over the matter before he did anything about it. In the great majority of cases, if he goes over his work thoughtfully, he will reach the right answer and will avoid getting himself and the company into an embarrassing position. More importantly, he will eliminate the waste that goes with thoughtless mistakes, and he will train himself to do a better job on everything new that he undertakes.

You have often heard the saying that the only man who does not make mistakes is the man who does not do anything. Mistakes will occur, but every mistake should be a serious lesson to the man who makes it. If he earns the reputation of thinking carefully about everything he does, the mistakes a man does make will be excused.

Every business needs more people who think. I cannot emphasize that word too strongly. Thinking is what makes our useful and profitable line of International Business Machines possible. Thinking is what makes well-rounded sales and satisfied customers possible.

Thinking is what really makes an organization.

24

The men who will go farthest in this business, or any other business, are the men who demonstrate that they are thinkers. They are the men who are able to stand on their own feet.

Every executive values and is looking for the type of people who are capable of relieving him safely of many of the things he would otherwise have to do himself. The more a man thinks about his job, the more responsibility he is able to carry, the more valuable he becomes to himself and the company and the more progress he is able to make.

The men who will go farthest in this business are the men who demonstrate that they are thinkers.

Point out to the men working with you and around you that we forgive thoughtful mistakes—that it is only the thoughtless mistakes that cause trouble. Tell them first to be sure they have thought about each proposition, then to go ahead. You will find there is nothing that will so surely help them eliminate mistakes and get ahead in The IBM than that one thing—and there is certainly nothing that will so surely help the business, and every individual in it, to go ahead and become more and more prosperous.

Thinking is what really makes an organization.

25

Look Your Work Squarely in the Face

Interview with President Watson
Forbes *Article*

April 1, 1930

To establish sales morale, it is essential to start building at the top of the organization. The old idea that those in administrative positions should be autocrats has gone. The day of the section boss in business has passed. Every manager in every department of business, in factory, office or field should remember that his duty is to help the men under his direction.

If cooperation is to exist in any business enterprise, if effort is to be stimulated to produce the results for which the company was organized, the people in it must be given the chance to become acquainted, to exchange views and to understand one another. Nothing is more productive of results than departmental meetings in conjunction with schools for salesmen, foremen and executives.

Every manager's first duty is to help the men under his direction.

Efforts should be stimulated occasionally, because it is natural for people to get into ruts or fall into time-wasting habits and very often be unconscious of the fact. To keep up and stimulate the efforts of those under him requires much thought and study on the part of the manager and department head. Arousing the desire to excel is a highly satisfactory method of bringing about this result. Sales contests and published records of quotas and accomplishments are the direct means whereby these ends can be attained.

Sound policy demands that every man in a responsible position have support from his superiors. We must prove our faith by demonstrating the dependence of the business on the men who run it, and, in turn, their dependence on the men who help them carry out their respective operations. Men at the head of business face the necessity and the opportunity of taking more men into their confidence and showing them the way, realizing that their knowledge will produce dollars in profit.

No one has to be a genius to succeed in business. One does not have to lie awake nights worrying about his job. Men must look their work squarely in the face as if to say, "This is the right thing to do." If we do what common sense dictates, nine times out of ten it will be the right thing.

I would advise a young man to pick two or three companies in a line of enterprise which appeals to him—companies which show a forward trend of sales and profits. He should make a careful study of at least three such companies. Then he should seek to get a job with one of them, going in prepared to work hard, learn all he possibly can about the business and the objectives of the management.

Then he should put himself in the hands of the management, relying on its good judgment and fairness to reward efficiency and merit.

We must prove our faith by demonstrating the dependence of the business on the men who run it and the men who help them carry out their respective operations.

Have Faith in the Future!

Tabulating Machine Sales School 56 and Service School 32

Endicott, N.Y.
May 20, 1930

Mr. Armstrong said you were being honored by my presence this morning. I would like to reverse that, saying instead that I am very highly honored at being here and meeting you. Nearly all of my time and thought is devoted, not to the past or to the present of this business, but to its future. Whenever I have an opportunity to visit a class of new men who are going into the sales or service branches of our business, I feel that it is a great privilege and honor.

I want to give you this thought. I want you to study and analyze our business. If you lack this faith in its great future, you should not go on in the business. I want to say to you that after all of my experiences with the various industries in this country (and I try to keep in touch with all of them), I know of no place where young men have as fine an opportunity to build a future for themselves as they have in The IBM.

Opportunity is the thing which interests you more than anything else. It is much more important for you to get into the right kind of business than it is for us to get one man who is going to be the right type for The IBM. We have so many men to depend upon that if one drops out we can take up the slack.

Nearly all of my time is devoted to the future of this business.

You young men who are going out to build a future for yourselves should take this seriously; you should feel that this business is the very best place for you to be. Then you can go on and do the things that you are told to do and, in addition, suggest other things for us to do that will improve the business. Then there will be no doubt as to your future success.

No man deserves any special credit for being an average man. It is the men who are striving to be above the average who are the men who build business—they are the men who build nations. They are the real builders in every line.

28

That is what I want you in this class to get fixed in your minds—that you are going to learn all you can here, and then you are going out and use everything you have learned to stimulate your minds and your thoughts along lines that will bring into this business new thoughts, new ideas and new principles that have never been heard of before. That is what has built this business. You cannot stay in one place—you either go forward or go backward.

You should feel that this business is the very best place for you to be.

We need men who can help others. That brings to my mind this thought: You often hear a man say, "I can go out and make my living anywhere in this world." Of course you can, but what does that mean? To make a living for himself is what is expected of every man. Some men are satisfied with that alone. But that is not the big point; that is just part of the day's work.

The big thing to keep in mind is to help create something that will aid in making a living for other people. That is where our real satisfaction, our real contribution to society, comes in—to help produce something that will extend through all of the seventy-seven countries in which our products are used, and to help all of the people who come in contact with our business. That is why this business has such a fascination for men who are eager to do something.

You often have heard of men who have had every advantage of education and training and yet do not seem to get along. It is because they have not taken into consideration wisdom, which is the power that enables one to use knowledge to advantage. Be sure that you use wisdom in connection with the knowledge you gain in IBM.

Different men will talk to you from this platform. Some will impress one man, some will impress another, and some men in this room are apt to get the idea that this is a very complicated business; that you must know a great deal in order to succeed. Some men, particularly young men, may become discouraged, thinking, "I can never present this proposition like Mr. Armstrong or like Mr. Braitmayer." You don't have to. You have only to figure on getting the good ideas that come to you from the platform and then on going out and presenting them in your own way.

Your own personality, backed by the knowledge you have gained here, will fight the whole battle. Your personality, combined with your product, is 90% of this business. There is no mystery. It does not require any genius to make a success. Honest effort combined with the knowledge of the products and what the products will do, backed by an honest day's work every day will enable any man in this room to meet with satisfactory progress and success in this business. This matter of selling is one of great simplicity.

Don't ever doubt the value of your own ideas without presenting them to the Sales Department or to the head of whatever department you are in. Carry out the instructions that are given you here and when you get a new thought, which we want to urge you to do, present it to the head of the department you are in. And if it is good, they can give the benefit of your idea to the entire organization.

I just want to mention one more very important point. The most im-

The most important element in the success of every young man is his health.

portant element in the success of every young man is his health. You are a healthy looking group, but always keep the importance of health in mind. Don't ever do anything that you feel will injure your health in the slightest degree. Sound health is your best asset. As long as you are healthy you can make a success in this business or any other business. Be careful and do the things that will keep you in fine physical, mental and moral condition.

If you do those things and carry out the teachings of Mr. Armstrong and the other gentlemen, I am sure that I will have the pleasure of seeing every one of you improve as the days, weeks and months go by, and that you will build yourselves up to a position in this business where we shall be very proud and thankful that we brought you into it.

Always keep the importance of health in mind.

Study – The Master Key to Future Growth

Editorial in Business Machines

June 2, 1930

During my visit to the Endicott factory last week, I again had the opportunity of witnessing the activities of our sales and service schools. In reviewing the work and meeting the students of Tabulating Machine Sales School No. 56 and Service School No. 32, now in session at the factory, I was impressed with the importance and value which our educational policy has developed.

IBM's policy of developing the business by developing the men in it through education is the main factor in our company's progress. In this day and age, education is the one Master Key we can depend on to open the door to future progress.

IBM's policy is to develop the business by developing the men in it.

Without our sales schools and the type of instructors engaged in our school work, it would be impossible to provide the quality of salesmanship necessary for the exacting standards required of IBM salesmen.

The future of International Business Machines Corporation, and of every person connected with the Company, depends not upon the amount of time we spend in study; but upon what we learn and upon our ability to transfer our knowledge to the newcomers in the business so that they may keep step with the pace of IBM—a pace which is constantly increasing!

Every member of The IBM organization should be both a teacher and a student.

The future depends upon our ability to transfer our knowledge to the newcomers in the business.

Study, Work and Progress

The IBM Sales School Students Number 67

Endicott, N.Y.
July 12, 1932

I was very interested to hear what Mr. Braitmayer had to say about the continued growth and progress of this business in the years to come and about the need for such young men as yourselves in our organization to take on constantly more responsibilities.

Character Rules Success

I should like to tell you why Mr. Braitmayer has stayed in the busi-

You become stronger men because you stand for the right principles in your business and private lives.

ness since its origin and why he has been successful. It is because he developed early in life one quality without which no man can make a success in this or any other business. Mr. Braitmayer did not ride through these years on his reputation. It is his character that has been the reason for his success. Character is the quality he developed early in life and that he has continued building ever since.

Without it, as I have said, no man can be successful.

Never be confused by the meanings of "reputation" and "character," because there is a great difference. Reputation is what people think you are; character is what you really are; what you know yourself to be. As you go through life and develop real character, you become stronger men from every viewpoint because you yourselves know that you stand for right principles in your business and private lives. That is the most important, the best advice that anybody can give you.

Look Into the Future

You heard me speak this morning of the past. You heard me express a little of the vision I have of the future. But check my statements later and you will find that I was wrong when I expressed them. I have made a great many predictions about the future of this business in the past eighteen years. The records prove that I have been mistaken every time.

When I predicted that this business would double in so many years some of my associates said, "Mr. Watson, it cannot be done." When I said, "We are going to increase this factory space a certain amount," some people felt that it could not be done. Every prediction that I have made about the future growth of this business has been wrong.

The reason that they have been wrong is that the business has gone far beyond any vision that I have ever expressed. The same thing is going to happen in regard to my prediction today, because the opportunity for the development of this business is so great that no man has enough vision to form a picture of what this company is going to be.

What is the most important thing for you to think about—the past of this business? No! Although it is good for you to know that, the most important thing for you to get into your mind in this school is the part that you, as individuals, are going to perform in the future development of this business. Keep that before you all the time.

Do not pay attention to the man who fails, because in every business and in every branch and walk of life, there are always those who fall by the wayside. You cannot afford to waste any of your time on subjects of that kind. Keep your eyes fixed straight ahead. Look into the future; always look up and decide that you, personally, are going to make contributions to this business that will be recognized by its heads.

Keep your eyes fixed straight ahead. Look into the future. Always look up.

There is no mystery about this business. Talk to the men in it who have made the greatest success; get acquainted with them. You will find that none of them has done anything unusual. They have simply developed character. They have followed the company's policies, although at times they may have thought that they were wrong.

All we ask the men to do is to follow the policies of this company and to follow them one hundred percent. If they find they cannot agree with them, they should not remain in the business. If you know, however, of any way we can improve a policy, we are always glad to consider suggestions. We know that we cannot conduct this business next year on exactly the same policies as we have this year. We progress because we are willing to change when we feel that

33

improvement will result. There is nothing in the world that holds people back like monotony, for it is monotony that kills both men and business. We want you to examine our policies and thus do better work.

I have never stood before a class since I have been in this business when I have considered the opportunity to be as great as I believe it to be for you today. Never mind what you read in the newspapers concerning depression or unemployment. Just make sure that you yourself are employed. You can do that by keeping busy.

Wisdom is the power that enables us to make practical use of our knowledge.

Any man who keeps busy, whether in depression or boom-times, will get somewhere. You cannot always go ahead as rapidly, perhaps, under certain conditions as under others. But the man who understands our business, who knows the fundamentals and is willing to continue to study, can go out during any kind of times under any conditions and get business. He can do so because he has something to present that will help all businesses.

In these times particularly, all businesses are looking for something that will aid them. You will have to explain more things to more people, but that is all to your advantage because in that way, you obtain more training. In connection with that point, do not forget that you are going to need something in addition to knowledge. You must have wisdom. Without wisdom, knowledge is useless. Wisdom is the power that enables us to make practical use of our knowledge.

I know the record of every man in this school. I know that every man here has had the proper start. You are all starting equal. There are no politics in our business. Every man has an equal chance. Friendship does not make any difference; nor does it matter from where a man comes or whom he knows in the business. Every man is judged on his merits and the quality and quantity of the results he produces.

I have no fear about any man in this class not making a success. I want you to get your eyes on the higher visions. There are going to be many new positions. As men grow older in the business, they are going to want to relax a little. We are looking forward to the development of younger executives. They are developing. They are

34

taking more work off our shoulders today. If they were not, we would not be able to carry on.

We want you to strive to do important work in this business. Help us make it a great business. We think it is big today. It is in comparison with the past, but five or ten years from now we want you to compare the business then with what it is today and realize what great growth we have experienced. Above all things, we want you to be able to say that you have contributed your full share toward building the business.

Always Continue to Study

Do not worry about your work. It is not necessary. It is not the type of work about which you have to worry. The only thing necessary for you to do is to study—to study not only while you are in this school but also when you are out in the field.

All of us know from our experience in the classroom that it is easier for some to learn than for others. If the man who does not absorb things quite so quickly will really apply himself with determination, he will eventually learn. And when he does, his information will stay with him better, perhaps, than with the one to whom it came easier.

I mention this because in every class and in every school some become discouraged when they do not seem to grasp things as quickly as the others. Do not let anything discourage you in this business. Everything about it is encouraging. No sales organization in the United States has had the encouragement and the good cheer in its work during the past two and a half years that our organization has had. Why?

Because we have had products to present to people who have been willing to listen, knowing that they would be benefited through the use of them. Keep that in mind. Do not let anything discourage you.

Do not let anything discourage you in this business. Everything about it is encouraging.

You do not have to be slaves. You do not have to break down your health through hard work. We do not want you to do that. We want you to work intelligently. We want you to keep an account of your productive and non-productive time just as accurately as we keep an account of it here in the factory. Before this school ends, you will have received a thorough training in what productive and non-productive time mean in the manufacturing phase of the business. Study that and apply it to your work, because it is even more important in the field than in the factory.

Your productive time is the time that you spend in the presence of a prospective customer trying to interest him in our products. The time you spend getting down to the office early in the morning, arranging and planning a number of things, is all non-productive time. You have to put in a certain amount of it. But always keep in mind that

Your productive time is the time you spend in the presence of a prospective customer.

the time spent at your desk is non-productive and that you will never draw any salary or commission as a result of it. Keep that in mind and make use of your time.

Maintain the proper balance between your productive and non-productive time. If you follow this advice you will find that it will mean more to your success than any other suggestion I can give you, because time is your chief stock-in-trade.

Be a Self-Educator

Follow the instructions that are given you in this school, and then learn to be a self-educator. That is the greatest education in the world. Study each individual problem with which you come in contact. Solve it for yourself. Every time you meet and overcome an obstacle, you become that much stronger. We expect and want you to have someone working for you; someone you can teach. You have something to pass on to other men.

There is no use of talking about bricks and mortar and machinery without backing them up with the strongest and best sales force possible. The high character and the fine standing of our sales organization have always been a source of pride to me. I have had the pleasure of coming in contact with and talking to our representatives in twenty-four different countries. They are all the same kind of people. They all have the same spirit. I find the same IBM spirit in Endicott, Washington, Dayton or wherever I go throughout the world.

I know that you are going to play a great part in building the future of this business. I congratulate you on coming into the business at this time. I congratulate the company on having you, because we need you more than you need us. We want you to feel that way about it.

We want you to feel that we are not conferring any favors upon you. When we gave you the opportunity to come into this business, we did so because we felt that you would be able to contribute something to our business. We are not philanthropic. We would not be taking you into the business unless we felt that you could help us. We did not give you a job because of the present economic conditions or the lack of employment.

There is no use talking about bricks, mortar and machinery without the strongest and best sales-force.

We have taken every one of you into this business because we have decided, after looking you over and looking you up, that you can make a contribution to the success of this business.

Do not feel under any obligation to us. Just go ahead and do your part and we shall both win.

We progress because we are willing to change when we feel that improvement will result.

Advice to Young Men Entering Business

Tabulating Machine Sales School Number 57

Endicott, N.Y.
October 29, 1930

I enjoy everything that concerns The IBM, but, most of all, I enjoy meeting with young men in IBM Sales Schools who are starting their business careers with our Company.

The kind of business in which you start your career, and the way in which you start, mean more to you than they do to this company. The company is made up of many individuals; if one drops out, we can replace him and go on, or we might even go along for some time without replacing his services. But if one of you makes a mistake in planning his career, it is likely to handicap you considerably.

Therefore, it is to your individual benefit to take this IBM business very seriously. I know that you are doing so.

The Right Kind of Business

Judge the character of a business by the usefulness of its products and the character of its men.

As young men starting your careers, you have many things to consider. You must consider the character of this business, the quality and value of its products, the character of the men in it with whom you are going to associate, and the character of the people to whom you are going to present IBM products. Each of these is important.

You have had an opportunity to judge the character of this business by the products it manufactures and their usefulness to the people we serve. You have also had an opportunity to judge the character of the men with whom you are going to associate because several of them have visited this school and have addressed you.

You have had the opportunity of judging the people and the business of IBM. In summing up the situation, I cannot think of any place that a young man could start where he would be surrounded by any higher type of men; where he would have a finer clientele or where he would find a higher class of products than you find here.

I feel that you, looking at it from your point of view, have chosen the right kind of business to enter because the big thing about The IBM is that it is not finished. You are not coming into an organization that has been built—we are just building it. You are not coming into a business that has succeeded—we are merely succeeding a little more each year.

Mr. Armstrong referred to our increase this year over last year. We are proud of that because it shows that the men in our organization are so interested in the businesses we serve, in their own personal welfare and in the welfare of their families, that they have put forth extra effort this year—they have worked harder than ever before to secure the increase of 11.3% which we show over the corresponding nine months of last year.

When we compare the first nine months of this year with the first nine months of 1928, we find that the increase is 42%. I mention these figures not to bring out the amount of money that we are making for our stockholders, but because it shows that you are in a progressive concern.

You must continue to study not only this business, but also business in general, and make the biggest place you can for yourself in IBM. There will always be many opportunities for the men who put forth an honest, intelligent effort. Knowledge is a wonderful thing. You cannot progress without knowledge.

We realize that education is important; all the businessmen of this country realize it. That is why we have so many schools and so many different kinds of schools in The IBM. We know they are necessary.

We even have Executive Schools. They are the most important of all because the executives are always called upon to teach others. We started the Executives' Schools many years ago when, realizing every man knows something the others do not, we decided that we would try to teach each other.

They have been the most profitable schools we have ever had, because the executives of this company are being called upon to carry greater responsibilities every year.

Wisdom Required With Knowledge

The young man requires wisdom as well as knowledge. You can acquire all the knowledge in the world, but if you do not back that knowledge with wisdom, it will be of no value to you. Wisdom is the power that enables you to use knowledge to advantage. Keep that in mind.

I want every man in this school to take great pride in his own record. Never be satisfied to be among the average. We do not deserve much credit for being average men, or an average business or an average nation; it is the people who stand above the average in the industries of the world who get the credit. It is the men who are above the average that count, because they take care of the ones below average and bring things to a balance. I want each one of you to make up your mind that, when you leave this school, you will be above the average in your records.

NEVER BE
SATISFIED TO
BE AMONG
THE AVERAGE

It is the men who are above the average that count, because they take care of the ones below.

You may not be able to do it every minute or every year, but you can do it over, say, a five-year period. That is what the executives look for when they have important places to fill. They look for the men whose records are better than average. I cannot emphasize too strongly how necessary it is for you to be better than average men. I tell you this from the company's standpoint, because I know we will need more men than are gathered in this room to fill executive positions in this company during the next five or six years.

One of the greatest problems in business today is to develop enough men to do the bigger things, and that is where you are going to fit in because I know you are all serious men. I know that all of the men who preceded you in IBM Sales schools are out in the field putting forth an effort to be better than average. I know that many of the other young men in this organization, and many of the older men also, are making good records.

Success Requires Character

In addition to knowledge and wisdom, to succeed, men must be of good character. They must be spoken of outside the business as men who stand for something worthwhile, men who are interested in public affairs. You owe an obligation to society outside of your work.

Try to get interested in something worthwhile in the territory to which you are assigned. There is always work for men of your type, something you can do to help others. Regardless of how much you work to help others, your efforts will help you most of all, because the man who is willing to help a community and help his neighbors always prospers and profits more than anyone else. Keep that in mind.

Strive to be outstanding citizens of your community and of your country. That is as important as being a good man in business and besides it helps you to become a good man in your work.

Learn to Supervise Yourself

Why do we need so much supervision in business? It is because the majority of men in business are always depending on somebody else. When you start out make up your minds that you are going to supervise yourselves, because self-supervision is the most valuable kind there is. You know what is expected of you, so just go out and do it.

Learn to supervise yourself properly, and that will qualify you in time to supervise other people. Take your orders gracefully. A man who cannot take orders gracefully will never be in a position to give orders.

Do not be afraid to be critical of us, if you think we are not running this business properly. But do not criticize us to your fellow workmen. Go direct to headquarters. We are always anxious to receive constructive criticism, but we do not care

Supervise yourself. You know what is expected of you, so just go out and do it.

for destructive criticism. That helps no one. Always make up your mind before you criticize that you are going to think out some plan that you believe is better, and then come and present it to us. You would be surprised at the number of good suggestions that we receive in that way.

You would be surprised at the number of changes we make in the handling of the affairs of IBM through suggestions we receive from men like yourselves. We want you to keep that in mind and be among the builders of this company. We want you to think of The IBM as it will be ten years from now when this factory will be twice as large as it is today and work with a view to placing yourself in a position to say at that time, "Well, I have helped build half of this factory since I have been with this company."

Genius Not Essential to Success

It is not the number of hours but what we do with the hours that count.

I want each one of you to have more confidence in yourself than in anything else. One thing that I never overlook in talking to a group of young men starting out in life is to call their particular attention to the fact that it does not require any genius to be successful. It requires only an intelligent, honest effort.

Make your minutes count. It is not so much the number of hours that we spend at work; it is what we do with hours that count. The point is to make those hours count for something. Do not waste your time on a prospect unless he is a good prospect. If a business is not large enough to use our machines to its advantage, do not waste any time with it.

Leave a good impression with such prospects so that when their business becomes large enough, they will remember you, your product and your company.

When you do place our machines in a business, be sure to give the customer the best possible service, because service means sales. Follow up your customers and let them know you are wholeheartedly interested in giving them service and giving them something for the money they are paying for your product.

I have touched on a great many different subjects because my mind is so full of the various things that come up in connection with the education of young men in The IBM that I do not know where to start or where to stop. I hope I have been able to leave a few sound thoughts with you.

You have noticed in our various offices our outstanding motto, the one word "Think." I want each one of you to take that as your motto. It has done more for me than any other one thing. Every one of us is capable of doing a job better if we will think before we start.

If we look back over our past, we will realize that the mistakes we have made have been thoughtless mistakes. We made the mistake because we did not think.

Let us resolve to think about our new job. As young men starting out think how you can do more for yourselves, how you can make for yourselves a better position in this company. If you will do that, the interests of the company will be well taken care of.

Think before you act, and then if you make a mistake you will be forgiven. We have another motto, "We Forgive Thoughtful Mistakes." If a man told me that he had thought a thing over and gave me his reason for doing it, I do not care how wrong it might be, I would never criticize him, because he had done his best—he had put thought into it.

But if a man tells me that he did not think, I do not like it. I do not like to overlook mistakes of that kind, because a man should think.

I do not want you to interpret this as coming from me merely in the interests of The IBM. I want you to feel that I have talked to you for your own good as individuals because that is my intention. We cannot hope to build this business unless we build the individuals in it.

If you can take what I have said as my contribution to your personal success, I will feel that I have accomplished a great deal in coming up here to talk to you.

I have talked to you for your own good and not merely in the interests of The IBM.

Strive to be outstanding citizens of your community and of your country.

THE "I" IN IBM IS INTERNATIONAL

Tom Watson delivered this collection of international speeches as he left for, traveled through and finally returned from Europe. It was a four-month excursion.

Although The IBM was one of the first businesses to use the new wireless telephone service between New York and London in 1927, this was not a time of instantaneous communication; rather it was a time when the boss was gone, he was unavailable. There was no dialing his cell, firing off an e-mail or sending a short Blackberry® message for his advice and counsel. From the day he walked up the ship's gangplank with his family and business associates in June 1930, until his return in September, he was, for the most part, out of touch.

Those left behind had to make decisions. The IBM still had to function. Under these circumstances, during the Great Depression, he expressed supreme confidence in his team.

The night before leaving for Europe, everyone communicated to Tom Watson how important he was to The IBM. He brushed aside their comments. He said it would be very unfair to everybody in The IBM if he did not tell them he had been a very small part in the building of the business; that in good conscience, the only thing he could take credit for was surrounding himself with men "like you who are representing our company throughout the world."

One has to wonder if in the back of his mind he was anticipating finding in Europe what he had found when taking over the C-T-R Corporation: very little enthusiasm, but maybe just enough for him to take it and grow.

In Italy though, he immediately found enthusiasm. He commented, "Italy has become a bigger part of me than it ever was before." Encouraged, he stoked the fires of that enthusiasm across Europe.

Keep in mind the international policy of helpfulness and cooperation with one another.

45

On this trip he would visit Austria, Germany, France, Czechoslovakia (now the Czech Republic) and England. He would speak of his determination to avoid being perceived as a "higher official." He desired to be their assistant, nothing more. To him, any executive who failed to be an assistant to his men would be of very little value "to his people or to his company." For Tom Watson's executive team, there was no need to read between the lines. They knew exactly what was expected of them. He was modeling the expected behavior.

He touched constantly on the subject of the stockholders who had invested in The IBM and the great responsibility he carried because they "have placed their confidence in our integrity and ability to conduct this business." He continued his lifelong habit of teaching, instructing and elaborating to inspire leadership throughout his corporation. On this trip, he focused on his international executives.

He regretted that the word "manager" had ever entered into the vocabulary of business. He developed and expanded his constant and reoccurring theme that all executives should be "assistants to men." He cited the need for cooperation, education and dedication.

In "The Basic Rules for Successful Supervision" he lays out in clear terms the straightforward rules of supervision in The IBM. Every executive must "employ the right kind of men, teach them the business properly, supervise them closely, promote them when you have an opportunity and discharge them only when it is necessary."

In "Aspects of World Trade," with his customary frankness, he says that the United States conducted an experiment on Wall Street. He says we tried an experiment of "making a fortune without working." Unfortunately, it exploded and "all went down to earth."

As he prepared to leave home from England, he touched on the issue of power, stating that some men, when

Our products are known and used around the world.

given power believe they "have been given authority to tell other men what to do. Consequently, they are not able to tell anybody what to do that will be of any value." He offered some insight into how he determined the quality of an individual. It is not the big things a man does but the attention to "little things."

Finally, home from his travels abroad, he summarized succinctly in a message to The IBM Organization that after all his travels and meetings with IBM representatives from nineteen different countries, "The only difference I found was language."

In Tom Watson's eyes, we were becoming more than a business. We were becoming what he believed was required to be successful—The IBM Family.

The business and the family were International.

We have ceased to think of The IBM merely as a business.

Give Me a Man with Vision

*Opening Address in Honor of Mr. Boucas and
IBM Executives Sailing for Europe*

New York, N.Y.
June 4, 1930

While Mr. Boucas said his territory was too large, he did not ask me to reduce it—he asked me, instead, to help him increase his organization. That is the spirit that builds IBM—not the cutting down of work laid out for you to do when you find it to be more than you can handle, but the development of more people to assist you in doing the job.

I have often said to you, and I repeat it again today, that there is no saturation point when it comes to education. Do not ever allow any

of the young men working with you to feel that they have studied this business enough to know everything about it.

It is the same with success. I always like to repeat that. I was congratulated only today on the success of this business, the success we have made of it—congratulated on the quarterly statement.

No matter what happens, keep in mind that we are merely succeeding.

Those things are pleasant to hear, but I do not honestly feel that we have made a success in this business. Do not allow any of our young men to feel that they have made a success; I do not want you ever to feel that we have succeeded. No matter what happens, keep in mind that we are merely succeeding.

Mr. Nichol said some very complimentary things about me. I would be ungrateful if I did not acknowledge with thanks the kind expressions he voiced, but I would be very unfair to myself as the chief executive of this company and to everybody in it, if I did not tell you that I have played but a very small part in the building of this business. There is only one thing that I can conscientiously take the credit for, and that is for surrounding myself with you men here and the thousands of others like you who are representing our company throughout the world. That is the only thing for which I might deserve some credit.

The remainder of the credit goes to and should be distributed proportionately among the men in the organization who have contributed in the various countries, cities and towns and in the various departments of IBM to the up-building of the business. That is the only way that any business has ever been built and the only way that it ever can be built.

Surrounding myself with you men here is the only thing for which I might deserve credit.

Mr. Jennings has been successful, too, not only in building up the company and the company's interests, but personally as well. He has saved a portion of his earnings from the beginning and invested it. His earnings and his investments have put him in a position where he can now retire and do anything he wishes to do.

It makes me very happy to know that when a man reaches the point of retiring from active service, he is in a financial position to do so without having to economize or make any change in his standard of living. That is the position Mr. Jennings is in today and we are all proud of it.

We know that you are not going to forget us because we feel that you are a real friend to every man in the organization and a man never forgets his friends.

It is the accumulation of these little things that men gather from each other that builds a successful business.

Take Full Advantage of Your Opportunities

*Opening Address in Honor of Mr. Boucas and
IBM Executives Sailing for Europe*

New York, N.Y.
June 4, 1930

I want you to feel that in working with me you are cooperating with a fellow worker rather than with a higher official of the company, because that is exactly the way I feel towards everybody in this organization. I firmly believe that an executive who cannot conscientiously feel that way about his organization can be of very little assistance to his people or to his company.

I want you to feel that you are cooperating with a fellow worker rather than a higher official.

Mr. Ford referred to the fact that I have often said I never worry about the business when I am away. That is true. Whenever I have made a trip to Europe or to any other place and have been away for any length of time, the organization has always produced more business and beaten all previous records for any corresponding period. They did it last year and four years ago when I went abroad. That to me is a source of great satisfaction.

It gives me the knowledge and assurance that everybody in the organization feels the responsibility of the business, as well as their individual responsibility.

*It is on the ability of the young men to take advantage
of opportunities that the future of this business rests.*

In Praise of Italy's Pioneers

Italian Convention

Florence, Italy
July 5, 1930

Our policy at home is that the man who is at the top of any branch or department of the business must consider himself an assistant. If he is not able to assist the men under him in carrying out the work, he is not a thorough manager.

I want you in Italy to feel that we are a part of you, because we feel you are a part of us. Do not look upon us as visitors from America. Look upon us as people who are engaged in an international business—just as much a part of you as we are a part of the people in the United States or any other country. Our policies must be shaped so that they will apply to every country in the world.

They are simple:

- Cooperate with one another.
- Give the best possible service to the users of our products.
- Continue to study and learn more about all business in general and our business in particular.
- Be loyal to your customers and yourself as well as your company.

If a man is loyal to himself, doing what his heart tells him is just, he is headed in the right direction and he will always do what is best for his assistants, his superior officers in the company and his customers.

If a man is loyal to himself he is headed in the right direction.

If we all keep in mind that international policy of helpfulness and cooperation with one another, we will come closer together and we will all be happier and accomplish better results for our country, our company, our families and ourselves.

If a man is loyal to himself, doing what his heart tells him is just; he is headed in the right direction.

51

Enthusiasm Is Man's Greatest Asset

Italian Convention

Florence, Italy
July 5, 1930

We have a motto at home that I have kept before me all my life: "We are a part of all we have met." That proverb has always meant a great deal to me. Now that I have had the opportunity of coming to your country and seeing a great deal of it, I feel that Italy has become a bigger part of me than it ever was before, and I hope that I have become to an equal extent a part of you.

We are part of all we have met.

Several things impressed me forcibly at your meeting today. The first was your enthusiasm. I have never attended a meeting where more enthusiasm was displayed, and that, gentlemen, is the greatest asset any man can have. We cannot accomplish much in life without work and enthusiasm.

That is what makes us want to work and enables us to enjoy our work. Your enthusiasm, I felt, was the outstanding spirit of today's session.

I noted, too, with great satisfaction, that our men are endeavoring to render proper service. We take people's money for the use of our machines and our duty is to see that in return the best possible service is given.

Otherwise, we are not entitled to the money.

We demand that you render proper service to our customers; you have the right to demand of us, in return, that we render proper service to you.

Those for whom we are all working are the company's 3,500 or more stockholders. The stockholders of the company have put their money into the business, entrusted it to our care, and we must guard that trust.

We are a part of all we have met.

52

Thinking Internationally

Banquet Address

Vienna, Austria
July 10, 1930

I believe that International is performing a great service to the world, in supplying machines of such benefit to business everywhere. Through the development of the family spirit within and among the different countries, we are promoting better understanding, thereby contributing toward peace and the betterment of the world.

We find that IBM people in every country are happy to cooperate with members of our organization in other countries. I am happier over that fact than I am over anything else in my entire business life. I see evidence of this friendly spirit and understanding when members of our worldwide organization come over to the United States. They are received by our people as if they were from some part of the United States. Likewise, when we of the United States visit you in the different countries, we are received as one of you.

We are all working together and as I have said many times, we do not want our people to feel that they are working for any one individual. The people for whom all of us are working are the stockholders of the company. We have more than 3,500 stockholders who have entrusted their money to us.

We carry a great responsibility toward these people who have placed their confidence in our integrity and ability to conduct this business, and I am happy to say that we have been able to give a good accounting to our stockholders on the investment they have made in The IBM.

It is our intention and purpose to do all we can to help our people make greater progress and more money. It is simply a matter of getting more people into the business. I urge every one of you here to look around in your territory and to find some young man who will represent you and work part of your territory.

Do not keep any man in your employ who does not sell, because you cannot afford to work and pay out money to him when he does not produce.

When you hire a man for the purpose of selling machines, you expect to make money as a result of his efforts. If you will follow those lines, every one of you can make a satisfactory income in The IBM.

Salesmen's Importance

The success of this business depends on what the men sell, and that is why I am interested in the salesmen.

We want to know what the people require and demand of you.

We want them to tell us the conditions in their respective territories and what the people demand.

We want to know from the men in the field what the people on whom you call require and demand of you, and we are going to endeavor to the best of our ability to meet those demands and requirements.

We carry a great responsibility toward our stockholders.

Look Beyond Today

Convention Address

Prague, Czechoslovakia
July 12, 1930

We are here today to learn what we can do to help you.

We do not want you to look upon us as your superior officers, or your managers or your directors; we want you to regard us as co-workers who have come over to find out what you need.

To the best of our ability, we shall give you the assistance you require.

We must find out from your customers what they need now, and then we must look beyond the needs of today to those of the future. Tell us what you think your country will require later on so that our engineering staff can build for the future.

We must never think that what we have today will satisfy the demand ten years from now, because the whole world is progressing and we must move along with it.

We want you to regard us as co-workers who have come over to find out what you need.

Although I am unable to understand all that you say at this meeting, I get the spirit back of your words.

It is The IBM spirit, gentlemen—the spirit that is found in every gathering of IBM people—the spirit that is generated by the merits of the machines we sell.

Confidence in the quality of its merchandise is the foundation of every successful business.

We must never think that what we have today will satisfy the demand ten years from now.

The Value of Exchanging Men and Ideas

Convention Opening Address

Stuttgart, Germany
July 22, 1930

We have always found Mr. Jennings to be very frank with us.

When he has not agreed with a policy, he has told us so.

Here is a fact, the full significance of which I want all of you to get firmly fixed in your minds and hearts: When you do not agree with the policies on which our business is conducted, we want you to talk frankly with us about it; and if, after we have explained the reasons for putting them into effect you cannot agree with us, in your own best interests you should resign.

The policies on which this business is conducted are not my policies; they have been built up from the experiences of a large number of successful people in our organization and have been carefully studied.

Not for one minute do we ever continue a policy after we have found it to be unsound and one that does not pay. Always bear that in mind.

Any of you who are selling, talk to Mr. Jones; you will find he understands the language of the salesman.

Salesmen have a language of their own as accountants and lawyers have. The salesman's language is the most important one in our business.

The salesman's language is
the most important one in our business.

The Forces That Produce Success

Convention Opening Address

Paris, France
July 28, 1930

I said "our company." Who owns our company? We executives do not: We own a little of its stock which we bought and for which some of us are still paying.

IBM is owned by more than 3,500 people—stockholders who are scattered throughout the world. Our stockholders have given us money to use in the conduct of our business. Of course, they are expecting returns on the amount invested.

But there is something else they have given us—their confidence. They have trusted our integrity and our ability to conduct this business along profitable lines.

We executives regard this trust very seriously, and whenever we are called upon to make disbursements it is not I who decides how much shall be spent and for what . . . such decisions are made

Our stockholders have given us their confidence. They have trusted in our integrity.

by a committee of five. We never spend money unless assured of proper returns. This is one of the policies of the company. We are not here in France for the purpose of laying down business policies.

All that we ask of you is that you do what we have done in the United States. We grant you that conditions here are different from those in America, but so far as that goes we have variations at home. Conditions in New England, for instance, are different from those in the Southwest.

Our success lies in developing men. We cannot build nor progress without more men in France and in other countries where The IBM does business. We must keep in mind the great amount of work that remains to be done.

Our success lies in developing men.

Our Work Is One of Service

Convention Banquet Address

Paris, France
July 29, 1930

When I visit our people in France and in other countries, I always feel just as much at home as though I were with our people in the United States. There is every reason why I should feel that way. My duties are not confined to the United States. Our business is an international one, and I strive to think internationally about it. When we shape our policies we think in world terms, whatever policies we formulate must apply throughout the seventy-seven different countries in which we are doing business.

It is more than a pleasure to be here tonight; it is a real privilege and one in which I take great pride. I have only one regret, and that is that all my family—I mean both the Watson family and the entire IBM family—are not here also. The IBM is one great family, and its spirit is developed the more we see of each other. We have representatives here from eighteen countries in addition to France.

I wish to welcome here tonight the representatives of the French Railways, Insurance and Public Service Companies and other large concerns. It is always a pleasure to have customers with us for we regard them as a part of our organization. Our work is one of service. We have no right to go to any business concern, either public or private, and ask them to pay us their money for the use of our machines unless we can render them a real service.

Look Beyond Personal Gain

I have often said that a man deserves no credit for making a living. We must render service beyond thought of personal gain. I could not be happy if I were connected with a business that did not render a service to a large number of people.

As I look over our organization and the records our men are making in seventy-seven countries of the world, I realize that we are doing something to make life easier and more pleasant for a large number of people because of the service we render our customers. I am really astonished that we are not doing more because there is so much more we can do through the medium of our organization. We should not think in terms of money but in terms of service.

When I realize the vast number of representatives we have throughout the world and the great family spirit they represent, regardless of nationality, regardless of religion or creed, it makes me feel that IBM, like other international organizations, is accomplishing a great deal toward building for the future peace of the world.

Growing Men

We cannot make a business grow without making men grow. That is the secret of every business success. People often speak to me about our successful business. I always correct them. We have not made a success, but I do feel that The IBM is succeeding. We want you also to feel that you have not succeeded. We want you to feel that you are aiming for success but that you are never going to catch up with it, for if you do, you are finished. Let us keep in mind that we are going to put forth our best effort to build a little more toward success for ourselves as individuals and in the interests of the stockholders.

You are not working for me or for any other executive. I have often said I regret that the word "manager" was ever injected into business. A man who can assist not as a manager but as an aide renders a real service. To render assistance one must be in a position to lead men; the men in the organization on their part must always pull together with the man at the top. I do not mean myself. Every individual in our French organization must follow Mr. Delcour, the leader, for he knows how to build an organization.

I have often said I regret the word "manager" was ever injected into business.

Before closing, I want to refer to an IBM motto: "A man is known by the company he keeps; a company is known by the men it keeps."

I am proud and happy to have our company known by the men it keeps. I never worry about our representatives. I know they realize their duties to their customers, to their officers, executives and associates, and that they will always carry to their customers the high ideals and dignity of The IBM.

We cannot make a business grow
without making men grow.

The Basic Rules for Successful Supervision

European Executive School

Paris, France
July 30, 1930

The chief advice I have to give you as managers is this: The first duty of every man is to keep his duties in mind.

I feel that everyone in our organization is desirous of doing his duty toward the company. Sometimes, however, men do not fully understand the responsibilities that go with their positions, and so I just want to point out five things that every manager must keep in mind and perform to the best of his ability.

Five Basic Rules

Employing Men – When you employ a man you must give great consideration to the type of man he is. The best kind to employ in our business is the young man, because it takes quite a while to train a newcomer. It rests upon the shoulders of the older men in the business, old either in years or in service, to pick out the right type of young men and to teach them.

Educating Men – The most important thing is to impress upon them their duty to render a full measure of cooperation to other men and the company. We want you always to keep in mind that we never discharge a man simply because he has violated a business policy of our company. Always be very fair. First, discuss the matter with him and explain to him the importance of adhering to the policy. We want you, likewise, to sit down with a man who violates a policy and go over matters with him.

After you have done your best and he still persists in doing wrong, the only thing for him is to get out of the business. This is fair both to him and to the company.

Supervising Men – After you have trained men you have to supervise them. Some managers put that first, believing they must supervise the young men who are just starting in the business. That is like asking a man to bring you orders before he understands the product you ask him to sell.

If you want to supervise a man, you must first teach him and bring him to the point where he can help you by means of a thorough knowledge of the business. He must always feel that you can help him. Each man will start with much more courage when he knows that you really can assist him.

If you want to be a leader, you must help those working with you to realize that they must not be afraid to come to you and discuss their questions with you. My advice to you in regard to supervision is, first, to make your men understand and believe that your desire is to assist them rather than to order them. When you have done that you have strengthened their ability and if they are ever in trouble they will come to you to talk it over.

You should always be fair with your salesmen because they are always alone in their field and meet people who have a great habit of saying, "No." Let them discuss matters with you and try to help them. Give credit where it is due. If a salesman has done something that is not right, talk the matter over with him and show him where he is wrong.

Promoting Men – Do not permit a young man to believe, however, that just because he has made a good record he should be promoted. A young man starting in our business must help you.

Discharging Men – Unfortunately this enters into every business. It is sometimes necessary to discharge a man, but never discharge one without a just cause. Always give him your reasons. Never let him feel that you let him go without good cause.

If you give enough thought and attention to the employment, to the education and to the supervision of men, you will have very little discharging to do.

Employ the right kind of men, teach them the business properly, supervise them closely, promote them when you have an opportunity and discharge them only when it is necessary.

Keep these thoughts in mind always and you will make a success.

Make your men understand and believe
that your desire is to assist them
rather than to order them.

Aspects of World Trade

American Club Address

Paris, France
July 31, 1930

We of the United States realize that our country is still a very new and a very young country. We are grateful to the European countries for the contributions they have made toward up-building the United States. We are particularly grateful to this country for her contributions.

In one respect the United States has a very great advantage over any other country, because we have had people come to us from all countries in the world, making us part of them and enabling us to build a very substantial nation in a short period of time. I always like to express my gratitude on this point when I speak in a foreign country.

We are grateful to the European countries for the contributions they have made to the United States.

Every day we hear of and look up foreign exchange. However, I have in mind another type of exchange that is very important. It is the "foreign exchange" of ideas and ideals, of methods and men, the exchange of students between our universities, the exchange of teachers and the exchange of men going back and forth between countries.

We read in the papers that conditions are bad in the United States. Conditions are not as good as they were a year ago, but they are getting better.

We have to experience little slow-ups in domestic and international business. It is a good thing that we do, because business is a great game. If you win all of the time, it soon becomes monotonous. Life would be dull if we did not have to readjust ourselves from time to time.

A certain group of people in the United States tried an experiment: They tried the experiment of making a fortune without working, of making a fortune through the stock exchange. They extended the experiment until it exploded and all went down to earth.

62

To expand world trade, it is every country's duty, every corporation's duty and every citizen's duty to put forth every effort to help build trade in the world. This should be done not only for the country, its business or its individuals, but for all countries, all businesses and all peoples. We must work together, we must all cooperate and we must do so agreeably in order to build up a proper condition in world business.

We are giving more thought every year to spending more money for education. We have 28 million pupils in our primary and secondary schools and junior and high schools and over a million students in our colleges and universities. As a matter of comparison, that is more than we find in the remainder of the world combined. We are thankful to foreign countries for their assistance and contribution in building up our educational work. Business hinges on that one thing: education.

An increased per capita consumption leads to high wages; and, of course, a high wage scale gives us buying power—buying power in the hands of the masses rather than in the hands of the classes. This is what makes trade expand. It cannot be done by keeping buying power in the classes.

Sometimes we read that a man is ridiculed because he is an idealist. We need more idealists because we must have vision. I have always found that my great handicap is not having enough vision, because every time I predict something, something better happens.

It is true of most of us.

*If you win all of the time
it soon becomes monotonous.*

We Must Do More Each Year

Convention Opening Address

London, England
September 1-2, 1930

The purpose of my talk this morning is to sell you something—not IBM products, however. I want to sell you the big idea of making this business of ours many times larger than it is today. The owners of the company—our more than 3,500 stockholders—are depending on me as head of this company to make more money for them each year.

You, as individuals, are giving us your time, which is your stock in trade, and we want to help you to make better use of your time and to earn more money for yourselves. That is the only way we can make money for the stockholders.

If every man who attends this convention starts with an open mind and determines that he is going to get something out of it, which will enable him to help every other man in this organization, then the success of this meeting is assured.

We want to be of greater assistance to you and your assistants than we have in the past. That is our real reason for coming over here—not to tell you how we are doing things in America, but to find out from you what we should do that we are not doing in order to help you and the business. We want you to feel that this is your convention, not ours. We want you to tell us honestly what you have on your minds, what you think we ought to know that will aid you and the other people, individually, in this business.

That is exactly what we want each one of you to do.

If you do not believe in our policies, we want you to tell us so. Then we shall hold a meeting to determine whether our policy or yours is right; if yours is the better, we shall immediately take steps to adopt it. I want you to follow that rule with me and with others in executive positions with whom you have contact. Only by so doing can we get together and cooperate. If we do not know what you are thinking about, we do not know where to start.

We want you to be frank with us; if you do not agree with our policies, tell us so. Our policies are not my policies. Every decision that has been issued over my signature has been gone over carefully by all of my executive staff in New York.

I would not think of arbitrarily telling people in this business that they must do thus and so. That is not the way to build a sound business structure.

A one-man policy is like an engine of only one horsepower or one cylinder; one of them does not get you very far. We often bring in our factory foremen and our factory executive staff when we consider changing a policy because those men are engaged in making our products and we, therefore, look to them for valuable information and help in the shaping of our policies.

When you give men authority it affects them differently. Some men think, "I have been given authority to tell these other men what to do." Consequently, they are not able to tell anybody what to do that will be of any value.

When a man is given a promotion his responsibility has been extended, and the first thing for him to do is to worry a little over it instead of taking a great deal of pride in his new power. His first duty is

Worry a little bit over your extended responsibility instead of taking pride in your new power.

to sit down and to think seriously about his responsibility and how he can aid his co-workers who in time to come will be doing bigger things in our business.

It does all of us good to worry a little about how we are going to take care of our jobs. Think over the responsibilities of your new position and then lay out a plan whereby you and the men under your direction will be able to accomplish results.

That is what will build an organization.

A one-man policy is like an engine of only one horsepower or one cylinder; one of them does not get you very far.

The Simplicity of Securing Orders

Convention Banquet Address

London, England
September 2, 1930

There is a group doing a very great work in promoting not only the future peace of the world but also the future prosperity and comfort of the human race. That group comprises such organizations as The IBM.

It includes other companies, the names of which I shall not mention because I might overlook some, whose aims are similar to ours and which put into operation the same business policies in every country, instill in the minds and hearts of the members of their worldwide organizations the same ideas and ideals, bring the men together and give them an opportunity to cooperate.

Cooperation Brings Personal Benefit

Every time I see or hear that word "cooperate," I wonder if I am doing enough in the way of giving The IBM people an opportunity to do so. It is a simple thing to tell men to help one another, but you have to do more than that. You have to prove to them that it is profitable to help one another. Show them where they are going to benefit personally by it. You are not going to have any cooperation unless you hold conventions and meetings of this kind. That is why I advocate conventions.

I want to tell you about a convention that made a great impression upon me. It was held by a Time Recorder man in St. Louis when we were starting the convention idea in the ITR. He had no organization but he had a meeting with himself.

If you have one man or ten men, hold conventions; sit down twice a month and hold a convention just the same as if you had five hundred. Of course you cannot send yourself a telegram, but you can send one to somebody else, asking him to help you. That one-man convention was profitable to the man concerned because of what he got out of it; we have used the idea in promoting the convention spirit throughout our organization to very good advantage.

Cooperation amongst members of a business, among businesses and among countries is a great factor in success.

To bring about this cooperation people must have the opportunity to get together. That is why I appreciate meetings of this kind; they give us the opportunity to visit with one another, advise one another and exchange ideas. I always learn something from every one of them.

Do not try to learn everything at once. A building is not completed in that manner; one brick at a time is put in place. Watch the progress being made in the construction of a building as you go to and from your work each day. See the care exercised in keeping the line straight. One brick at a time but in a short period a beautiful building is completed. That is the way an organization builds its business, the way an individual builds his education and character.

The quality of a business is judged by the quality of individuals who compose it. The way to judge the quality of the individual is to observe the little things he does, not the big ones, because no man performs an outstanding feat until he has gained experience by doing a lot of little things.

Taking Advantage of Opportunity

Remember that opportunity is of no value unless used to advantage. Someone can show you an opportunity but you yourself must make use of it, whether it is a way to make money or a way to distinguish yourself. If you do not take advantage of it, then the opportunity might just as well not have existed.

The quality of an individual is in the little things he does, not the big things.

Looking back and realizing how many opportunities I have missed, and how much more I could have accomplished if I had taken advantage of each one of them makes me want to give advice in this matter to every young man I meet, for there comes a time in every man's life, and I do not care what his position is, when he looks back and thinks, "If I had taken advantage of every opportunity presented to me I could have accomplished so much more than I have."

That is all any country or any corporation can give people—an opportunity. Giving a man an opportunity means more than giving him a position. The men higher up in the business have to do more than give a man a territory and say, "There is your opportunity."

An opportunity means, first, your territory, if you are a salesman; second, it means the help that your managers and supervisors extend to you; third, it means the policies of the company laid out on sound lines, which you are expected to follow.

So let us all, regardless of our positions in The IBM, make up our minds that from now on we will take this matter more seriously; not in the interest of the stockholders of The IBM, even though they do furnish us the money to run the business and consequently are entitled to the first consideration, but in the interest of each individual.

I am asking every man to consider himself first of all—to take advantage of the opportunities offered in this business in his own personal interest, because if every man in this room can increase his earnings next year 25 or 50 percent over this year's earnings, he will automatically take care of the stockholders' interests.

Make Use of Experience

Now a word to you older men!

Are you making proper use of your experience? Are you using the experience, which required years to gain, simply to get as many orders as you can? If you are, it is a mistake. Every man of experience in this business, if he is not already doing so, should determine now that he is going to use that experience in teaching those who work for him to produce more business. That is what we want our supervisors to do and they are planning to do it.

The individual salesman does not feel he should make a lot of demands on his supervisor, so he does the best he can with what he already knows. Instruct your men, find out what is troubling them and help them smooth out their difficulties. Show them the way to secure more business with less effort.

Every supervisor should endeavor to find out what his men are thinking. Talk with every man, not just to make conversation but with the view of working shoulder to shoulder with him and rendering all possible aid.

I worked for four years under Mr. Range, an agent for the National Cash Register Co. When I started, I was not able to sell a thing. I would call on many people during the day and come back to the office at night tired out but with no orders.

Mr. Range once said to me, "Well, young man, how are you getting along?"

I answered, "I'm not getting along at all. I cannot find anybody who wants to buy a cash register."

To that Mr. Range said, "If the people you have been calling on already knew how valuable cash registers are in running a store, we would not need you to go out and tell them. Now you and I will go out together and find someone you think is a prospect. If we fall down we will fall down together, and then I cannot complain."

That, ever since, has been my motto in the supervision of men. I am willing to go out with any man and fail with him. I try to work shoulder to shoulder with my executives. I am willing to fail with them and take my full share of the responsibility for the failure.

In our work as supervisors and directors of men we must keep that in mind. We must consider ways of helping salesmen to get more business. The majority of salesmen, you know, work on commission; their supervisors work on a salary basis and are paid for one reason only—for their ability to supervise, not for the privilege of carrying a title.

It is the same in my case.

The directors of our company do not pay me just to be its president; they take into consideration what I am doing in the way of helping the other men in the organization.

I am not paid just to be president but to help the other men in the organization.

We must all help one another.

I want each of you to feel that everyone above you is your assistant and to know that the company expects every man in an executive position to consider himself an assistant.

That is our policy of supervision.

When Benjamin Franklin was asked how he acquired such a complete knowledge of so many different subjects, he replied, "I was never ashamed to ask about anything I did not understand."

There is always someone to help us if we but ask. Sometimes we hesitate to do so because we do not want the other fellow to know of our lack of understanding, and we remain in ignorance.

Opportunity is of no value unless used to advantage.

—

Home Again

Message to The IBM Organization in
Business Machines

September 18, 1930

I am glad to be home again, following a visit with our European organization, and to express my appreciation to those who carried on the responsibility of the business here in my absence. While abroad I had an opportunity during the several sales conventions, to meet and talk with the company's representatives in nineteen different countries. The only difference I found in them was their language.

Though the many new high records that were made were intended as a tribute to me, they were, in reality, a tribute to the men who made them and to the business. I extend my sincere thanks to all members of the European organization who contributed to the success and pleasure of my visit abroad and to all members of the home organization for their efforts during my absence and their warm welcome on my return.

*We have ceased to think of The IBM
merely as a business.*

THE "B" IN IBM IS BUSINESS

The Industrial Revolution had ushered in a "machine age" that, it turns out, would never let up. Glorious machines and the means to power them were being created—automobiles, cameras and electricity. Thomas Edison exemplified the new American pioneer.

Some attributed the Depression-era unemployment to the productivity gains from machines displacing men. Some wanted to remain at a standstill; some, even worse, wanted a return to a past of manual production and manufacturing.

Watson, however, championed his belief that the Machine Age would eventually make "men dear and their products cheap." By staring intently into the future and questioning what was next, he envisioned a "Man Age," where the creativity of men would form the basis for a company's success.

Tom Watson loved pioneers and he envisioned a new type. Instead of pushing westward, these new pioneers would change the financial system, business environment, society and government for the better. FDR was a pioneer in government, and in the coming Man Age a successful corporation had to hire the right individuals, educate them, supervise them, encourage self-study and self-improvement and retain the best for a lifetime of service.

The secret of business is to develop men and expand the business as they demonstrate their ability.

This futuristic view would set in stone the foundation of The IBM: a corporation designed to attract and retain the very best employees. We have touched on this already in earlier chapters. In the coming chapters we begin to explore it in earnest.

IBM itself was a machine company. Starting as the Computing-Tabulating-Recording Company (C-T-R), it sold a vast array of devices. But, fundamentally, it came down to three critical divisions that sold tabulating machines, time recorders and computing scales. Putting together a coherent story around this menagerie of devices pertinent to a business took some salesmanship. If there were ever a primer written by Tom Watson to a Chief Executive Officer on how to establish, grow and maintain a business, this is his treatise. He believed that business is, "a vast school, parading its problems before our eyes and waiting for an answer."

Business is a vast school, parading its problems before our eyes and waiting for an answer.

The IBM's foundation in business, its stamina and endurance are captured in this one article printed in *Business Machines*—The IBM's revolutionary magazine for employees and customers. Within this article, Tom Watson outlines the philosophy and benefits of The IBM's products to the 1930s businessperson and society. He gives powerful, industry-specific examples that would serve today's salesman well to read, learn and practice. These examples culminate in the detailed analysis of the evolution from the first U.S. Census in 1790, executed without automation, to the 1900 Census when "the Bureau of the Census first was able to do what Congress had requested: complete its reports within three years."

Of course, Tom Watson, being the preeminent salesman of his time, added, "This was done without a proportionate increase in the office force."

Such a statement, in the midst of the Depression, would not have been received lightly. So he searched for a balance in his writings and speeches. He positioned this new "Age of Machinery" to be the vanguard of an improvement in employment, working conditions and pay. He offers an example of a company saved from bankruptcy, returned to profitability and handed back to its owners as a healthy concern.

Jobs were saved.

He strove within The IBM to constantly hire and educate men around these new machines. He invested in his employees. He invested in his customers.

This was his ultimate business model. "The whole secret of business seems to me to be: Keep on developing men and expanding the business, as they demonstrate their ability to fill more important positions."

Watson launched a philosophy that would endear him then as now to all IBM Caretakers—he believed in the dignity and worth of every man and woman. He believed that the coming "Man Age" would expose that truth to all businesses and he was not going to just watch it happen.

He was going to exploit it.

He gambled the future of The IBM on it—and won.

The secret of business is to develop men and expand the business as they demonstrate their ability.

The Development of Modern Office Methods

Published by the Alexander Hamilton Institute
(Reprinted in Business Machines)

July 31, 1930

A few months ago, a large manufacturing concern adopted new methods in handling its payroll. Something like 12,000 men and women are employed by this concern. Payday comes twice monthly. The department heads, the employees in the office, sales department and factory staff, are paid on a salary basis. All other employees are on a piecework basis.

Of course there isn't any more joyous event in any company than pay day. Yet in this company, for years payday had been almost a nightmare. There were so many last-minute figures to take into consideration; so much piecework; so great a percentage of variation from week to week.

It all required figuring, and that took time and cost money. There were mistakes, of course. There were complaints from men and women whose pay didn't check with their expectations. There was grief and delay and criticism. What should have been the happiest day of the month became a source of considerable worry.

So the company, after careful investigation, introduced new equipment into its payroll and accounting departments. This equipment represented a variety of new machines; each intricately designed to do a task almost human but to do it with mechanical speed and accuracy. And it worked.

This new equipment did more than save money. It brought together the necessary figures on costs and produced statistics on which the management could operate the business many days sooner in the month than previous methods had done. It ironed out causes for error and complaint. And in direct labor expense alone, this new equipment was able to show a saving of $125,000 the first year.

That's the keynote of today in selling office equipment.

Everything must pay for itself and earn a profit besides. There are some things machinery can do better than men, but the machine must demonstrate an increase in efficiency and a saving as well. Only by demonstrating their superiority to rule-of-thumb methods can business machines win their way.

Sometimes a demonstration of this kind verges on the dramatic.

There was a company, for example, which had fallen into the hands of a creditors' committee. The outlook was discouraging. No one was quite certain how a profit could be dug out of that uncertainty. Yet profits should be there.

The answer came at the introduction of new office machinery that put the whole office-end of the business on an efficient basis. Leaks were detected, profitable products were noted, salesmen were graded according to profit rather than mere size of orders or length of expense account and sales programs were outlined on a basis of definite fact rather than guesswork.

As a result of this analysis, the company was converted into a profitable and growing concern. It was saved from bankruptcy and was handed back to its owners a healthy, even rejuvenated, concern.

Spending Money for Overhead Often Produces New Profits

Some businessmen of the old school will tell you that profits are made in the field by the sales force; and that an office exists merely to perform some dull clerical work. That's the old idea of an office, just a tail-end feature of the sales department, for which indifferent help was good enough.

You'll find some businesses today where low-grade help runs the office and where action is actually slowed down because the office force never is encouraged to use its initiative. But businessmen today realize that supervisory expense is a definite economy. Money spent for management is as much an investment as money spent for equipment. Whatever tools management needs to keep itself posted are a practical and sensible expenditure and should be so regarded.

Money spent for management is as much an investment as money spent for equipment.

For example, another company, which had not been doing any too well, modernized its methods. Previously it had very little in the way of cost figures and facts. But by means of equipment which analyzed the business, it was able to reduce scrap losses $40,000 the first year.

A large steel company similarly created a new profit through new office equipment. Direct savings of $15,000 a year were recorded. In addition, the company's financial statements were completed by the fifth of the month instead of the fifteenth.

In still another company, a change in office machinery made it possible to derive a statement by departments covering the previous day's work and have it posted in the shop every morning by eight o'clock. Thus the company was furnished up-to-the-minute data and each worker was given a report on yesterday's production to encourage him to do better work today.

Offices Are Just Catching Up

Offices are slow in adopting labor-saving machinery as compared with factories.

You might think that offices would be first to adopt labor-saving machinery. But a survey shows that offices are slow in this respect as compared with factories. The reason is that factories had to adopt labor-saving equipment to stay in business. Any efficient factory today knows the cost of each operation. Each step is constantly being studied to find a shorter and cheaper way of doing that operation.

But in offices, the cost of the whole job is just averaged up. You can't say definitely what any one step costs, because each man's work dovetails into that of the next. Everything is generalized and bulked. And since an office is not trying to produce anything at a profit with competition constantly bearing prices down, the introduction of labor-saving equipment into offices has been slower than efficiency has sometimes suggested.

So was invented the first electric tabulating machine. It was a crude affair, as we view it today, but its basic ideas, although new, were fundamentally sound. Facts and figures were recorded on punched cards, each punch-hole through its position indicating some fact or figure in conformity with a predetermined code. Electric currents, contacting through these perforations, flashed an instantaneous message to the counting apparatus as each card came into position.

Thus any classification could be recorded and counted at will. Any information punched on the cards could be assembled, collected and analyzed quickly and accurately with a minimum of human aid.

As might be expected, however, office methods are getting in step with the most modern ideas of factory work. Machinery has been perfected to supplement the work of human hands and human brains. In addition to the typewriter, the adding machine, the filing cabinet and other accessories of modern business, we now have machines doing tasks that, in many cases, were not possible before. The mechanization of American business is a fascinating subject to write about.

Most interesting of all of the stories of modern business, I believe, is that concerned with the development of the electric tabulating machine.

The Need Created an Invention

In 1880, a quiet, studious engineer, Dr. Herman Hollerith, was employed as a special agent in the United States Census Office. By reason of his technical training and his interest in machinery, he was placed in charge of the compilation of statistics of steam power used in manufacturing.

Census data was written on large cards. To compile the necessary information the cards had to be sorted under one classification, counted, and then sorted again and again under other headings. The work was tedious, cumbersome and costly, for there were millions of cards. There was every chance of error, with few possible checks for accuracy.

The fact that this was the way a census always had been taken did not prevent a few thoughtful individuals from seeking a better and less tiresome method. Dr. John S. Billings of the United States Army and Dr. Hollerith talked things over. They agreed that some mechanical device to do the counting and sorting would be a wonderful advantage. Dr. Billings was in charge of vital statistics. Dr. Hollerith, who was an inventor, took the idea and put it to work. A government commission recommended the adoption of this machine, and its use brought to light the need for further refinements, as is always the case.

In those days every sale was an experiment, every new use was a departure from industry practice.

Then came a wider application of the idea. It seemed a pity to have a machine able to do an almost human task and then use it only once in ten years. If the tabulating machine could solve the problems of census tabulation, were there not problems in business that could similarly be analyzed and handled? The answer seemed indubitably to be, "Yes."

New uses began to be discovered; new customers won. Along with this came the problems of building these machines so they would be economical and durable, so that any person of average skill could operate them and so that they could be put to work in various places without requiring constant factory supervision.

These developments brought our infant company into contact with the problems of cost accounting. This field was later to prove a fertile one for a device capable of such analytical work as the electric tabulating machine had demonstrated.

New Uses Found

In those days every sale was an experiment; every new use was a departure from what had hitherto been the practice in that industry. Progress was slow, as is always the case with a pioneer idea. But as fast as one company after another demonstrated that the tabulating machine was a success, it became possible to apply the same use throughout a whole industry.

For example, insurance companies found that tabulating machine equipment could be used for analyzing their risks under various classifications. Railroads used it to classify freight accounts. Sales managers were interested to know what their sales problems were; how many prospects in a given classification they could count on; what types of merchandise were their best sellers and what lines were the most profitable.

With growing demand came marked developments. At first the cards were placed in position by hand, one by one, and a registration obtained by pulling a lever down. Improvements were made so the machines were able to handle a steady flow of cards, swiftly and accurately. Automatic sorting machines were devised.

Today's electric tabulating and accounting machines, however, represent dozens of sub-patents and are almost uncanny in their speed and accuracy.

Analyzing Needs Overcome Prejudices

Most people are familiar with the time clock. At first glance one might say that the recording of time would be a benefit purely to management, since it enables those who pay wages to check the time of employees and more closely figure costs. Yet experience shows that the time clock idea is of value to the employee as well as to the firm.

It prints an accurate and unchangeable record of the time each man puts in on his job. It ensures punctuality. It assures fair handling, and removes any chance for clerical error. It is honest, impartial and fair.

EMPLOYER   EMPLOYEE

The whole tone of the job is raised and work becomes more self-respecting.

In its early years the idea of a time clock was resented. Yet it is only fair to say that devices of this kind have removed the necessity for espionage in industry. When you can put men to work and let them record their own time, on and off each job, the whole tone of the job is raised and work becomes more self-respecting.

Thus machinery has promoted a better spirit in business. There is less spying, less arguing about how much work each one did and more regularity in attendance because every minute counts and is automatically counted. A man knows he gets credit for what he does. Any prejudice has long since been lived down.

Working closely with our customers, we found a need for other devices connected with time.

Instead of letting each department have its own clocks, all pointing at random, factories and institutions now have a dozen or a hundred clocks synchronized from one master clock. Stores have time-recording clocks to let headquarters know that the store was opened on time. Hotels and other businesses have time stamps to note the hour and minute that mail is received.

As new needs have brought new challenges to our inventive genius, the field has been broadened and growing confidence has made it possible for customers to find new uses for this type of equipment.

Modern Retailing Represents New Developments

One phase of our business throws us directly into the field of the retailer. There too we find the effect of new ideas. The scale is the office of the small retail store.

Just as a factory or office sells the time and labor of its workers at a profit, so also a store must know the exact price of what it is selling. So scales have been developed to do all the figuring for the proprietor. This speeds up the service, since a machine-made answer is quicker than multiplying with paper and pencil. It creates a greater friendliness between customer and clerk because prices are less subject to human error.

In an inconspicuous way, the systematizing of the retail store has played as large a part in the development of today's business as the systematizing of the office. Without more accurate weighing devices, a storekeeper could not exist on the margins of profit obtainable today. He needs a better system to ensure his success.

We have a deep realization of the part these various recording, measuring and analyzing devices that we market have played in the growth of modern business. Our own company only recently was a small concern. It has grown as it has been able to ascertain a new need and supply a new answer.

The retailer needs better systems to insure his success.

In our sales work we have helped many a small customer organize his affairs in such shape that profits were certain. It has been a pleasure to watch small companies grow.

How Our Company Developed

A successful company needs a marketable product; policies that are adjusted to changing conditions; new ideas as they can be utilized to advantage and a growing body of efficiently trained men.

Perhaps the last factor—manpower—is first in importance.

When I joined this company sixteen years ago, our three divisions were not disorganized; they were unorganized. There were plenty of ideas lying around, but many of them seemed too big for the organization to handle. The directors told me, "You'll have to go out and hire outside brains before you can build up this company." I told them, "That's not my policy. I like to develop men from the ranks and promote them."

All of our major executives today were once minor employees. All of our department heads have been promoted from the ranks. Our salesmen are always started in at the bottom and brought up to where they can compete with the rest of our sales organization for the best positions.

The whole secret of business seems to me to be to keep on developing men and expanding the business as they demonstrate their ability to fill more important positions.

The secret of business is to develop men and expand the business as they demonstrate their ability.

Studying the Needs of Business

Early in our work we learned that business is a vast school, parading its problems before our eyes and waiting for an answer. You have but to glance through any trade paper or business magazine to find problems that executives are facing. How can we reduce our selling cost? How can we eliminate this waste? How can we maintain uniform efficiency and quality? All businesses are asking these questions.

The man who would supply the answer must school himself in the routine of that industry or trade. He must learn the language of that type of business; learn its specific problems.

Take, for example, a fire insurance company. The actuaries must be able to visualize instantly any city and get a picture of its risks. Huge books, giving in colors a chart of the streets and houses, are kept miraculously up to date with daily changes. The whole business is one of analyzing, arranging and classifying. The records of each policy are placed in punched cards, ready for instant tabulation. Thus the company knows how many garages its policies cover in Baltimore; how much insurance it has written on houses in Duluth.

If any risk becomes greater than experience shows to be safe, the office reinsures part of it with another company. This is being done all the time.

When any new type of danger appears—such as the explosion of x-ray films in a hospital—the company can learn instantly how many hospitals are insured with it and what the total risk is. From this it can decide what to do next; whether to raise its rates, require more careful inspection, or what. The data is all there.

When you learn how an office is run and what its problems are, you begin to see how to fit your message to the ears of those who must understand it if the sale is to be made. For this reason we maintain a complete business library. Here we keep constantly immersed in the problems of the many industries our salesmen serve.

Business today is so interrelated that what helps one often helps others. If we find the answer to other people's problems, we also find something we ourselves can benefit from knowing. This, of course, is the essence of salesmanship.

The Day of Higher Pressure Selling is Gone

Sales today, of anything other than day-to-day supplies, are seldom made merely because the seller wishes to make a sale. Mr. Public may buy a low-priced magazine at the door because the magazine is thrust at him; in a case like that it is almost easier to say, "yes" than "no," and the amount is inconsequential anyway. But on more permanent merchandise, the buyer seldom buys on impulse. He waits to be shown a definite advantage to him in making this purchase. He buys only what promises to earn him a genuine profit.

The essence of salesmanship is finding an answer to other people's problems.

More and more we find that office equipment such as we manufacture is sold on the basis of research. He buys only what promises to earn him a genuine profit.

We say to a businessman, "Wouldn't you like to know the profit your salesman, in Phoenix, Arizona is making—and know it while the information is still news?" Then if he is interested, we show a way of deriving that data for him.

Often we say to an executive, "Let us make an analysis of your office methods. Perhaps we won't find a thing worth changing; in that case you'll have the satisfaction of knowing that your system can't be improved upon. We will make no recommendations unless we find a definite use for new equipment, for it would be of no advantage to us to supply you with equipment unless it can be used at a profit."

Businessmen find it hard to resist an appeal like that.

It places the brunt of the argument on us. Instead of our employing strategy and eloquence, we prove our case with facts; and what's more, with facts concerned directly with his business.

So sales are made on the basis of a survey, followed by an analysis, backed up by recommendations. Obviously, the man who can secure business in this way must have a clear understanding of business fundamentals.

Planning for the Future

Today, 90% of our business is on machines devised or improved in our own company during the past sixteen years. New devices have been added. New uses have been found for present equipment. New ideas have been embodied to keep our merchandise ahead of any present or future competition.

Sixteen years ago we appropriated not a cent for experiment and research.

Sixteen years ago we appropriated not a cent for experiment and research. Today our Research Department is constantly taking machines apart, studying to perfect them and testing out new ideas, as well as inventing new machines. We are constantly striving to make our company more useful to the firms that rely on us for business aids.

This policy represents both a responsibility and an opportunity for our entire organization. Men in the factory and sales organizations and on the accounting staffs are all urged to make suggestions that will improve our product and our service.

Research, we tell our men, is not merely a matter of searching for something. We must find something! A man can go around searching for the rest of his life, but everything depends on what he finds and then on what he does with it.

We must find more things as a result of our searching, and then put those things to use.

Along with the bringing in of new ideas, we must constantly make better machines at a lower cost. To do so we must buy to better advantage; sell on a closer margin; get new customers and think of future possibilities. The demand from the American consumer is constantly for something newer, something better.

Always we hold before our men and ourselves that we, as a company, are succeeding, but we haven't yet made a success. Any time you feel you have arrived and have accomplished what you set out after, that moment you begin to travel downhill.

The Place of Study in Industry

Anybody in business today who thinks he can get along without study is going backward. There is no saturation point in education. This fact cannot be too strongly emphasized, especially in its application to business. We of The International Business Machines Corporation are studying all the time.

We of The International Business Machines Corporation are studying all the time.

Some are studying languages to fit them for export and foreign duty. Some are studying engineering and salesmanship. We have schools, not only for salesmen and factory employees, but also for our office people. Then we have one of the best schools in the country just for executives. Every man in the class is a teacher. Each one knows something the others don't know, and each helps all the others.

Take the purchasing agent, for example. His work is not merely buying lead pencils and raw materials. His buying schedule must coincide with the requirements of the factory. If any season of the year represents a peak load of sales, buying must prepare in advance for this. If any item faces a rise in price due to shortages, wars or other disturbances, he must safeguard his requirements by placing advance contracts. Today's purchasing agent should be a student of economics.

The office manager—the factory superintendent—the treasurer of the company—the man who places our insurance—the man who selects new employees each has a viewpoint and a fund of information from which the rest of us can benefit. They make up our Executives' School.

In addition to this company schooling, many of our men are going to night schools; many are taking correspondence school courses.

In any job there are two things to learn: first, the routine methods to be gone through; and second, the reason for it all. Many men fail because they never learn the mechanics of their work properly. But a greater proportion fail because they never truly find out what their jobs are all about, and how their day's work ties in with the big plan of what their company is trying to do.

There is so much to learn that we find it well to keep employee and official both going to school. This promotes a harmony of interest through our organization and equips us anew to carry our message of efficiency to the businesses whose interests we serve.

American Office Methods Lead the World

It has been said that the typewriter introduced women into business. No one knows how many positions have been created because of business machines and better accounting methods.

The neighborhood shop today can set up and maintain a better accounting system than a big business concern could have had two generations ago. Every firm, large or small, can now have an efficient bookkeeping system with machines to do the routine work of listing and adding and a few better-paid men and women doing the brain-work that only humans can do. This is so much an everyday part of our lives that we cease to wonder at it. Yet when we speak of the efficiency of modern business we pay silent tribute to the usefulness of office machinery.

It is interesting to take a single striking example of the change that has come about within the past fifty years. We can select one of the greatest business offices in the world—a portion of the United States Government at Washington.

The Application of Machinery in U. S. Census

The most spectacular instance of the value of office machinery to supplement human hands and brains comes, of course, in the United States Census.

The first Census was taken in 1790. Life in those days was beautifully simple. Women were either housewives or spinsters; not stenographers, salesladies, filing clerks, telephone girls, advertising writers or owners of their own businesses. Jobs for men were chiefly those of the tradesman, the farmer and the merchant; there were not the myriad kinds of brokers, salesmen, manufacturers' agents, magazine editors, garage repairmen and other occupations that we have today.

And yet, in spite of the comparative simplicity of the facts from which that 1790 Census was compiled, seven years were needed to separate, add and classify the figures. This pioneer task of tabulation filled a volume of fifty-six pages.

By 1830, forty years later, city life had not yet become complex, but the country was growing. There were more people to count and more classifications to figure. This time the work of analyzing the returns was not left to the field force, as in 1790, but was turned over to an office staff of forty-three people. Their calculations required six full years and resulted in a volume of 214 pages.

Jumping ahead to 1880, we find the ten-year Census had grown to 21,458 printed pages, requiring the work of 1,495 office workers. This was the Census which Dr. Hollerith helped work on. It was the last time that hand tabulating was done on this tremendous job. For in 1889, a government estimate, printed in booklet form, showed that if the new Hollerith electric equipment were installed to do the mechanical counting, a saving of over $500,000 would result on each Census; and this in spite of the fact that government workers in those days were paid only $15 a week—$2.50 a day.

The 1890 Census then was a much more comprehensive analysis of population figures and industries than had ever been obtainable before. The data swelled to 26,408 pages, with an office force of 3,143 persons.

In 1900, the Bureau of the Census first was able to do what Congress had requested: complete its reports within three years. This was done without a proportionate increase in the office force. 3,447 people did the work. Because of a keener analyzing ability brought about by the machines, permitting a more compact survey, the tables were reduced from over 26,000 pages to 10,925 pages for the 1900 Census.

The 1930 Census will be much more complete than any of the others, giving a summary of home owners, of proprietors of business, of owners of radio sets, of proprietors of businesses and employees, as well as the total of single, married, divorced and widowed persons of each sex. This data will be obtained without an increased office force because of the improved efficiency of the machinery doing its part of the work.

Not Fewer People – More Facts

Thus the task of collecting, reviewing and analyzing more than 120 million cards and totaling their information under thirty or more classifications is done with dependable accuracy.

It is estimated that the use of office machinery in the Census Department reduces the tabulating time 60% and the office cost 50%, as compared with the old pen-and-ink days. This type of saving is of interest to every business, for everywhere the demon of overhead expense is an enemy to fight. Yet the achievement of office machinery is not entirely in cash savings; there is also a benefit of new clearness of information, a new thoroughness and a new accuracy.

Because of the clairvoyant ability of a machine to interpret facts punched on cards, sales managers weigh one territory against another on a basis of concrete information. It is possible to grade salesmen impartially and fairly. The control of a business becomes a matter of reading charts and reports that give the business picture up to a few days before.

All of this is a development that has come with the use of labor-saving machinery in offices. So for the most part we do not regard office machinery as putting people out of work; rather, it supplements human eyes and amplifies their usefulness. The same office force that formerly worked without modern machinery can, with machinery of the right type, produce a quantity of new facts that formerly were so buried as to be unattainable except at a prohibitive expense. The fact that machines are able to do this extra work at a cost so low as to pay for themselves is an added feature which ensures their welcome.

Can We Make Business Depression Proof?

As business gains an understanding of the fundamental laws of economics, there is hope that we can look ahead and make business more and more depression-proof. Instead of relying on guesswork, management today gets figures that tell their own story.

We have not yet attained perfection, but it is safe to say that much of the danger of old-time panics has been removed. Business grows steadier with each generation. Today businessmen have a better idea of where they stand than ever before in history. As a result of this new analytical attitude, factories budget their production over a twelve-month period with a uniform output each month instead of the old-time peaks and valleys.

The recent business depression would have been more serious than it was had not business generally been following a permanent policy of low inventories and frequent buying. As it was, few firms were forced to meet heavy inventory losses. And any improvement in demand is promptly reflected back to the source of supply.

The heightened efficiency of the railroads has helped to bring about this policy of frequent buying. This is not only a benefit to industry but also helps the railroads by maintaining a more even demand for transportation.

Looking toward the future, we hope that superior management will make unbroken prosperity the normal course of business. With supervisory equipment of the highest type at its disposal, management is growing daily more far-sighted and accurate.

There is hope that future downward swings will be short-term recessions without widespread suffering and that business will grow more capable and eventually depression-proof. That will be the supreme achievement to credit to the score of modern American office methods.

Business is a vast school, parading its problems before our eyes and waiting for an answer.

THE "M" IN IBM IS MACHINES AND MEN

The International Business Machines Corporation was based on leading-edge products that raised the wages of workers, profits of corporations and efficiency of back offices. The IBM provided machines of speed, accuracy and economy. This was the image projected to the outside world for customers, press and consultants.

Although new products positioned The IBM for the growing productivity of a new machine age, Tom Watson knew that this was only half the equation needed to equal success. More critical was manpower. To him the "M" in IBM could have easily stood for "Men." He believed the people of The IBM were its revenue-generating engines. People drove the company forward, inspired it, maintained it and kept it growing.

All the machines in the world will not bring success unless manned by the right kind of men.

Success, therefore, equaled machinery plus men—men infused with enthusiasm. Unbounded enthusiasm powered them. The mission of his executive team was to unleash that enthusiasm.

Manpower as the other half of the equation—educated, trained and dedicated salesmen, factory workers, researchers, sales managers, factory foremen, executives and president—would staff every level of The IBM. His organization, The IBM, was going to lead business into the coming "Man Age."

In "We Are Going to Greater Heights," Watson stresses that The IBM is judged by its representatives. He and his executive team could not be in front of every customer, but he had eliminated that need; he had men of character representing him and they were bound together by a common goal to achieve greater heights. Those greater heights could only be achieved by a sales force standing in front of the customer with character. He trusted in his sales force to accept and carry this responsibility.

In "IBM Filled with Opportunities," he expounds that The IBM is full of opportunities for his men, both young and old. Watson wanted to retain each man's knowledge, experience and wisdom within "The IBM." He spoke to their future career opportunities. He spelled out exactly what was expected from his older men to achieve an executive position—it was not about products and processes but preparing and promoting people.

In "Quota Men Contribute to IBM Success," Watson shares with "all due respect and feeling" for the others in the audience that it was the One Hundred Percenters in the sales organization enabling The IBM to build a business and set new records. As always, he shows sensitivity and concern to even the salesmen at the back of the room who didn't make their quota numbers that year. He says he sees in each of them the kind of "knowledge and heart" that will put them in the front row the following year—no one could sway him in his belief that every man in The IBM was "One Hundred Percent Club" material. He told his salesmen to:

- Expect "no"—no just starts the selling process.
- Believe that in The IBM there are no rocking chair positions.
- Seek to contribute to company, community and country.
- Hang tight to good thoughts.
- Become executive material by listening and learning.
- Act out of self-initiative with unrestrained enthusiasm bounded by self-supervision.
- See The IBM as a real family proposition.
- Seek out a supervisor if you are a "round peg in a square hole."

This section closes out with "You Have Only Begun to Learn." Standing before those he loves the most in this IBM family—a room full of eager sales school graduates—he projects his heart, saying these men are The IBM's greatest assets. They should be people of good character, take pride in their work, be enthusiastic, have a strong relationship with their supervisors and always look to a future within The IBM.

The impression you make on a prospect
is the impression he receives of the company.

We Are Going on to Greater Heights

Sales Convention Banquet Address

Chicago, Illinois
February 1931

We are proud of everything connected with The IBM. I am more interested in the way you represent our company than in anything else you do, because the company is judged by its representatives.

You cannot take the company, the officers and the executive staff with you as you call on your prospects. The impression you make on a prospect is the impression he receives of the Company. I know that the reputation, the character, the high standing and the integrity of our company are in good hands.

I know that the reputation, character, high standing and integrity of our company are in good hands.

You members of our sales organization deserve much credit for helping to keep the pay envelopes of our factory people full during the past year when we were able to employ more instead of fewer men. That was due to the efforts of our sales organization, and we thank you for it. All the people in the factories, needless to say, appreciate it.

We have had depressions before and we have come out of them. What has happened afterward in every case? We have always gone to greater heights, because during the depression people think harder and straighter. They devise new methods, new products and new inventions. The result is greater heights. That has been the case following every depression this country has had.

I wish for every one of you greater success during this year than you have ever had in any previous year of your life.

I am more interested in the way you represent our company than in anything else you do.

IBM Filled With Opportunities

1930 One Hundred Percent Club

January 26-30, 1931

We talk much of young men coming into the business. Sometimes the older men may get the impression that we are going to fill this organization with young men and crowd them out. If you stop to consider for a moment, you will realize how we appreciate the men of long-term service.

You older men will realize that these young men are brought into the business to help make bigger men of you. When we discuss promoting a man from the field to an executive position, among the first things we take into consideration are:

- His attitude toward bringing young men into the business
- His treatment of those young men
- His teaching
- His supervision of them

The man in this business who can demonstrate his ability and desire to bring young men into our organization, to train them and to supervise them properly, is building for himself an important executive position in this company.

I wish to say a few words to the young men who are just entering this business. You come to this convention and you listen to the various people who have been in the company many years. You may get the idea that IBM is a big organization in which it may be a long time before you will get your opportunity. If you observe the various executives, you will find many young men occupying high positions. They have come into this business with the decision to do their best and to remain in IBM. That kind of young man can gain promotion rapidly in this organization because we have great need for more executives every year, not only here but in other parts of the world.

I give that word of encouragement to every young man. You have a great opportunity, a greater opportunity than I see in any other organization.

**Young men are brought into the business
to make bigger men of us all.**

92

Quota Men Contribute to IBM Success

Opening Address
1930 One Hundred Percent Club

New York, N.Y.
January 26, 1931

I thank every Hundred Percenter here, not only personally, but on behalf of all the officers and directors, especially on behalf of each and every stockholder of The IBM.

It is, after all, the stockholders who count most with us; they are more important than the officers or the directors or the Hundred Percenters or all of us combined, because they have furnished us the money with which to carry on this industry.

We have today more than 4,000 stockholders in our company. A matter came to my attention just a few months ago which made me realize more keenly than

Most of our stockholders are small stockholders. That is our great responsibility.

ever before the great responsibility which rests upon the Hundred Percenters, the officers and directors of The IBM; and that, gentlemen, is the fact that more women than men are stockholders in our business.

This would indicate that our stock is looked upon as a safe and profitable investment. I think there are very few companies that can show more women than men on their stockholders' lists. I mention that as I consider the circumstances an added responsibility. Most of our stockholders are small stockholders, as you can judge by the fact that we have more than 4,000.

So that is our great responsibility.

Mr. Nichol referred to my contributions to the company. I regret that I am not able to contribute much more toward the building of this business. I perform my duties in New York to the best of my ability. I can say that also about every other official of the company.

Without you Hundred Percenters, however, out on the firing line, sending orders in to keep the factory wheels turning—orders on which we can make a profit and, in turn, pay dividends to our stockholders—where would we be? Where would I be? Where would all the other officers of the Company be?

We would not be here.

It does not make any difference how much ability I or the other officers of this Company may have or how much we might be able to increase our efficiency; we could not build this business, we could not produce the records, without the Hundred Percenters.

I say that with all due respect and feeling for all other members of the organization. Every Hundred Percenter is above the average in the organization. Every non-Hundred Percenter in The IBM throughout the world is below the average. As I came on this platform my eyes rested first on the Hundred Percenters with the highest records who sit down in front, then they came to the Hundred Percenters with the lowest records—above one hundred percent—who sit in the next rows; and then I looked to the rear of the room where the non-members are seated.

I want to say to you, in all sincerity, that it is impossible for me or any other man to come on this platform and draw any line of distinction between you so far as appearance is concerned. As I looked around, I realized that we have in this room men who possess the kind of knowledge and the sort of hearts that will make them determine this morning to come back to the next convention a year from now wearing red badges of membership.

I have commented upon records because they are the only things by which we can judge; we have to judge men in every walk of life by the results they achieve. There is no one in this room who can convince me that all of the men in this business are not Hundred Percent Club material.

I realize that some men have sound reasons for not being in the One Hundred Percent Club this year. Some have been handicapped by illness, either personally or in their family. Some perhaps, have met handicaps in their territories that they could not overcome, but on the whole, gentlemen, the reason why more men are not Hundred Percenters is that they did not apply their knowledge and abilities in the same way that the Hundred Percenters did.

I know that every Hundred Percenter in this room is not only willing but anxious to help all other members of the selling organization to become members of the Club. As you Hundred Percenters come in contact with other men in the field, point out to them the many advantages of membership. Explain to them how such membership entails not only great honor for them but also more money, which is important to their wives and their families.

Let us start off this morning with the determination to exert all our efforts to assist more men to become members of the One Hundred Percent Club.

In erecting the standards and frames which carry the names and records of the Hundred Percenters along with a group of IBM mottoes, you will note that the men who arranged this convention allowed for several more rows of cards.

That is why they made the standards so high.

When you come back here next year, instead of two rows of cards, you will see four rows around this room—which means doubling the number of Hundred Percenters.

Every Hundred Percenter
is above the average in the organization.

Walk and Talk

Scale Division
1930 One Hundred Percent Club

January 26–30, 1931

I wish to say something to you regarding long-term service in this business. Every one of you older men can double your incomes this year if you will get young men to go out and work for you. It is essential, however, to see that they work; do not allow them to waste time while you do all the work yourselves.

If they were all ready to buy our products, there would be no necessity for salesmen.

You can find out in one week whether or not a young man is capable of making good as a salesman of Dayton products. It does not require genius to find the people who need these machines. Walking and talking are all that is necessary. These are the two things we must do. Most of us can talk but some are a little shy on the walking. Whether you use a motorcar or your feet, the main thing is to cover ground and keep moving from the time you start out in the morning.

There are a great many new men here. My advice to them when they go out is to expect their prospects to say, "No." People would simply telephone to the office and tell us to send them a machine.

Fortunately, real business is not done that way. Those which do get their orders without effort inspire no interest and certainly provide no futures for those whom they employ.

Walking and talking are all that is necessary.

How to Increase Your Earning Capacity

Time Recorder Division
1930 One Hundred Percent Club

January 26–30, 1931

We have no rocking chair positions in our sales organization. I have been selling goods—or trying to help other people sell them—all my life, but I have never yet found any other way of doing it except by getting out into the field and talking to the people who could use the product.

Spending actual time in the presence of prospects talking about your products and trying to get orders is the only way you will ever get anywhere. It is not enough just to get to the office early in the morning. It is what you do after you get there that counts. The man who takes time to read the paper, visit with everyone in the office and dally around with nonessential things is not going to get ahead.

The only time that counts, in dollars and cents for you, is the time that you spend in the presence of a prospect, talking. You salesmen must watch your non-productive time, and under that heading put all the time of your working day that you are not actually talking to someone about buying your equipment.

When you go back to your offices from this convention, start the time clock system on yourselves. It is not necessary to report to anyone but yourself. At the end of each week, figure out how many hours you have spent trying to sell Time Recorders. You will be amazed at the small amount of time you will have to your credit.

Spend time in the presence of your prospects talking about products and taking orders.

With that knowledge before you, start out the next week and try to increase that number of hours. Just as soon as you increase the number of hours you spend in the presence of prospects, just so soon will you increase your earnings.

The only time that counts in dollars and cents
is time in the presence of prospects.

The Importance of Outside Activities

General Session
1930 Hundred Percent Club

January 27, 1931

I am particularly proud of all of our men who do something worthwhile outside our business. I was especially pleased and proud three years ago when the directors of a trust company in Binghamton invited Mr. Venner to be president of that bank. They were so anxious for him to accept that they arranged for an assistant to do all the work so that it would not interfere with his work in The IBM. They said, "We want your name as president of that bank because it means so much in this community."

That is real service. That is service even to your own company. He has been interested in the educational program of Binghamton. He has been interested in the spiritual life of that city and in everything else in which a good citizen should be interested.

I mention the fact, gentlemen, because it brings out the point that we all owe a duty to the community in which we live, to society at large. It is a fine thing for a person to participate in things worthwhile outside his business so long as they do not interfere with his work for his company. I find wherever I go, not only in this country, but throughout the world, that some of our people are recognized as men who can be counted upon to do big things in their communities.

I want all of you to resolve to stand for something big and fine outside of your business life. That is the way to grow; that is the way to develop; that is the way to become real leaders in the company, in the community and in the state.

Resolve to stand for something big and fine outside of your business life.

98

Our Outlook Is Based on Sound Judgment

Convention Banquet Toastmaster
1930 Hundred Percent Club

January 29, 1931

I now come to my hardest task in the convention—that of bringing it to a close. I always regret the closing of our conventions. I get so much real pleasure, so much information from them, that I lose sight of the fact sometimes that we must draw to a close.

We are going from this convention and we are going to hold tight to the good things that we have learned here. We are going to hold on to the good, sound thoughts that have been presented as to why we ought to go forward. We are enthusiastic in this business, we are optimistic; but our enthusiasm and our optimism are based on good, sound business judgment, and we never shout about our opti-

Hold on to the good, sound thoughts as to why we ought to go forward.

mism nor our enthusiasm until after we have made a very close canvass of the whole situation, because we do not like to make predictions that will not be fulfilled.

And while I am not boasting about your records, gentlemen, you have never yet fallen down on anything you have told us you are going to do.

You have told us this week that you are going to produce more business in 1931 than you did in 1930.

I know you are going to do it.

How We Can Learn from Each Other

Eastern Sales Convention Address

Endicott, N.Y.
February 19–21, 1931

We who find ourselves in executive positions in The IBM can perhaps remember sometime in the past when we felt that we knew a great deal about the business but we found that we can always learn something through contact with the men in the field. We fully appreciate that the only way in which we can add to our knowledge and be of assistance to other men in the business is to come in contact with the men from the field as often as possible.

IBM SALESMAN | **IBM EXECUTIVE**

We improve the business by getting honest criticisms and constructive suggestions.

We have long since learned that there is a great deal of knowledge to be gained from the men who have just started in the business. We welcome the ideas of the young men who are new in this business because we are always seeking new viewpoints.

We want everyone in this meeting, whether he is a manager, a sales agent, a salesman or a student, to feel that this is his convention. We expect all of you to feel it your privilege to tell us what is on your minds.

It is impossible for any company to devise a policy for running the business or a curriculum for the conduct of its training schools that is perfect in the beginning. We must gradually but constantly improve in all these things. The only way that we can improve is by getting your honest criticisms and constructive suggestions and then building our policies around them.

There is one good reason why it is going to be better than any other—that is that you are going to hear less from those on the platform and more from those who are actually active in the field. Every man out in the field, at some time or another during the year, meets with something that to him is difficult. More often than not, the difficulty is imaginary and disappears as soon as he looks at it with a different perspective.

That is why we are here today to talk over all the little things that may have been bothering us. You can tell us the things that you feel handicap you. Perhaps some man thinks his territory is too small. Perhaps another feels that his territory is too large or that he has not had enough assistance. Whatever it is, tell us all about it and we will do everything we can to correct the situation.

Our time this week is to be devoted not to telling you what to do, but to listening and learning from you the things you want us to do that we have not been doing.

I am speaking for the entire executive staff. We are very earnest about this. We want to do more, and we will when you have told us what you want us to do.

When you talk you teach. When you listen you learn.

Double Manpower to Double Business

Time Recorder (ITR) Sales Convention

Endicott, N.Y.
February 19–21, 1931

In building up your sales force, keep only the men who show an interest in the work and an ability to produce. Use careful judgment when you employ a young man. Get him started the right way, supervise him properly and you will get excellent results. Try to see him every day. Make him report to you at a certain time every morning and tell you what he did the day before. Have him show you a list of the people he called on and tell you how he handled each call. That is all you need to do.

The best of men will not be valuable to you unless you supervise them.

If you will spend a little time every morning with a new man, you will be able to determine inside of one week whether or not he is capable of being an ITR salesman. When he tells you about his work the day before, you can easily judge from your own experience whether he is really interested and whether he is working properly.

In training new men you must strictly supervise them. Be sure that they work the territories that you assign them. That is your responsibility. The more thoroughly your territory is covered the more it will benefit everyone concerned.

Never hesitate to hire men if you are willing to supervise them. Remember, however, that even the best of men will not be valuable to you unless you supervise them.

I know that you are interested in making more money—whether or not you do so depends upon yourselves. There is no limit to what you can earn if you do the things you should do.

Use careful judgment when you employ a young man.

Steps in the Ladder of Success

270 Broadway IBM Club

New York, N.Y.
May 18, 1931

I want to thank you gentlemen for the interest you have shown in IBM by becoming members of this Club. We have here a great many young men tonight who are attending their first gathering of IBM people.

I want to welcome those young men and to say to them that there is room for promotion in The IBM during future years for every member of the organization. I also want to say, as a word of encouragement, that it does not require any special genius for a man to succeed in our business. It simply requires an earnest, honest, conscientious effort and a willingness to study the business.

The forerunner of all progress is education. You have all finished your schoolwork and have gone into business, but you must continue to add to your education. Once a man stops studying, stops adding to his stock of knowledge and information, he does not stand still—he starts to go backward.

There is no saturation point when it comes to education. Our country, I am proud to say, is making very great progress along educational lines. I was looking up some statistics recently on the growth and development of education and what we are spending for it. I found that fifty years ago we were spending $1.56 per capita on education and now we are spending $19 per capita on it. I never heard a taxpayer complain about his school tax. He may complain about all other taxes, but every American is always willing to go out when the school election comes around

Success simply requires an earnest, honest, conscientious effort and willingness to study the business.

and cast his vote in favor of further appropriations to develop education.

As a result, we have improved and increased all along the line and we now have 28 million young men and women in the two lower schools and one million young men and women in our institutions of higher learning.

That represents a greater number than the remainder of the world combined. So we have something to be proud of along that line.

What does all that progress mean to you who are confining your efforts now to The IBM Corporation? It means that the greater the progress of this country, the greater will be the progress of The IBM and consequently the progress of all those connected with it who do the things we know they ought to do.

IBM Supervision

On that point, I would like to say this: We are all working under supervisors.

You young men coming into the business have the head of your department who is advising you directly and supervising your work. He is giving you instructions and he is criticizing and encouraging you. You must realize that that man is being supervised and criticized and praised by someone else, by someone higher up—and so it goes until you get to the president's office.

Some of you may think that is where supervision starts. But it is not, because the president of your company gets closer supervision and more of it than anyone in any other department. The president is supervised by the board of directors and supervision does not stop there. Members of the board are supervised and carry more responsibility than anybody else, because they are supervised by the stockholders and the stockholders are the people who own the business.

So as you go up the line in our organization, travel the whole route, you realize that you are working for the owners of the business— about 4,000 stockholders, more than half of whom are women. We are very proud of that fact. We are proud of it, and we take it seriously because it makes us realize our great responsibility, whether we are officers of the company or office boys.

We have in our care the money of these more than 2,200 women who believe in us.

104

IBM is International

I would also like to bring to the attention of the young men in the business this fact: We have ceased to look upon IBM as an ordinary business. We look upon it as a great institution, a great world institution that is going on forever, as long as the business world turns round.

In Mexico, our next-door neighbor, where we once did not make much effort to get business, we have an organization now running better than 100%. Our business is growing; it is growing in foreign fields as well as in the American field. It is growing because we have the right kind of products and the right kind of men. The personnel of an organization is what counts and as I look out over the faces here tonight, I feel proud to think that every year we are getting more and more young men who are IBM people all the way through.

The personnel of an organization is what counts.

Do Right and Take Action

We want you to keep this in mind: We want you to do right in this business, not because I ask you to or because some other executive asks you to, but because you know that it is the best thing for you to do.

There is not a man in this room who needs to ask his supervisor whether he should do this or that. All of you are thinking men and we are all working together. I appeal to you young men to use your own initiative. Self-supervision is the most valuable asset any young man can have. Do not wait for your supervisor to tell you to do something.

You know what the work is after you have been in the organization a certain length of time; and whatever job is assigned to you, do that job to the best of your ability. If you keep on doing that, you will not only gain a greater command of yourself and greater knowledge, but you will develop initiative and ability to supervise others and gain promotion.

That is the only way a man will ever gain promotion in this business.

IBM Family

Someone's eyes are on all of you all the time; not for the purpose of playing detective and telling somebody that you are not doing your job well—the eyes of the officials of this company are on you for the purpose of picking out those of you who can do bigger jobs in this business. Just keep that in mind. We want all of you to feel right at home because this is a real family proposition. We do not want you to have any fear of anyone.

I meet most of the boys who come into the business at some time or other. I do not always remember names, but I do remember the faces. Whenever you meet me, I want you to come up and talk to me about anything that is on your mind, and that goes for all of the other executives in the business. The best way for you to learn more about this business is to talk to people who have been in it longer than you—perhaps who know more about certain angles of it than you do.

That reminds me of the answer Benjamin Franklin made when asked how he acquired such a wonderful knowledge of so many different things. He said, "Because I have never been ashamed to ask about anything that I did not understand." If there is anything you do not understand, ask somebody about it and you will find everybody willing and ready and anxious to give you information.

IBM Mobility

Another thing that I want to mention tonight is that when men start in a business as large as ours, with as many different departments and different phases of work, it is not always possible for the supervisor to place them in exactly the spot they should occupy.

We often get a round peg in a square hole or a square peg in a round

If you feel that you are not a proper fit, talk to your supervisor.

hole and cannot make them fit. So if you feel that you are not properly fitted in, talk to your supervisor, ask him what he would think about moving you into some other department. If a man is not functioning 100% in one department it does not mean that he has to get out of The IBM. It means simply that he should look the ground over, talk to his supervisor and get placed where he will fit.

106

IBM Enthusiasm

My message to you tonight is this: When I talk with a young man who has been in the business a short time, I ask him one question, "Do you like the business?" If he says, "Yes, I am enthusiastic about it," I say to him, "All right, do not worry."

I never worry about a young man who in his heart loves this business. It is just like any other proposition. You have to be enthusiastic about it and enthusiasm comes from only one source— knowledge. That is why I started out by talking to you briefly about education. Keep on studying this business! You will never learn The IBM!

I started out one time, as I thought, to really master this business and learn all about it, but I gave up a long time ago because the business is bigger than we are. That is the kind of business we are in. The IBM is bigger than anybody and everybody who is in it, and that is what makes it interesting. There is always something for us to learn, something more for us to do.

I want you men in this IBM Club to make your club a vehicle that will carry you on to the greatest possible heights in this business.

The best way to learn more about this business is to talk to people who have been in it longer than you.

You Have Only Begun to Learn

Time Recorder Graduates
IBM Sales School Number Sixty

Binghamton, N.Y.
May 19, 1931

It is a great pleasure and a privilege to meet with you tonight. You are all very fortunate in that you are starting in a business that is a pioneer in its field. As you know, our Company is made up of three Divisions, each of which started more than forty years ago and is a pioneer in its field.

Each of these Divisions is the leader in its particular line. I mention this because it could not have been possible had it not been for the sound principles upon which the pioneers built.

IBM Education

Pioneers built this company on sound principles.

Concerning the schooling you have received here, I believe education is the most important element of all those which contribute toward the progress of the world.

It is the most important thing also in connection with the progress of this or any other business. I feel, therefore, that we are very fortunate in having our educational program and in having with us on our executive staff men who thoroughly believe in education.

For the past several years, we have had Professor T.H. Brown of the Harvard School of Business Administration assisting us with our educational program. Since the first of this year, through the courtesy of President Lowell, we have been able to claim more of Professor Brown's time in connection with this work. Mr. H.W. Limper of our New York staff has also had considerable experience in the teaching field, as master in a boys' school, one of the best secondary schools in the country.

All down the line we have men who appreciate what education means to this business, and I am sure that you graduates of this school also appreciate what it means to you to have a proper foundation on which to build your future in The IBM.

There is no saturation point in education. That fact has been brought out here tonight by several speakers. This means that in completing your school work here you have only begun to learn. It means that you must study not only this business but every important business in the United States.

You must study not only this business but every business in the United States.

Incidentally, I believe that is one of the most interesting and valuable things this Company has to offer you—the opportunity to contact with and procure knowledge of every industry, large and small, in the United States.

Life Speeded One Hundred-Fold

I have spoken of traveling at a fast pace. Coming up on the train tonight I ran across a little article in the Scranton paper. It pointed out that one year of life now equals one hundred years in former times. Living one year in this age is worth living more than one hundred years in any other period of the world's history. We have witnessed a great many events and changes in the last twenty-five years. Many new things have come into our life. We have seen many things develop into great industries that were hardly more than ideas twenty-five years ago.

Take the greatest industry of our country today, the automobile industry. What was it twenty-five years ago? Then the motorcar was considered, and it was, a luxury for the rich only. Today it is the servant of the masses. This great evolution has been due to improved machines, which have made it possible to build automobiles to sell at a price within the reach of every one.

We hear of the "Machine Age."

That started only about a hundred years ago. Our country is only a little more than 150 years old and the age of greatest development and progress has been during this time. If you will look through your history and refresh your minds you will find that it *is* only during the last hundred years that the masses in this world have lived with any degree of comfort.

That is because during this time we got started in this era of development—doing things by machinery that were formerly done by hand, relieving the human race of the great burden of drudgery, bringing down the hours of working time and raising wage scales, which have meant greater comfort to all of the people.

IBM Sales Force

Our aim is higher each year.

We have a fine factory and a splendid organization of men operating it; we have the finest type of officers, executives and workers in all departments of the business, at home and abroad, but our great asset is our sales force.

During the past eighteen months, when many people were complaining and saying that times were hard, our sales force increased our business, and I have enough confidence in our sales organization as a whole to say to you tonight that in my best judgment it is going to do that again this year.

I have been in this business seventeen years, during which time I have made a great many predictions. I have made at least one every year, in which I predicted what we would do in that particular year and during the next five years. I have always made those predictions based on firm belief and I have been wrong every time. In every instance our accomplishments have exceeded my prediction.

I am going to predict here and now to you and to everyone in this business, that in the next five years The IBM is going to be far greater than in the last five years, and the last five years were the greatest in the history of the Company. Our aim is higher every year and we always reach the mark. Why do I say this? Just to have something to say to you men tonight, just to paint a beautiful picture for you to look at? No! I base that prediction on faith and on what we have done in the past.

I know we are going to do better and bigger things in the future. We have more and better products that can do more and better work for the people we serve, and we have more and better men to go out into the field and tell people about them. That is why I can stand here and say, with absolute confidence, that you are going to make good on it, that The IBM organization as a whole is going to do better and bigger things this year and every year. As representatives of this Company, you will serve a useful purpose in the world.

The value of the product and the service it gives are the big things in a business. We, in this particular branch of The IBM, the ITR Division, are dealing with the most valuable commodity in industry and that is TIME, something which, once lost, can never be regained.

I have often heard a salesman say, "I had a bad month last month, but will make it up this month." He can never make it up.

Every minute the clock ticks off yields something beneficial or something detrimental to every one of us. The more you think of that, the more impressed you will be with the importance not only of making use of your time, but of teaching the business world to appreciate its value also. As a result of such teaching, you will sell more of our time and money-saving products and that is what we are in business for.

Knowledge Begets Enthusiasm

There are so many things to talk to young men about that I hardly know where to start or stop, but one thing I want you to think about every day is the matter of education—studying your business and keeping your enthusiasm up. That is the thing that is going to build success for you as individuals.

You are starting in this business as salesmen. There are and will continue to be

**Study your business
to keep your enthusiasm.**

opportunities for every one of you to secure higher positions, because we have not yet begun to do our big job of serving the industries of this country and all other countries. We want you to go out into the field and do everything you have been told to do, and in addition, to figure out other things you can do in the way of serving the business world.

The executives of this Company will extend to you the fullest possible cooperation and we want you to do the same for us. We want you to cooperate with your associate salesmen, not only in the ITR, but also in the Tabulating Machine and Scale Divisions; because you can all help one another.

You have the advantage of working with men who can help you get entree into many businesses because they have been there before you.

Wherever you go, whatever office you are assigned to, the first thing to do is to get acquainted with the Tabulating Machine men and the Scale men in that territory and work with them. You will find them glad to work with you and to give you real cooperation.

Work for Own Good!

You have been told a great many things to do. Why should you do these things?

Do them for your own good. Do them because you know they are right and not just because somebody asked you to do them. Never do anything that will not measure up to the standards of The IBM. If you do you will despise yourselves for having done it. You will regret it not solely because of its having displeased us but also because of its being unworthy of the standards of the Company you represent.

Wherever you go and present yourselves before businessmen, you

will be presenting The IBM, and everything that we have is going to be judged by the way you conduct yourself. That means character. You have that to start with.

Remember, you are not only going to do the right thing yourself but you are going to do everything you can to see that everybody else with whom you come into contact in The IBM does the right thing; it will pay you as an individual to do that.

Everything that we have is going to be judged by the way you conduct yourself.

Importance of Pride

Another thing I want to call your attention to is pride—pride in your record, in doing a good job for the company you represent. I would not give fifteen cents a year for a dozen men who do not take pride in doing a good job for their company and making a good record for themselves. I want you to learn to stand on your own feet, to do a good job, to supervise yourselves and teach yourselves from now on, and in that way qualify yourselves to teach and supervise others. If a man cannot teach and supervise himself, he is never going to be of value in teaching and supervising others.

You know what your job is. Have absolute belief and confidence in the management of this Company, and when your supervisors tell you to do something, do it to the best of your ability. Never figure that they are wrong, because there is no one-man policy running this business.

I have never made a decision without first consulting as many members of my executive staff as were available at the time,

Titles mean nothing in this business.

because I do not think any business can be run successfully on a one-man basis.

We want your suggestions and criticisms if they are constructive. We do not want destructive criticism, but we do want constructive criticism. What I mean by that is if you criticize us for the way we are doing a certain thing, qualify it with a suggestion as to how you believe we can do the same thing better. Whenever you get to your superiors with that kind of criticism, you will be welcomed.

Bring Troubles to Supervisors

Never keep to yourself anything that bothers you. If you believe we are wrong in directing your work, tell us, not someone else, about it. Tell your troubles to the man above you just as quickly as you can and whether they are real or imaginary you will receive consideration. If they are imaginary they will be cleared up, and if they are real they will be adjusted satisfactorily. That is the policy of The IBM.

We want you also to know this; titles mean nothing in this business. Every executive in The IBM considers himself an assistant to all other men in it.

Naturally, we have to put in more thought and time on the sales end of the business than on any other because we have to sell machines to keep the factories going, and I am very happy that we have been able to keep the wheels turning at Endicott during the last year, particularly, and that we employed more people in 1930 than any other year in our history.

We built one new building here in 1930, and Mr. Ford has just been checking up plans for an addition to another building which will be started very soon. Because in spite of what you hear about depression, we believe in the future not only of our business, but of our country, and we are going right ahead with our plans for the future.

New Expansions Planned

We are planning more for the future today than we ever have. We are planning to expand the work of our engineering department. We had a meeting on that only yesterday. That is why Mr. Ford and I could not get up here. Some of the inventors had ideas they wanted to talk about at once, and we could not put it off.

That is the kind of work that is going on behind the scenes in IBM, and you are going to be backed up with everything we can give you. We are going to try to develop you and break you into this business in a sane, slow and common-sense way. This is the way we believe in training young men and we want you to depend upon us until you are able to stand on your own feet.

I am going to have the pleasure of seeing you from time to time, and the greatest pleasure I am going to have in the future will be meeting you at the One Hundred Percent Club—some of you next year and others the year after as you develop in the business.

I feel, in looking you over tonight, that you are one-hundred-percent One Hundred Percenters, and I know you are going to produce one-hundred-percent results.

Do the right thing. Do everything you can to see that everybody else in The IBM does the right thing.

THE GREAT AGE OF MAN

Some men collect art. Tom Watson collected men—excellent men that he intended to keep. He believed the future of his company depended on finding and retaining the best people for The IBM.

In "The Value of Experience," speaking at the induction of eighteen new members into The IBM Quarter Century Club he states, "It is a good company that can interest a man to stay with it that long."

He worked at creating an environment in which there was always a balance and a win-win relationship between employee and employer. In win-win relationships,

It is a good company that can interest a man to stay this long.

the employee and employer are in a mutually beneficial relationship that establishes, encourages and supports long-term relationships.

Watson believed that every year a man decided to continue to work for The IBM was a vote of confidence in the business he was building—and his leadership.

As he elaborates in "The Reason for IBM's Progress," he says that The IBM's success is due to an organization of men who are always forward looking, staffed by men who believe in the business and a trained, educated sales force that has enabled The IBM to employ more people at a higher wage.

This "organization" was Tom Watson's personal quota. His goal was never a revenue target but rather to build "the best organization in the world." How personally he took this goal is expressed in "Teachers Just Point the Way." He says, "I have to assume the responsibility for everybody and everything in this business, and I appreciate what that responsibility means." But, as he looks around the room and realizes that those men are spending time away from families, studying at night to be better employees and better individuals, he finishes with this observation: "It makes me feel that my responsibility is being shared by all in the organization, and that is a very great source of satisfaction to me."

Almost every article in this section contains perhaps his most powerful and emotional discussion, focusing on dispelling what he considered the myth that the world was entering a new Machine Age.

With that he disagreed—strongly.

He saw a different age coming—A Man Age.

This is not the Machine Age but the Great Age of Man.

He felt that the Depression, as both men and business came out of it, would accelerate the development of new and creative technologies that would ultimately lead to a life far better than was experienced before the Depression.

He wanted a company that inspired commitment, dedication and loyalty. Even as he asked for that loyalty to his company, he believed a person must first be loyal to himself.

He was positioning The IBM to take advantage of the coming Age of Man.

This is the Great Age of Man.

The Value of Experience

In Honor of Eighteen New Members
Quarter Century Club

Atlantic City, N. J.
May 23–24, 1931

I wish to extend a welcome and the thanks of all our stockholders, directors and officers to the members of The IBM Quarter Century Club. The greatest pleasure I have in The IBM is to attend a meeting of this club. We organized this club seven years ago and I am sure that there is nothing that has created so much interest in the business.

We try to teach all our people the value of experience. If a man is the right kind of man and is in the right kind of business, there is nothing like experience in performing his duty. Experience makes a man valuable to the company, not only in his own individual task but also in setting an example for and directing others.

That is why we place so much reliance on the man of long service in our business.

We place reliance on the man of long service in our business.

The Quarter Century Club is growing fast and we have another club that is growing, too. That is the 40-Year Club, which has four members at the present time.

Three of those members are unable to be here tonight. Mr. Saum is here tonight, and he represents both the 40-Year Club and the 25-Year Club.

Continuous service builds valuable experience.

Pride in IBM's Citizenship

Quarter Century Club Banquet

Atlantic City, N.J.
May 23–24, 1931

I am not going to say any more except to thank you, personally and in the name of the company, for the fine cooperation you have given us, the work you have done for the company and the inspiration that you and the other Twenty-five Year men are giving to all of us, who are looking forward to qualifying for membership in this club.

It is my ambition, and I am sure it is the ambition of all others who have been in the company's service for any length of time, to become a member of this club. I do not believe that there is a single man in The IBM who does not look forward to the day when he will qualify for membership in the Twenty-five Year Club. We are to be congratulated from the standpoint of both the individual and the company on having an organization such as this.

It is a good man who can stay with a company for twenty-five years, and, on the other hand, it is a good company that can interest a man to stay with it that long. We feel, therefore, that we are representing one of the finest businesses in this country, and I personally feel that, with the cooperation and assistance of our organization, we are going to make The IBM not only bigger, but also better from every standpoint, every year.

I am proud of The IBM organization.

I hear so many fine things said about our people and what many of our men stand for in the communities in which they live, that I do not believe there is any place in the country today that can boast of a finer citizenship than we have represented in our company.

That, to me, is one of the biggest things about The IBM.

I want to thank you—those who are here and also those who are absent—for the fine character you display at all times.

It is a good company that can interest a man
to stay with it for twenty-five years.

The Reason for IBM's Progress

Home Office Annual Outing

Roton Point, Connecticut
June 15, 1931

Because our business has continued to increase during the past two years, I think that on an occasion like this, when we are all together having a good time, it is a good thing to reflect on the reason for that condition. It is a very plain simple fact that we have products that are useful to the people who buy them, and are even more useful and more needed now than ever before.

We also have an organization of men who are always looking forward, never backward, and that is the real reason why we are making greater strides every year. It is due entirely to the people in our business.

I want to say just one word here in praise of our sales organization. I wish to convey this message from all of us. They are the people who have kept the factory wheels turning and I am proud and very happy because of the fact that last year, when so many organizations were reducing the number of working hours and the number of people employed, we found work for more people than ever before, and at a higher average wage.

Every year as we gather at these little outings you will find more people.

I think that is the greatest tribute that could possibly be paid to a sales organization, because it was the sales organization who made possible this enviable record.

Every year we gather at these little outings, you will find more people. I wish to pay my tribute to all the people in the organization and especially to the sales organization, which has kept the factories going and kept everyone employed.

Everything depends on the results accomplished by the sales organization.

Reasons for Pride in IBM

Metropolitan Sales Organization

New York, N.Y.
October 1, 1931

My thoughts are now directed towards the great burst of enthusiasm I have just witnessed and heard. It occurs to me that perhaps there is more enthusiasm in this room than in any other in this part of the world this morning. You who are working in the metropolitan area of New York are really under a handicap that does not exist to the same extent in other parts of the country because there seems to be more gloom in New York than anywhere else.

But what has that to do with our business?

Nothing!

This is the Man Age

We have no right to talk or think pessimism because the first eight months of this year have been better than the corresponding period of any year in the history of this business. We are all proud of that record. We are so proud of it that we are going to keep it up and make this year the greatest year in all our history. Why are we going to do that?

Manpower is more important than machine power.

Because we not only have manpower in this business but we have the right kind. You have heard me talk a great deal about manpower and its importance in business. Manpower is more important than machine power, not only in the sales force, but also in the factory.

Some people have the idea that because we have improved machinery in the factories we do not require high-grade manpower, but the exact opposite is the case. The finer the equipment one puts into his factory the higher the grade of men he must have to run it.

The history of improved machinery proves that it makes men dear and their products cheap.

120

That is an argument that you have to meet in visiting your customers. We hear a great deal about it now. Some go so far as to say, "Why this is the machine age! That is the reason for the Depression!"

This is not the machine age!

This is a Man Age—the greatest Man Age the world has ever known.

If it were not a Man Age, we could not have these wonderful machines that you are selling and that your customers are using, that other people are making and selling and that we and everybody else are using. Let us get that fixed in our minds. We are not living in a machine age. We are living in a Man Age.

Why have we been able to make the fine record we have made—because of machines? No. We use various machines to make our product, but

This is a Man Age. The greatest Man Age the world has ever known.

we have made this record because of the fact, in my judgment, that we have the best body of men that can be found in any business in the world. I make no exception to that statement and your record proves its truth.

We All Have Quotas

You salesmen have various quotas to deal with in IBM.

First to be considered is the general IBM quota. Then there are the divisional quotas—Tabulating Machine, Time Recorder, Industrial Scale and Dayton Scale quotas. Mr. Battin has the financial quota to keep in mind all the time. Everybody has a quota in this business.

What is my quota?

None of those I have mentioned, because I cannot contribute directly to the securing of any of those quotas. But I have a quota, and that quota is "the best organization in the world." That has been my quota ever since I have been in this business and I feel that I have made my quota because we *have* the best organization in the world. What does the best organization in world mean?

It means that we must all work together and continue to get more people into this business as time goes on. That is the quota that I have before me all the time.

No one could feel more proud than I do this morning because in IBM, we have the finest organization to be found anywhere. I say that without reservation because you have carried on through a period of depression, not of one month or two months, but of two years.

Always Looking to Improvement

There never has been a single occasion during all that time when any man or any group of men has come to my office and talked about business depression, or about hard times or indicated that we could not do this or that. Every proposition presented to me has gone something like this: "Mr. Watson, we believe if we do so-and-so, it would improve this business."

Another reason why I am so proud of this organization is that I have to give it less supervision that most chief executives are required to give their forces. I never worry about what you are doing when I am away because I know that every man in The IBM is always doing his best.

In business, not all men can have high records at the same time.

I know when I look at the records, that the men who have not made much good ones have done their best nevertheless. That is how much confidence I have in you. Not all men can have high records at the same time. It does not work out that way in business; but individually we keep in fairly good balance, sometimes up and sometimes down.

Pride in his record is the greatest asset a salesman, an office man, an engineer, a factory man, a service man or an executive can have. The man who is not proud of his personal record cannot even get joy out of life, to say nothing about becoming prosperous. I stand here this morning more proud of my record than anybody in this room could possibly be of his.

I am proud of you, and by you I mean all of the men and women in IBM scattered throughout the world who comprise this organization.

Thankful to Members

You have my thanks and my appreciation to a greater extent than I am able to express. You have kept the factory wheels turning. You have kept every IBM employee working on full time. You have done more than that; you have made it necessary for us to build additions to our factories during the past two years of so-called depression. That, in turn, has furnished employment to a large number of people outside The IBM organization.

You have reason to be proud of what you have been and are doing to improve the employment situation. You have been helping employment by keeping sales up and enabling us to keep all our people employed on a full-time basis.

I am not only proud of that, but I am very, very thankful, because it is hard to have to lay off people, and when there is no work for them we are obliged to take steps toward protecting the business. In

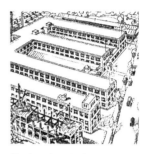

You have kept the factory wheels turning and every IBM employee working on full time.

our business we must constantly think of protecting the investment of its more than 4,000 owners, many of them represented right here.

There are so many big things you have to be proud of this morning that it would take all day to recite them in detail. I am touching only on the high spots. Take real pride in your records. It will help you in your sales work.

I want to repeat what I said to some of the executives at a meeting yesterday. My time is yours. I will go anywhere with any man if it will help this business, because we executives, as you know, look upon ourselves not as managers, not as chief executives, but as assistants.

This is the greatest morning I have ever had in this business—to be able to talk to you proudly and honestly as I am doing now.

Take real pride in your records.

Teachers Just Point the Way

Opening Session
The IBM "Owl School"

New York, N.Y.
November 12, 1931

I think I am very fortunate to be here. In looking over the group in this room, it appears more like the convention of a One Hundred Percent Club than a club meeting or school session.

It occurs to me that this School and Club can be compared with the research laboratory and the assembling department at the factory. In the research laboratory they seek out ideas. In the assembling department they assemble the parts into the finished product. I think that in your work and in your study of this business, such a comparison is the best one that I could make. You are, in your daily work, searching consciously or unconsciously for better ways of doing things. That is what we are all doing. That is what life is.

Then you meet in groups, conventions, schools, clubs or whatever it may be, and through your combined efforts you assemble these ideas into some concrete form for the purpose of making them a constructive force for the betterment of yourselves and the company you represent.

Life is about constantly searching for better ways of doing things.

We have done a great many things in IBM to help build the business. We have organized to sell our machines throughout seventy-eight countries of the world. We have sales managers, district managers and executives—all the titles that were ever used in any commercial organization. All those things have been very useful and have helped to build this business.

But the thing that I always have depended on more than anything else is our schoolwork and our research work. To me, these factors are of far greater importance than all our other activities, and I want to congratulate you young men who are willing to use a little extra time each week to study your work.

Interested in Company

The reason why you are willing to do this is, first of all, that you are interested in this company. Men will not put forth extra effort unless they are really interested, and you are interested in this company because you believe that it holds an opportunity for your future. You may not have thought of it in that light, but that is the reason you are interested.

You believe you are with a company that is manufacturing and distributing the right kind of products, the kind that you can stand behind wholeheartedly. That is why you are interested. You believe that a

You are interested in this company because you believe it holds opportunity.

company that has the products that we have, a company in which all of its people are so deeply interested, is a good place for young men of your caliber to cast their lot and make a place for themselves for life.

The reason for its constant growth is not due so much to the fact that it has any special genius in the management, as it is to the fact that we have a business that enables us to produce and sell machines that are useful and beneficial to industry as a whole. Those are the things that inspire men to work and to study.

I hope that in the research and in the assembling work which you are undertaking in this school and in The IBM Club you will keep in mind that as a result of your efforts in research and your assembling of ideas, you are going to build for yourselves and for this company a great constructive force that will be added to what we already have, and it will enable us to continue to build this business and to make it bigger and better each year.

You are interested in the company; you are loyal to the company; and you are going to continue to be interested and to be loyal. However, I want to impress one thing upon you.

Be loyal to yourselves first of all.

If you are loyal and true to yourselves, you can never be false to your company, your family or your friends. What precisely do I mean, some of you may ask, by being loyal to yourselves in this business?

I mean simply to do the things that you know you ought to do in the position you are filling. Do not try to see how *little* you can do, but try to see how *much* you can do, not only in your own particular job but in the department in which you work. Furthermore, see how many things you can do that will help this business as a whole.

See how much you can contribute to helping the men who are working alongside you and all others who work for the company.

Teachers Just Point the Way

No matter how good your teacher is, no matter how much knowledge he and the people who assist him may possess, one or two men cannot hope to teach you very much about this business in the length of time they are going to be with you as instructors during the course of your school. They can only give you the ideas and point the way. Then you must go on and continue to build up your knowledge yourselves. There is always something you can learn.

It is unnecessary for me to talk to you about the value of knowledge. You know how valuable it is. However, I do want to call your attention to the value of wisdom. You often see men who you know are possessed of full and complete knowledge of a subject, but who still are getting nowhere. Why is it that, with all their knowledge, they are not successful? It is because they lack wisdom—the power that enables them to use knowl-

Teachers can only give you the ideas and point the way.

edge to advantage.

Apply Knowledge to Gain Wisdom

Therefore, as you go on in your studies and acquire knowledge of your subject, see that you develop wisdom along with it. Find out how to apply your knowledge; because unapplied knowledge is useless. It becomes excess baggage if you get too much of it. If you have not acquired with it sufficient wisdom to enable you to use it to the best possible advantage, it is of no value to you or to anyone else.

You will be given every opportunity in this school in the way of instruction. That will be very helpful, but remember that self-education is the very best kind of education that you or any other man can ever possess. So keep in mind, in starting, that you must not depend too much upon your instructors to teach you the business. The most valuable part of your training will come from your own efforts to learn the business.

We have taught enough in our company schools to make every single individual in the business a hundred-percent success. However, I am sorry to say, not all our men are Hundred Percenters, although we have an unusually high percentage of such men. Why is it that not all of them are Hundred Percenters? It is because a great many people do not absorb the knowledge to which they are exposed. There is not much use in teaching unless somebody learns what is being taught.

Self-education is the very best kind of education.

Deep Interest in Schools

I am very glad to have had an opportunity to be here this afternoon, because the work that you are doing in these clubs and in these classes means more to me, personally, than any of you realize. I have to assume the responsibility for everybody and everything in this business, and I appreciate what that responsibility means. For one thing, it means responsibility to the more than 4,000 stockholders who have entrusted their money to our care.

When I see these various groups of men who are studying our business and applying themselves in an earnest endeavor to do better each year, it makes me feel that my responsibility is being shared by all in the organization, and that is a very great source of satisfaction to me.

I want to thank you young men, especially those who are coming into the Owl Class for the first time this year, for giving up your time to extra study. I assure you that every one of the executives in this business realizes that it is his duty to contribute something to this school during the course of your study.

If you are loyal and true to yourselves, you can never be false to your company, your family or your friends.

Education and Machines

City College of New York
Reception in Mr. Watson's Honor

May 25, 1932

I never lose an opportunity to be with people who are interested in education, because education is the one thing that we must depend upon at all times in the building of this civilization in which we are all so deeply interested. Furthermore, there is no saturation point in education. When you leave this school and go out into the world of business, keep on studying, because when any of us stop studying we are lost.

When any of us stop studying we are lost.

There always is something to learn because conditions change so fast that we have to know more about the things we are going to do next year than we know this year in order to keep abreast of the times and also in order to keep pace with others. I happen to be interested directly in tabulating machines, but I am also tremendously interested in all kinds of machines because progress depends so much upon the machines we invent and perfect.

Machines Lengthen Life

In order better to appreciate the benefits that people have derived from machines let us go back to ancient Greece and the old Roman Empire. They depended entirely upon animal power and manpower. It is true that they accomplished much, but think of the time and effort and the shortening of men's lives which this involved.

In England before the days of either water or steam power, and in many other countries as well, a board was made by placing a log on an elevated platform with a man below and a man above to work the saw up and down. It took a long time to make one board. The men engaged in this work, we find from the records, were old and broken at forty. These things make us realize more forcefully the benefits derived from water, steam and electric power and present day machines.

Perhaps it is true that most things being done today by machinery could be done by hand. Perhaps it also is true that this would involve the employment of a great many more people. But there is another side to the coin. Men without the aid of machinery might produce an automobile, but it would take them so long and cost so much that the price of the finished car would be prohibitive. Only a few could be sold.

In other words, if we start considering how many men could displace a machine, we must also consider what the result would be and what the cost of the finished product would be when produced by manpower. When we do that, we begin to realize the part that machines are playing.

Present Is Greatest Man Age

We frequently hear, particularly in these times, that we are living in a machine age. I disagree with this. I feel that we are living in the greatest Man Age the world has ever known; that men today, individually and collectively, are doing bigger and better things than ever before in history.

The machines we speak of are really only tools that men have devised to assist them in doing a better job. In all industrial and all agricultural production we find that these machines, these tools which men have created out of their own ingenuity, have made it possible to cut down the working day and at the same time to increase wages.

Moreover, I believe that as we devise better machines and better ways of doing things we will be able to still further reduce the working hours of the day as well as still further increase wages paid to workers. To my mind, that is one of the greatest things at which we can aim. We are building a great country. In spite of all the handicaps and setbacks, we are going to do a good job in the end.

It is unfortunate that so many of our people are at present out of employment, but it is due to the fact that we got a little bit out of balance in our ideas and allowed our general structure to get out of adjustment. But we are now busy trying to find out why that happened so that we can correct it.

Machines are only tools to assist
men in doing a better job.

Individual Thinking

Personally, I think that one of the things that had most to do with our present situation was that we got away from individual thought and individual action. We drifted into mass thinking. We were all getting the same kind of news about the same things at the same time through our very efficient publications, over the radio and through other channels and allowed ourselves to drift away from the very important habit of individual thinking.

But now we have to get back to it.

A lot of advice is being given these days by a great many people as to what someone else ought to do. We have to give more thought to the things we know we ought to do ourselves. I think we have made a good start in that direction already. As more thought is developed along those lines, particularly as more of us think about the things for which we are personally responsible, greater progress will be made in pulling out of the Depression.

Machines and Work

Just one more word on this point: While it is true that machines of all kinds, including accounting and recording machines do more work with fewer people, it is also true that the designing, building, selling and shipment of such machines provide work for a lot of people.

And I would like to repeat that machines enable us to manufacture things at a lower cost. This brings the selling price down to a point where more can be sold, greater production is necessary and more employment is provided in their manufacture and distribution.

Three Important Points

Speed is of the greatest importance in practically every business.

As to machinery for accounting work, there are three important points that we always consider. They are speed, accuracy and economy. The machine must do the work in a shorter time, it must do the work accurately and the operation must be economical in order to make it a good business proposition.

Speed is of the greatest importance in practically every business.

For purposes of sales analysis, it is very important that records and reports be available quickly so that executives will know how to direct their salesmen, how to correct their shortcomings, how to encourage those who need it and praise those who deserve it. The same holds true of the factory. In cost keeping it is very important to get accurate records and get them quickly, of what it has cost to make the goods. In either case, if the records and reports are too long in coming, they are about as useful as last week's newspaper.

As you travel about this world you will find that the countries making the least use of improved machinery are the poorest countries and are making the least progress. Wherever you find a nation that is taking up improved methods and working to further improve these methods, you will find a progressive nation.

Result of Education

Our leadership in mechanical progress I regard as a direct result of education, and I also believe that we have made greater progress in education than any other country in the world.

People in foreign countries sometimes speak of us as giving no attention to education, yet we have more students in institutions of higher learning than all the rest of the world combined. We have

We are living in the greatest Man Age the world has ever known.

today some 28 million students enrolled in our two lower schools. At present we have only 3.5 million of these 28 million in secondary schools, and our present attention is being devoted to the task of increasing the registration at the secondary schools. We are going to make even greater progress in education in the future.

I am sure that you young men and women who are enjoying and profiting by the advantages of this school fully appreciate that you are more fortunate than many others located in other parts of the country where there is no such school as this.

There is no saturation point in education.

A New Business Era

The following interview with Laura Vitray
was published by the New York Evening Journal

November 24, 1931

"The spreading of work, as an emergency measure, will help to solve our present unemployment situation." Thomas J. Watson, president of the Merchants' Association of New York, made that statement today in an interview with the *Evening Journal*.

The association has already endorsed the principle of "spreading work" and has urged its members to take such action whenever required to prevent layoffs. Work the full force part of the time, rather than part of the force all of the time, is its advice. As a result many of the large employers in the New York district are adopting either the six-hour day or the five-day week.

A New Business Era

The employer must give thought to those things that will benefit his employees.

Mr. Watson, who heads The International Business Machines Corporation, with thousands of employees in the United States and Canada and throughout the world, sat and talked today of a new business era that is not only coming, but is already here.

"I regard the six-hour day only as a temporary measure," he explained, "because I am inclined to think that after this depression we will need everybody in the United States working full time, to take care of the immense volume of business that will be ours.

"The recent action on the part of the government and the bankers in establishing the National Credit Bank, together with the president's plan to assist home-builders, should encourage all of us to plan for 1932 along constructive lines looking to an increase in business.

"The fact that 175 firms in this country showed a larger volume of business for the first nine months of this year than for the same period of last year is proof that some businesses have already started to improve.

"When prosperity returns, I believe it will also be a more substantial prosperity. What do I mean by that? Well, not so much foolish speculation, perhaps."

Then Mr. Watson went on to tell his reasons for seeing ahead a period of tremendous industrial activity. This country is now suffering the consequences of the war, he pointed out, by a depression long artificially deferred, but which was obliged to come. Meanwhile, American psychology, fundamentally democratic, will eventually force the pendulum of industry back to higher production.

"The American idea that is at the root of everything we do," he said, "is that everybody wants something better. Moreover, we are anxious to give our masses the chance to enjoy everything that life holds in the way of comfort and enjoyment. We regard it as every man's right in America to have a home and a radio and an automobile and a thousand and one other things that formerly were luxuries available only to the rich.

"This spirit of mass enjoyment of the good things of life can be realized only through mass production. Add to this the fact that standards of living are on the upgrade in almost every country in Europe, with a corresponding increase in per capita consumption in these countries. This eventually will exert a marked influence on the volume of America's foreign trade."

Machines Only Tools

Do we live in a machine age, in which workers' rights are flaunted, human happiness forgotten in the ruthless warfare of competitive commerce?

Mr. Watson smiled at that. His corporation turns out many types of business machines that aid and abet the human brain. "Why, this is no machine age," he said, "This is the Great Age of Man. Machines are just the small tools, the creations of men, that help them do their work. How can they replace men?

"Manpower is the real progressive force in the modern world. Improved machines make men dear—their products relatively cheap. They destroy drudgery and create jobs. And this is the

Manpower is the real progressive force in the modern world. Machines make men dear—their products cheap.

133

Man Age for another reason. Organizations have changed their attitude toward men in the past decade. Today it is a far more human attitude.

"I know of no large corporation today whose heads are not vitally interested in the welfare and security and happiness of the men and women they employ. This was not always so.

"But it has come about through close contact and more intimate acquaintance between employer and employee, and the contact of industrialists one with another . . . through the talking over of employment and labor and financial problems and the educating influence of trade associations, chambers of commerce and other business organizations to which most of the large concerns belong.

"Every individual employer today is giving thought to those things which will benefit his employees . . . nor is any change of policy adopted without careful consideration of its effect upon the workers."

Employing More Now

Briefly, Mr. Watson gave a few details of his own corporation. It has plants in Toronto, Canada; in Paris, France; Stuttgart, Germany and in London, England. A larger number of people are now employed in these plants than in 1929.

"We are not the only ones," said Mr. Watson, "who have succeeded in accomplishing this. The trouble is those who stand by their employees are so seldom talked about. New York firms, and concerns throughout the country, are putting forth much real effort to combat depression and to maintain employment at as high a level as possible.

"With the present close cooperation of the Government, the American bankers, employers and employees, I believe we have every reason to look forward to better things for all in the future."

This is the Great Age of Man.

THINK

No compilation of the words of Tom Watson Sr. could ever be complete without his reflections on the word THINK.

Watson expected every individual to THINK. He was very forgiving of thoughtful mistakes. He was very unforgiving of thoughtless ones—and in fact, if a mistake resulted from a lack of forward vision or thought, it could ignite a volatile temper.

In this editorial published at the end of 1931 for all employees in *Business Machines*, he asks each individual to THINK of new opportunities, THINK of the engineering advantages they have in the market, THINK and plan and apply untiring effort to increasing their personal income. Most of all he wants each individual to THINK with the utmost confidence and PLAN how to move ahead.

At the beginning of a new year, he wanted everyone to have a moment of positive reflection on what was good about the economy, business and their personal lives but then act as "thought and plan transcend reflection in usefulness to business."

Think of what intelligent planning and untiring effort can do.

Keep in mind that this was shortly after the second anniversary of Black Tuesday. To lead The IBM out of this depression, his thoughts, practices, habits and direction for 1932 involved thinking, planning and applying his untiring efforts.

From his perspective, he was inviting The IBM Caretakers along on the journey. He believed that reflection, thinking, planning and action would apply beneficially in both corporate and personal lives.

It was a journey The IBM team was on together.

THINK to participate in The Great Age of Man.

Things to Think About

Business Machines *Editorial*
The Company's Newsletter

December 31, 1931

The beginning of a new year is a good time to reflect for a moment, then to THINK and PLAN. Reflection is worthwhile only as it provides inspiration for future action. Thought and plan transcend it in usefulness to business. But The IBM has made splendid progress in the passing year and in that fact lays a world of incentive for our employees in 1932.

Reflection is worthwhile only as it provides inspiration for future action.

THINK of the enormous volume of production and distribution that is absolutely necessary to keep the immense population of our country provided with the essentials of life, to keep a fair proportion of our national wealth constructively employed and to lay the basis for continued progress in American standards of living. It is imperative that business in the United States shall continue to increase and to progress.

THINK of the New Year as one that offers unprecedented opportunities to salesmen in every division of The IBM in every section of the United States, for progress is the essence of successful business and there are many evidences that this axiom will be appreciated in 1932 as never before. There is some application for one or more products of this company in every progressive business in the country.

THINK of the engineering ingenuity The IBM has put into the production of every item in its various lines to the end that they might serve business with a maximum of efficiency and economy, and of their demonstrated value in virtually every field of commerce.

THINK, then, of what intelligent planning and untiring effort can do to increase your personal income and enhance your prestige among your business associates during the coming year. Every individual who represents The IBM in any capacity is in a position to confer material benefits upon many business enterprises in 1932, and there are many evidences that business will be receptive as never

136

before to plans and equipment to promote speed, economy and efficiency.

THINK of the story The IBM has to present to business in every line, of the many enterprises right in your own territory that have never had an opportunity to get the full import of this story, of what it means to their profit showings and to the accuracy of their records.

THINK how many of these businesses a more determined canvass certainly would bring into the prosperous and progressive fold of IBM equipment users, of what it would mean to your own income and to the comforts and luxuries enjoyed by those dear to you.

THINK with the utmost confidence of the products you have to offer business. They have all been tried and tested. The advantages of their use have been thoroughly proved. Demand for them is increasing and it is up to you to make capital of this fact in 1932 for yourself and your company.

Mental inventory time for all of us arrives
with a New Year.

LAYING THE IBM'S FOUNDATION

The IBM Basic Beliefs were not written down until almost 1965, more than thirty years after these articles, when Tom Watson Jr. captured, summarized and distributed his and his father's basic tenets.

These beliefs and principles can be seen in their formative stages in the following articles and speeches of Tom Watson Sr. These principles from the founder of The

The foundation has been securely laid and it is up to us to build the proper kind of structure.

IBM would become its impenetrable foundation for almost a century.

Watson Sr. believed it was always easier to build after the foundation was laid. He constructed a foundation—a new type of foundation for a new type of corporation—based on fundamentally eternal principles.

From these articles it is clear that The IBM:

- Was interested in procuring a true picture of the business. Executives encouraged constructive criticism.

- Hired the right kind of men; educated, supervised, promoted and, when necessary, discharged them with respect.

- Defined education as training the individual to exercise their capacities to their fullest extent.

- Didn't stop educating people at the university or IBM schools, but continued to offer self-improvement through self-study guided by self-supervision.

- Based advancement on merit. Those who worked achieved greater opportunity than those with the right background who didn't.

- Promoted managers based on being pushed up from below by those they assisted. No one moved up by pull from above.

- Made its managers assistants to men.

- Ensured its executives, when standing on stage, saw before them the faces of those who were most directly responsible for the company's progress.

- Invested in new product development for growth.

- Worked for every salesmen to attain a "One Hundred Percent" sales and customer service record.

- Sought a balance between personal and work lives. Employees knew within themselves where that balance was. Personal health was a primary concern.

- Learned from its mistakes.

- Held its duty to its stockholders as its greatest responsibility.

- Cooperated with and helped other businesses succeed.

- Expected perpetual change.

- In spite of its outward appearance of white shirts, wing-tip shoes and blue suits, it outlawed mass thinking. It encouraged, expected and demanded individuality of thought.

Finally - You must THINK!

The principles of this business are fixed.
They are lasting principles.

Investments for the Future of IBM

Tabulating Machine Students
Mechanical Service School Number 40

Endicott, N.Y.
January 12, 1932

It is a great pleasure as well as a privilege for me to meet with you this morning and to look into the faces of so many young men who are going to play an important part in the future growth and development of our business. Everything is new to you now.

You probably have never seen a factory just like this before. Those of you who have seen factories before and who are familiar with other businesses will find many things here that are different, many things that you have not come in contact with in any other plant. One of the things you will find that is different is the importance we attach to the educational phase of our business—the way to teach men about our business.

Make Constructive Criticisms

As you go along in this business you will sometimes see things that appear to you to be wrong, but keep this one thing in mind. When Mr. Ogram or anybody else tells you what to do and how to do it, you accept their judgment until you have had an opportunity to study that particular point and are able to come to them or to your other instructors and make a constructive suggestion of some way that you think will be better.

I told Mr. Vernier and some other gentlemen in a little meeting this morning that if we carefully study our methods of doing things we can usually find a way to improve them. When you get out into the field, you are going to have an opportunity for real service.

When you get out into the field, you are going to have an opportunity for real service.

This brings me to this point: You students are starting in the very best place in this business for young men who want to learn the business and succeed in it.

Started at Bottom

On my right here is Mr. Venner. You have been here long enough to know all about him, what his position is, how he is recognized and what he is thought of by our company. Mr. Venner started in the mechanical end of the business. He did not have the advantage of a school such as this in which to learn about the business. He had to start in at the bottom and work his way up step by step.

His business education has been self-education all the way through. Mr. Oldroyd, Superintendent of all IBM manufacturing here at Endicott, also worked his way up to his present high position with the company.

Conditions are different today. You have the benefit now of this school and the help of all the men in this plant. You get the benefit of their years of experience. In this school we will try to the best of our ability to give you a working knowledge of this business.

We know all about you. Every man's record has been looked up. You have been passed on by several people in our business as being young men of IBM character and ability. That comes first with us; that comes ahead of your education or your ability, because IBM is not an ordinary sort of manufacturing business. We look on IBM as a great world institution engaged in the manufacture and distribution of machines that benefit mankind.

Represents Lifetime Work

What you see here today represents the efforts of a lifetime of many people. We owe more to the pioneers—the people who conceived the idea of doing accounting work through punched holes, of mechanically and accurately recording time, of weighing goods in the store and computing money value without the necessity of the clerk having to figure it—than we will ever be able to repay, for without their ideas none of us would now be working for The IBM.

We are making a wonderful line of machines. We know they are wonderful because of the value their users place upon them. The record of our business during the past two years, when our users have demanded more from us than they ever did before, shows what that value is.

That is an important thing for you young men because your connection with this company is more important to you than it is to anybody else and you cannot afford to make mistakes. We do not

142

want to make the mistake of getting men into our business who are not the right type and who are not qualified.

A Career in IBM

Starting in this business marks the turning point in your career. You are not here for a short time. I am sure every one of you has in mind building a life's position. I can say to you young men truthfully and honestly that I cannot think of any place in the world that can possibly offer you as good an opportunity as The IBM.

We want constantly more and better manpower.

The reason I say that to you is because less than 55% of the accounting work of the world is done by machinery today. That gives you some idea of what you have ahead of you.

As I stated to some of my associates in New York the other day, reviewing the past two years, we all ought to be ashamed because we have not done more in that period.

That is the spirit of IBM.

We try at all times to keep a true picture; procure a better perspective of this business. We do not want to fool ourselves. We do not want to tell each other how good we are. We want to look ahead.

We want you gentlemen to look ahead not only so far as our present machines are concerned but as to other kinds of machinery which we might develop to help the people we want to serve to do a better job. That is why we are making plans for an engineering laboratory across the street. We are going to put up a building there that will be 200 x 70 feet and four stories high, a building for the express purpose of investing money in the future of IBM.

We will never get any direct return from the things we do in that building because nothing will ever be sold that is built over there. Machines will only be developed there and then we will bring them over here to the factory to be manufactured. We plan to spend a million dollars in research work this year. We have spent over $800,000 each year in research work in the last two years.

We have absolute faith in the future of this business.

In an organization such as we have representing 4,000 stockholders, if we can stand before the board of directors and ask them to authorize an expenditure of over $800,000 in one year simply for research and development work, it means that we have absolute faith in the future of this business.

We are going to spend a great deal every year in research for the future. Twenty years from now you who will still be comparatively young men may look back and realize that the policy of this company in constantly investing in research has been responsible for its growth.

Extra Effort Counts

All you have to do is an honest day's work. We do not want any of our people to work to the point of endangering their health.

We want young men who are willing to do an honest day's work and we do not have to tell you what that is—you know! Not only that, but we want you to see how much help you can extend to your fellow workers. We want you to make constructive suggestions as to improvements of our present products. We want you to think about the invention or development of new machines because you, who are coming in contact with the customers, are going to have a real opportunity to find out what other things we ought to do.

You will succeed in proportion to the effort you put forth, and, gentlemen, it is the extra effort that counts.

Above all things make up your minds that you are not going to be an average man. It is men who are doing more than the average. They make up for the fellows who are below the average. Never be satisfied when you look at your record and say, "I am up with the average." Many young men fail just that way.

Being in the average class means you are way below the men who have made the records that have built this business.

Importance of Study

Some of you have had the advantage of technical training in universities. Others have had the advantage of a common school education. But, gentlemen, if you will take advantage of your opportunities in this business, it does not make any difference where you left off with your studies in the classroom. It will just be a help.

It may mean that you will have to work a little bit harder and take a little bit longer, if you have not had the university training, but you can still procure just as fine an education and just as thorough a technical training as you could have obtained in the universities.

I do not want you to misunderstand me. I am not talking against the universities. I am proud of the fact that I am a trustee of two of them. I recommend that every young man seek training in a university if he can. However, knowledge comes from study, from no other source.

Every man has the opportunity to study if he is willing and for the young men who feel that possibly they are handicapped because they did not receive university training, I would say that they should make up their minds to work and study. Say, "I am going to catch up with those fellows." Put in a little extra time each day. Just as soon as you begin to add to your stock of knowledge, it whets your appetite and you want more.

Knowledge comes from study.
No other source.

So my advice to you who feel that you ought to have had college training is to study, and we will apply that to everybody in this room. I have to study myself. I have responsibilities that are increasing all the time. I would not dare to even think of giving up my studying.

This Business is Different

Let us pursue this course of study with a feeling that this business is different from others; that this is not just an ordinary business. We speak of it as a great world institution. We are merely in it temporarily—just during the term of our lifetime—but the principles of this business are fixed. They are lasting principles.

The principles of this business are fixed. They are lasting principles.

No one in this business ever got anything through pull. Mr. Ford's father entered it in the very beginning. Mr. Ford's grandfather put the first money into this business. But did Mr. Ford get his position as vice president because of that? Check up his record. You will find him starting over here in the factory; doing service work in the field; working as a salesman, not for a little while, but for years, and then being moved from one small territory to a little larger one; then landing out in the northwest where he sometimes had to travel a thousand miles to call on a prospect.

No one ever did and no one ever will get anything from IBM through pull. It must be on merit.

In closing I want to leave this thought. This work that you are taking up is not difficult. It does not require any genius. You will see things, at first that you will think difficult to understand. You will hear people talk from this platform and you will say, "I will never be able to talk like that," but you can.

It is very simple. It requires nothing but honest effort and the use of ordinary common sense.

We do not want to fool ourselves.
We do not want to tell each other how good we are.
We want to look ahead.

Proper Use of Time and Effort

Opening Session
1931 One Hundred Percent Club

New York, N.Y.
January 18–21, 1932

It is always a great pleasure for me to be with any group of IBM people, but I consider it a special pleasure to meet with the Hundred Percenters, because the Hundred Percenters are better than average producers.

During the past two years, as you may know, many stockholders have heard a great deal about hard times and depression. Many of them have had it brought home to them in the shape of reduced dividends and in some cases, unfortunately, the elimination of dividends.

It is a source of very great satisfaction to me that our stockholders have had no such message brought home to them. Our operations have been increasingly, rather than decreasingly, profitable each year.

More women than men are stockholders in our business.

Executives Proud of Club

I suppose some of you salesmen are wondering why there are so many executives here on the platform. I can assure you we did not ask these men to come up here so that you might see how handsome they are, or even just to hear them talk. That includes me also.

The reason they are here is that we want to give the men at headquarters an opportunity to look into the faces of the men who are most directly responsible for our company's progress. All of us up here are more interested in the One Hundred Percent Club than we are able to tell you.

I am also very glad to have some members of our organization here this morning who are not in the Hundred Percent Club. I want them to be, and I am sure they will be impressed with the fact that they have not carried their full share of IBM responsibility during the past year.

There are, of course, some cases where men have been ill, or where they have had unusual conditions to contend with in their individual territories that made it impossible for them to make the One Hundred Percent Club.

We must appreciate our individual responsibility to the stockholders.

On the other hand, we know that there are a great number of the territories in this country that are not represented in this club from which we had every reason to expect Hundred Percenters; and in these instances we are disappointed. However, we are not going to present our case to you this morning in a critical manner. We do want every non-One Hundred Percenter in attendance at this convention to appreciate more than ever before his individual responsibility to the stockholders of our company.

There is one man here who started out with a determination to make the very best possible use of all of his talents, and of everything that IBM has to offer in the way of service to customers. He announced last year at the 1930 One Hundred Percent Club of which he was a vice president, and put his announcement in the form of a challenge to all of the men in all divisions that he would be back this year as president of the 1931 club.

I cannot tell you how proud I am of the man who made good that promise and is today to be installed as president of this club. He represents a division of this business whose prospects had every reason to feel the trend of the times more than any other class of prospects we deal with. The people to whom they were selling goods in many cases were not able to pay promptly. In other cases their customers were forced to curtail purchases.

Mr. Owens was transferred to a new territory at the beginning of the year so that he had to start the year without a long list of prospects partially worked up to the point of closing.

He had to go out and develop new prospects and then turn them into customers. He started as soon as he got back from last year's One Hundred Percent Club and he never stopped until the last day of the year.

He was determined to represent you as your president. By his achievement he has set a standard for all the divisions of this business. Incidentally, his territory was scattered over a large area. He was working provincial territory. He had no opportunity to secure large orders.

His record is made up of an accumulation of small sales. It was simply by everlastingly keeping at it and believing in his own ability and in the goods he had to sell that he won for himself the enviable honor of being your president. Thus there is no secret as to how Mr. Owens not only qualified as a member of the 1931 One Hundred Percent Club but also attained its presidency.

Look over the records of the leaders. You will find among them some young men, young in years as well as in terms of service. You will also find among them some of the oldest men in terms of service as well as in years. Mr. Pollack and Mr. Pick, of the Scale Division, for instance, are old in terms of service though not in years. They have never missed coming to a One Hundred Percent Club meeting.

Everything that we do is along the line of service. Every man in the organization is, in effect, a service man. We want to give perfect service—one hundred percent service. Some of our salesmen give better service to the company, to themselves and to their customers than others. Our ultimate aim, however, is to have every man a one hundred percent man in his record of orders and in his record of service to our customers and to himself.

Every man in the organization is, in effect, a service man.

That is why we have Professor Brown and Mr. Limper and many other men devoting all or part of their time to our educational program. We are going to enlarge that program every year just as we propose to enlarge our engineering and research department every year and expand and develop our sales organization every year.

In spite of all the talk that you hear about the machine age, this is the greatest Man Age ever known. We in The IBM organization claim to have a finer group of men than we ever had before, and more of them. Moreover, we intend to keep on improving and expanding our organization from month to month and from year to year. We want constantly more and better manpower to be used in making machines and selling machines so as to lighten the physical burdens of other people and enable businesses served by us to do a better job in their individual industry.

We have a finer group of men than ever before, and more of them.

That is the mission of every organization that is building and selling machinery of any kind. It must relieve the burdens of mankind and the more done along that line the greater are the opportunities for men because men use machines merely as tools to help them do a better job.

In spite of the fact that many companies in this country feel their business is not quite up to standard, every company can look forward to better results in the future. This is so, because in no line of business has development even remotely approached perfection. Until it does there is plenty of room for growth.

Praises Business Leadership

All of the well-regulated businesses in this country are succeeding from year to year. They are doing more planning, more thinking, more developing along every line. The businesses of this country are in good hands in spite of what you many read in the papers about lack of leadership. There is fine leadership in all of the legitimate businesses of this country—industry, transportation, distribution and finance. Let us never lose faith in the leadership of any of these great businesses that we see around us. Behind them are people who are studying and planning and developing for bigger and better things, not only for their own business, but also for greater contributions to industry as a whole.

We of The IBM want those of our men who are so fortunate as to stand out among our leaders to appreciate and realize fully that we have a real responsibility to other businesses. We must extend to them the full and hearty cooperation of our organization wherever it is possible for us to do so.

We want all businesses to be prosperous because that means prosperity for our country and for all our people.

What I say about cooperation with other businesses in this country applies equally to other businesses in the seventy-seven foreign countries in which our machines are used.

150

Several of these countries are represented on this platform this morning, and during this convention we want you One Hundred Percenters of the United States to get well acquainted with every one of our foreign representatives who is here. We want you to know them and we want you to learn from them the things that will help us make greater progress in this country. In turn we want you to teach them the things that will help them.

Learn From Overseas

One of my greatest sources of knowledge concerning the conduct of this business has been my travel in foreign countries, where I have seen men make records under conditions that would be very discouraging to men in the United States. You men in our sales organization today have never experienced the hardship of going into a territory where the people had never heard of your machines and where, after you had explained their purpose, the prospects shook their heads and said, "No, we have no use for that." But that is the experience of these men who have done and are still doing pioneering work in foreign countries.

Remember that less than one-fifth of our business can be credited to all of the seventy-seven foreign countries in which we are engaged in business. That is why I say that our work in the foreign field is still in the pioneer stage.

But that is not at all discouraging. It really is a source of great encouragement for the future, because when you compare the total population of the seventy-seven

One of my greatest sources of knowledge has been my travels in foreign countries.

other countries with the population of our country and then *realize* that out of those seventy-seven you are getting less than one-fifth as much business as you get out of the United States, you cannot help but throw out your chest and glow with enthusiasm at the future in our foreign field no less than at the future in the field at home.

Lack of Faith Dangerous

You have never heard me stand on a platform, since I have been connected with IBM, that I have not predicted to you that business would be better next year; that next year would be an improvement over last year. There has been only one year in the eighteen years that I have faced connected with this company that we have not shown an increase in net profits over the previous year.

We need to hang on to our courage and our belief in IBM and IBM men.

That one exception was in 1921. I am ashamed of it. I am ashamed of that record because it was not necessary for us to show even the slight decrease in our profits that we did show in 1921. It was because we did not have enough knowledge of what we ought to do. Although we thought we had, we had not given enough attention up to that time to our educational program. We had not realized the great field and the great opportunity before us, and when things went to pieces, late in 1920, we threw up our hands, so to speak, with the rest of the country. We said, "Yes, business is bad." We just didn't hang on to our courage and our belief in IBM and in IBM men. That was the only reason why in 1921 we fell behind a little.

By 1929, however, we had carried our educational program to a point where, when things suddenly changed, and more trained men were needed in the field, we were able to put forth the additional effort needed to keep our factory workers employed so that they might support their families and do the things that they had always done.

That is why we have exercised closer supervision over you men in the field. That is why you have heard so much talk about putting on more men to help you do your job. That is why we have spent more money during the last two years in the Research Department than during any other two years in the history of the business.

I shall be here throughout the convention and if I or any of my associates can help you in any way we are at your service.

Every man in the organization is a service man.

152

Prosperity Depends on Work

Twenty-first Annual Convention Opening Session
The National Retail Dry Goods Association

New York, N.Y.
February 1, 1932

It is a very great pleasure for me to be here, and I will try to leave you with some thoughts that I have in mind in connection with your work of dry goods retailing. I am familiar with your business through contact for a great many years with various kinds of retailers.

This organization is of immediate and vital importance because in administering to our wants and supplying our necessities it touches our daily existence in a more intimate and direct way than any other business organization. The daily messages contained in the advertising of the individual members of this association are an unfailing source for the study of economics in millions of households.

The volume of business that you have been able to maintain during the past two years leads me to say that the great retail organizations of this country have dealt with their own problems in a most creditable and constructive way.

It is the part of business leaders to determine the needs of the future.

My interest in retailing began back in the nineties when I first started in business as a salesman for the National Cash Register Company. At that time the entire business of the NCR Company was done with retail merchants, and I had the opportunity and the privilege of studying retail business, large and small, from personal contact with many concerns. Since 1914 I have been in another line of business and in this also I have enjoyed the privilege of doing business with the retailers as well as with all other concerns that keep records.

You are not simply opening your stores and waiting for people to come in and purchase goods. You are advertising, creating a desire on the part of the people to have things which they ought to have; you have injected into your business real fine salesmanship of an honest quality, and that is why your business is progressing and why it is going to continue to progress.

You have spent many years in improving your methods. Study has resulted in large reductions of cost through the elimination of waste. There is still need for improvement in distribution methods. Selling and distributing costs are too high and the attention of leading engineers is now directed toward this problem. Those organizations that are earliest to adopt improved methods are certain to profit most.

The World is Constantly Changing

The only thing we can be sure of is perpetual change.

Life is never static. The only thing we can be sure of is perpetual change. In our time changes are taking place rapidly; today's methods will not be suitable for tomorrow. It is the part of business leaders to determine the needs of the future. Tomorrow's methods must be planned today. Constant and careful research is a necessity no less urgent than the regular flow of daily business into your stores.

I believe thoroughly in the value of group meetings and conventions such as this one. They make possible in a short time an interchange of ideas and a spread of knowledge that would require considerably more time if attempted by the individual concern. The individual assimilates the benefits of the knowledge and experience of others in the group. Each man returns to his own problems with a better perspective. The enthusiasm and good will created by personal contacts act as a stimulus and give everyone new energy to meet the daily task.

Group meetings and conventions, however, are only an incentive to individual endeavor. The idea of the group cannot always be applied to meet successfully the needs of the individual. There has been in the past too much mass thought and action. You must learn to think out your own problems. The problems of each retailer are unique, not exactly duplicated in any other concern. Their solutions can be hastened, they will be more wisely considered and more satisfactorily settled, if due attention is given to the ideas and opinions of your own fellow executives.

A few years ago we acquired the habit of mass thinking. I think that is one of the things that caused a great deal of the trouble we have had. We were all thinking the same about almost everything, particularly the things that were going on in the speculative world.

Today, fortunately, the individual thinker is getting back on the job. The president of the United States is in the lead and he is thinking out ways and means to assist all of us. It is up to us, individually and collectively, to back him in every constructive movement he starts and I am sure that we all want to do so.

Individual thought and action will meet the individual's needs. Every man who has greatly served the world has done so by independent and fearless thinking. Edison, Bell, Eastman, Ford, Schwab, Rosenwald, to mention only a few of our own time—these men were pioneers in spirit, each one self-sustaining.

We are living now in a difficult time, facing unfamiliar conditions. The pioneer viewpoint, the pioneer abilities are necessary for 1932. Our country is a dominant force among the nations of the world. A great portion of its prestige and power is due to the pioneer efforts of our predecessors. We have a great inheritance. Its possession places us under obligation to preserve and increase it. The foundation has been securely laid and it is up to us to build the proper kind of structure.

This Is a Man Age

We often hear it said that this is a machine age. The term leaves a wrong impression. I say this is not a machine age but a Man Age. Machines are merely tools that men have devised to enable them to do a better job. The immediate effect of the machine is the saving of human time and energy in performing the work of the world. All the machines in the world will not bring success unless manned by the right kind of men.

It is manpower, not machine power that makes you successful. Men are doing bigger and better things today than in any other age recorded in history. There is more need today than ever before for trained and efficient manpower. We are only beginning to perceive the extent of the force concealed in our undeveloped manpower. When this latent power is released, the effect will be astounding.

When this latent manpower is released, the effect will be astounding.

Education is the greatest force at our command. Education is always the forerunner of progress.

The job of this generation is to learn the best way to use the means designed to further the end. Education is the greatest force at our command for the attaining of our purpose. Education is always the forerunner of progress, and it is a great satisfaction to note the increased interest business people are taking in educational work. We used to consider education as a walk backward into the past, a review of other people's minds, but business people and research people have interested themselves in it, and now, though we still take into consideration all of the good things of the past, we are reaching into the future and finding out what it is going to demand.

Business Man Must Educate

The man at the head of a retail business must be an educator if he is to progress, because he must always be educating people to go ahead. That applies in all other businesses. Modern education is defined as "training the individual to exercise his capacities to their fullest extent." It is the duty of business leaders today, first, to make available to the rank and file knowledge of the business and second, to expose men constantly to new opportunities.

The past two critical years have challenged the resources of our country and of all countries. I consider that we, as a country, are growing in stature as a result of those experiences.

Your problem is in the future. I do not know what the future holds, but you are looking ahead. My belief is that your future and the future of every business and every individual who is privileged to live in this country, are going to be far better than anything we have ever seen in the past. I am not going to tell you that prosperity is just around the corner, but I am going to tell you that prosperity is out there somewhere. How soon we are going to get back to what we call American prosperity depends on how fast we go and how hard we work.

It is the part of business leaders
to determine the needs of the future.

Launching a New Era of Progress

Breaking Ground Ceremonies for Company's New Laboratory

Endicott, N.Y.
July 12, 1932

This is a very significant event in the history of our company.

The turning of this shovelful of earth marks the turning point to a new era of still greater development, improvement and increased business for The IBM. This will mean more employment for the people at Endicott as well as in our various offices and territories throughout the seventy-eight countries where we sell our products. It also will mean better returns to our stockholders in the way of increased dividends in the future.

Praises Engineers

I want on this occasion to express my appreciation and the appreciation of the directors and stockholders of our company as well as to the engineering and research departments that have con-trib-uted so much to the growth and development of this business. It was the development work of the men in these departments during the preceding years that made it possible for us to carry on during the past three years of stress.

No business in the world can hope to move forward if it does not keep abreast of the times.

We have been able to carry on and keep our people employed because the men in our engineering department are constantly giving us new and better products as well as improvements on our existing products. These additions to our line have enabled us to put on more salesmen and broaden our field of activity.

We have realized from experience that the future of our business largely depends on the efforts, brain and ability of our engineering department. There is no business in the world, which can hope to move forward if it does not keep abreast of the times, look into the future and study the probable demands of the future. That is why today we are breaking ground for this new building, which will be devoted entirely to research and engineering work. We propose to have the very best equipped laboratory for a business such as ours

157

that it is possible to have. Having such a laboratory means a great deal for our company because the world is going to demand more of us in the future.

Machines Increase Employment

We sometimes hear it said that improved machinery causes unemployment. Anyone who makes a study of the actual situation, however, will find that this is incorrect. Every industry that has installed improved machines and which has kept its machinery up to date has expanded and employed more people year after year. Thus we are in a business that not only takes the drudgery away from office workers but that also helps to expand all business and increase employment throughout the world.

I have expressed our appreciation to the engineering department for its contribution to our success. I wish to express our appreciation and thanks also to the men in the factory for the quality of work they have given us in turning out the best machines of the kind that ever have been manufactured. I wish also on behalf of the factory people and office employees to express to the representatives of the field who are here today our deep appreciation for the extra effort put forth throughout the sales organization of The IBM world to send in orders to keep this factory going during these trying times. Everyone in the office and in the factory deeply appreciates the efforts that the sales force has put forth.

If I have accomplished anything in this business worthy of mention it is not due to my personal efforts and any personal ability. It is due entirely to the wholehearted support and cooperation that I have had from the men who have spoken to you this morning; from others who are not here, from you people confronting me here and from the salesmen and other employees of the company throughout the seventy-eight countries of the world where we do business.

When any man tells you that one man alone can do a big job he knows he is not telling the truth.

When any man tells you that one man alone can do a big job he knows he is not telling the truth; and when any one man listens to a group of men telling him that he did everything, he knows it simply is not so. That is why I want to say that all the success of The IBM is

158

not due to me or to any other man or small group of men. It is due rather, to the fine support, cooperation, brainpower and ability in every department of this business.

This has been a wonderful morning for me. I hope you people have enjoyed it a tenth as much as I have. I want to thank you all again not only for coming out here this morning and attending these ceremonies, but also for all you have done in the past. I particularly wish to thank the men and women of this business who were here before I came here and who did the real pioneer work. These men and

It is always easier to build after the foundation is laid.

women laid the foundation for our present business and made it possible for the rest of us to come in and build on that foundation. It is always easier to build after the foundation is laid.

I also want to pay tribute this morning to the people who have been in this business but who are not with us this morning, to the late Mr. Harlow E. Bundy, who founded the Time Recording Division, and to the late Dr. Hollerith, who founded the Tabulating Machine Division. They both have departed, but they have left monuments that will live on and will be cherished in the hearts and the minds of the people in this business today and all the people who are coming into it in the future.

I wish to pay tribute also to Mr. Edward Canby, who founded the Scale Division of our business, and who is still with us taking an active interest and advising us in the business.

Our business's future depends on the efforts, brain and ability of our engineering department.

A Great Step Forward

Editorial Published in Business Machines

July 14, 1932

The breaking of ground last Tuesday at Endicott for the erection of our new laboratory building and schoolhouse was a great event in the progressive development of this business. The laboratory will be used exclusively for engineering research, and the development of new and better machines for the future needs of industry. The schoolhouse will be used exclusively for educational purposes and the development of more and better salesmen to present these new machines to industry.

The progress of this business, particularly in the last few trying years, is not due to any outstanding genius in its management. It is explained by just two factors: research and education.

Today our company has more and better time and money saving machines to serve business than it ever had before; and more and better-trained representatives to sell them. When these two latest additions to our Endicott plant are completed and in operation, we will develop a great many more products to add to our line, and we will have a greatly expanded educational program for the benefit of the members of our organization and our clients.

The progress of this business is explained by just two factors—research and education.

I cannot place too much emphasis on the value of education. If our business and financial leaders had possessed the proper knowledge, this country would not have experienced the difficulties it has during the past three years. Our great industrial leaders, of which there is no dearth in this country, must take a more active interest than they have in all educational work. All of our people must give more thought to business and financial economics. To that end, the curriculum in our schools and colleges must be extended along practical economic lines.

There is no saturation point in education. No man ever goes so high that he can afford to say, or even to think, that his education is completed. No young man starting in business can afford to overlook the necessity for increasing his knowledge. That is why we are conducting and expanding our sales schools, service schools, foremen's schools, executive schools and office schools. That is why we hold meetings and conventions. And all this forms only a part of our educational program.

Every day brings added opportunities to IBM men to learn more about this business. Times and conditions change rapidly, and if a business organization does not change with them, it cannot make any great progress. Education is a most vital factor in enabling us to keep abreast of conditions.

Education is the most vital factor in enabling us to keep abreast of changing conditions.

Our new schoolhouse will provide us with the best educational facilities there are for a business such as ours. The acceleration in the work of devising more efficient machines which our new laboratory will make possible and the comprehensive courses of study which our new school facilities will enable us to adopt will put us in a position to render a better service to our customers and to our company than ever before and to produce a still greater return for our stockholders on their investment.

Every day brings added opportunities to IBM men.

WORKPLACE SAFETY

In the 1930s, the safety record for most United States businesses was abysmal—and deteriorating. Men and children were dying in factories, canneries and mines. Women in New York were working in sweatshops in unsafe conditions. Thos. J. Watson Sr. stated with rigor and conviction, as he always did on topics near to his heart, that the workplace should be safe.

Why should a business spend precious money on safety during a major economic depression? There were two main reasons: economic for those who needed a business justification and ethical for those who made decisions on a higher plane. Thos. J. Watson Sr. was both the pragmatist and the idealist.

First were the very real, tangible business reasons to act. He was, after all, a businessman and he knew that there were executives in corporate America who would only act if an idea had a positive, bottom-line financial impact. In this article, he points to the ability to reduce insurance costs. Employee productivity is a second factor—injuries waste a lot of time and manpower, which we've already established was, according to Watson, the company's chief asset.

We were prodigal of human safety, as we have been of many of our great natural resources.

The second reason to ensure workplace safety was a matter of ethics. It was that indefinable something that couldn't be captured directly in a profit-loss statement; intangible benefits such as shared cooperation, mutual trust and building a deep loyalty between Chief Executive Officer and the rest of his corporation.

He knew that by being a conscientious leader, "his workers would lend him their every cooperation." Cooperation was always top of mind. No business or government, he felt, could be successful if it was at war with itself. An optimized corporate financial statement required every individual's focus, attention and cooperation.

Tom Watson Sr. concluded that to be effective, the executive must *centralize* direction, focus and urgency in the corner office. But to be efficient, the executive must *decentralize* record keeping, responsibility and watchfulness to the foreman and individual worker.

The executive will be portrayed as a conscientious leader. His workers will lend him their every cooperation.

This book explores how Tom Watson Sr. balanced the financially tangible and intangible, the roles of pragmatist and idealist, the centralization and decentralization of authority. This article is a wonderful example of his approach and style.

It would seem that we were prodigal of human safety as we have been of many of our great natural resources.

Safety Measures in Industry

Third Annual Greater New York
Safety Conference

New York, N.Y.
February 24, 1932

Available records indicate that industrial hazards were first noted in those industries that, on account of the prevalence of dust particles, gave rise to diseases of the respiratory organs. It is entirely reasonable to believe that any interference with the vital functions of the respiratory organs would be the first to be noticed.

More than eighteen hundred years ago, the famous Roman commander, Pliny the Elder, made probably the first mention of the use of protective devices for workers in the so-called "dusty" trades. He observed that in the preparation of vermillion pigment, ancient workers covered their faces with bladder skins, which eliminated the possibility of breathing dust yet permitted them to see what they were doing.

One might think that this and similar observations regarding human welfare would have borne fruit in precautions in later generations. But, as age succeeded age in the march of time, we find that little attention was paid to the prevention of accidents until a comparatively short time ago.

A Shocking Picture

Looking back to the beginning of the present industrial era, when manufacturing became a factory process instead of a neighborhood or hand trade, we are shocked at the picture of industrial conditions, the lack of sanitation and safety devices and the frequency of fatal accidents and maiming injuries.

Executives must recognize a direct relationship between efficiency of the factory and welfare of the worker.

In some respects, it would seem that we were prodigal of human safety, as we have been of many of our great natural resources.

Factory legislation, civil service and trade unions have improved working conditions; but not until major executives fully recognize a direct relationship between the productive efficiency of the factory and the safety and welfare of the worker will the desired progress be made.

Flaws in Legislation

Prior to 1837, the common-law relation between employer and employee was no more than the legal relation between strangers. Following that year, however, a vast mass of special legislation developed governing the relations of employer and employee. The adverse character of these laws from the employee's standpoint is indicated by the doctrines of practices of:

- "**Contributory negligence**," which meant that an employee must prove that he was not negligent;
- The "**fellow-servant**" rule, which provided that an injured employee could not recover damages from the employer if the injury was caused by the negligence of a fellow-servant; and
- The "**assumption of risk**" rule, which was to the effect that an employee entering employment was assumed to consent to the ordinary and obvious risks incident to that employment.

With the application of these harsh rules, various statutes were enacted for the protection of employees. The good effects of this legislation were soon counteracted, however, by the development of the privilege of the employer to request his employees to contract away their rights under the law, thus relieving the employer of all liability for injury.

Little Financial Redress

Under this system, it naturally followed that little financial redress was obtainable for injured employees. The fault was in the system of law that forced upon the employee the burden of proof and made compensation possible to only a very small proportion of injured employees. This system led to excessive delays, due to the slow operation of court trials, and proved exceedingly wasteful in time and attorneys' fees to employer and employee.

In view of these shortcomings, the public demanded a more definite and rational system of law with respect to employers' liability for industrial accidents. This was accomplished through the passage of the Workmen's Compensation Laws, and within the decade 1910 to 1920, practically every industrial state in the Union enacted such legislation.

Accident Death Rate Increasing

Even with efforts to improve safety measures, the accident death rate per 100,000 inhabitants in the United States has climbed from seventy fatally injured persons in 1922 to eight-one persons in 1929, an increased toll of 15% in the seven-year period.

In order to check that upward trend and to reduce accidents and fatalities to the lowest possible number, a decided change in our attitude toward safety must be brought about. The safety movement has been in operation for somewhat more than two decades. The interest in safety measures, however, has spread largely as a result of humanitarian consideration. During this period, manufacturing production has increased more than three-fold.

Greater progress in accident prevention will be brought about through executive consideration.

The efficiency of the worker in factories, on farms, in mines and on railways has increased one-third in the past decade. How do we account for this progress? Much has been due to the systematic study of problems of production and efficiency. These problems have had the benefit of organized and continuous study by management. Systematic efforts have been made to economize on materials and labor and to solve factory problems in general.

But in the reduction of accidents we have not made the progress that we should have made. The factor of safety as compared to production is not commensurate. Sufficient stress has not been laid on the fact that greater progress in accident prevention will be brought about mainly through executive consideration, as is the case with the other major functions of management such as financing, engineering, production and marketing.

Management Policy Recommended

Through executive consideration, there should be formulated a specific company policy and plan of organization indicating definite activities and responsibilities for each department in its relation to accident prevention. It should recognize that safety operation has a bearing on good will, sales, production volume and general results.

Safety—prevention of accidents and health of employees—should be very definitely a part of every corporation's business policy.

The factors that make for greater safety should be definitely recognized, defined and expressed in a business. Executive policy should indicate likewise the specific channels of responsibility of all concerned and provide for such reports as will give to management a simple means of measuring results and instituting the proper measures of control.

Such a program parallels the recognized management approach to problems of finance, production and marketing, and recognizes that accident prevention is, in its final analysis, an integral part of operating procedure.

Executive Attention Needed

Considerable administrative attention is given today to economy. Financial statements are scrutinized with high-powered glasses to magnify any traces of wasteful operation, the fluctuating upward movement of unit costs and many other flaws in the industrial picture.

That same executive attention should be given to safety, which involves as much, if not more, responsibility than is given to other problems of plant operation. Since the average executive spends considerable time in the analysis of financial reports, I believe that the logical approach to a safety policy lies in the statement of income and expenses.

The same executive attention should be given to safety as economy.

The passage of the Workmen's Compensation Acts, beginning with 1911, introduced a new element of expense into the financial summary. This, in turn, necessitated an extra charge to manufacturing costs.

As executives, we are intensely interested in controlling our costs. A great number of corporate accounts have been analyzed and drastically reduced, but inadequate attention has been paid to the possible reduction of compensation insurance costs.

168

Safety Program Important

Once the executive's interest in the economic and social aspects of safety is stimulated, he will be ready to consider organization plans. Safety, however, does not differ from any other executive policy. But unless it receives the sincere and wholehearted cooperation of management and labor, it will not progress.

For that reason, the foundation of the safety program should be laid with the utmost care. Responsibility for the safety organization should be centered in the executive province, but the same supervision should be exercised in the execution of its regulations as in the case of the production schedule. A general committee type of organization should be favored so that equal representation might be had for executive, manager and employee.

With this all-embracing plan of organization, the employee's interest automatically becomes the interest of his employers.

Foreman Familiar with Needs

An effective approach to the execution of the safety program is through the foreman. In his daily contact with men, machines and material, he is in a key position to observe and correct unsafe practices found in the manufacturing processes. Moreover, he should be held responsible for the preparation of monthly reports summarizing the number and severity of accidents of each man in his department.

The inadequacy of accident reports now available is appalling.

Those who have attempted the study of industrial accidents will agree that it is almost impossible to obtain an accurate idea of the extent and cost of fatal and non-fatal accidents in American industrial establishments. That, however, is not the fault of our fact-finding institutions; it is due entirely to the lack of united and uniform assumption of responsibility on the part of industrial executives.

When a rough estimate, based upon studies of the National Industrial Conference Board, discloses that there are between ten million and eleven million injuries in the manufacturing industries annually, the necessity for executive action in accident prevention is apparent.

Every executive in the United States, whether he directs a large or small establishment, should see to it that accuracy and promptness govern the compilation of accident and inspection reports. Then,

169

with these records as an index to the productive efficiency and accident control in the plant, he can easily compare the position of his company with that of other organizations with reference to safety progress.

Executive Responsibility Continuous

But even when safety is written into the general policy, the executive has not discharged his entire obligation. It remains for him to keep the safety policy active and productive of satisfactory results. The ultimate success of the executive in that direction will be reflected throughout the whole company. He will be portrayed as a conscientious leader, and because of the spirit that he manifests in this direction, his workers will lend him their every cooperation.

Safety is a matter of individual responsibility for each factory or establishment; for each president; for each executive; for each foreman and for each worker. Only by a full realization of this responsibility on the part of each individual will safety be instituted and maintained as a specific executive policy, which will contribute immeasurably to a broader and sounder industrial program and add to the happiness—and improve the welfare of—the worker.

Safety is a matter of individual responsibility for each factory or establishment.

CHARACTER AND RESPONSIBILITY

So many times we hear of celebrities, sports figures and business executives speak of protecting their reputation—their good name. To Watson there was a person's reputation; and then there was personal character.

The two stood apart.

Although he definitely cared about protecting his reputation, ultimately it was character that defined any path for him,

Character is what you really are and what you know you are.

his people or his organization. It was unacceptable for him or anyone associated with The IBM to stray from that path. To him character was preeminent and intimately linked with responsibility. He felt that it took moral courage and spiritual strength to "accept responsibility."

Today Chief Executive Officers can sit before Congress and claim plausible deniability—that they could never possibly know what is going on within the vastness or complexity of their corporation. It is hard to envision that Tom Watson would have ever used such a legal tactic to hide from his responsibilities. He internalized his responsibility for his company's actions. He spoke words of individual responsibility for himself and demanded it of his team, constantly stressing the need for each individual to initially adhere to and understand corporate policy; but if in doubt to bring questions to the executives—even to him if necessary.

Watson accepted personal responsibility during the Depression. His character—the essence what he really was inside—was determined to stabilize and increase employment; to collect, retain and promote good men; to increase wages; to improve safety conditions and to pay consistent and growing dividends.

He held up The IBM as the model, an example of humanity's ability to cooperate not just domestically but internationally. To him, "strength of character is the one basic trait which will be found in all people who achieve greatness." There is no doubt that he desired greatness. Greatness, though, could never be found down a path of irresponsibility. For him, greatness was only found down a path bounded on one side by character and on the other by responsibility.

In 1914, when his company's Board of Directors wanted to extract short-term profit by "pumping and dumping" the stock (a practice that, leading up to the Depression, was very legal and very widely practiced), he stood toe-to-toe with them and won. For him, business was a matter of ethics. He was building a corporation that would go on forever; something lasting, enduring and beneficial to man; something people could trust and would want to invest in.

He expected individual strength of character within community, business and government. Of the government, he said, "It is our problem as individuals because the government is our government."

He was a Citizen of the United States of America.

He was the Chief Executive Officer of The IBM.

He was, in his heart and soul, an IBM Caretaker—an IBMer.

To him, there were no greater positions in life—no greater responsibilities. Because of his strength of character, he achieved greatness.

It is the rank and file of an organization that counts, and enlightened executives today fully realize this fact.

Character and Responsibility

Members of the Oxford Class of
The First Methodist Episcopal Church

Endicott, N.Y.
April 10, 1932

At my office in New York, I ring a time recorder six days a week, but I usually make Sunday a day of rest. However, I was very pleasantly surprised when I arrived here this morning and found not only that I must ring a time recorder to attend this class but that Mr. Johnson and all the other members of the class must do the same thing. I feel that your use of one of our time clocks is a very real complement to our company, to say nothing of its advertising value to The IBM.

None of us can ever hope to get anywhere, to be of any real use to ourselves, to our community or to our country, unless we have the character, the moral courage and the spiritual strength to accept responsibility. Strength of character is the one basic trait that will be found in all people who achieve greatness.

When I say character I do not mean reputation. Character is what you really are and what you know you are. Reputation, on the other hand, is what people think you are which does not necessarily bear any resemblance to what you really are.

I had an excellent illustration of just this point last summer on my farm. After a severe local storm I went out for a walk and found one of the largest limbs torn off what looked to be one of my finest maple trees. Its outside appearance had been excellent but to my amazement I found it decayed inside. Its beautiful foliage and fine bark were not able, unsupported by a sound heart, to withstand the stress of storm—just as

Its beautiful foliage and fine bark were unable to withstand the stress of the storm—just as some men.

some men, with fine clothes and important reputations, conceal black hearts.

Strength of character I regard as the most important thing in life.

A Business Saved

You all know the history of the Endicott Johnson Corporation; how the old company of which it is formed was about to leave the community when Mr. Johnson stepped into the breach. He undertook to rehabilitate that business in spite of the fact that rebuilding is sometimes harder than making a fresh start. But he was not afraid of the responsibility; and how well he has succeeded, how completely he has been found worthy of that responsibility, is a matter of international knowledge. Today the products of the Endicott Johnson Corporation are distributed throughout the world and everywhere they go they carry with them the influence and the real character of George F. Johnson.

Enlightened executives realize it is the rank and file of an organization that counts.

Rank and File Counts

I was very happy to hear Mr. Johnson refer to the importance in any business of the men who do the actual work. Generals would be powerless without armies. Executives are useless without the wholehearted cooperation of loyal workers. Your pastor could not accomplish anything worthwhile without the support of the members of this class and of this church. It is the rank and file of an organization that counts and enlightened executives today fully realize this fact. Moreover, I would like on this occasion to reiterate that I am proud of the rank and file of The IBM.

Coming back to the main theme of my talk, right next to character in the list of invaluable human traits I would place personality. Particularly in times such as the present, we need real outstanding personalities. It is not some fancy panacea or new economic theory that is wanted, but courageous and compellingly convincing personalities such as many financial, mercantile and other industrial leaders possess, to carry us on to still greater progress and achievement.

The reason there are not more such men is that we have acquired the habit of mass thinking. We got off the main track of original and creative individual thought. We have to get back to it, not only to individual thought, but also to individual action. Every one of us must put his shoulder to the wheel and do his bit. Out of such individual effort will come great achievements.

Personal Responsibility

I would like to enlarge a little on the idea of personal responsibility of which I have been speaking. If we are working for Mr. Johnson, for instance, personal responsibility means that it is definitely up to us to make a personal contribution to the success of that business, not simply to make more money for Mr. Johnson—which consideration does not enter into the problem at all—but to bring more payroll into the City of Endicott.

It is our problem as individuals because the government is our government.

This can be done by each one of us if we put forth every effort to make better products at the least possible cost. Decreasing cost means increasing distribution, which in turn means increasing production and higher payrolls. That is what we must think of as individual workers.

As citizens let us think more of what we can do as individuals in the community. The big problem facing the country today—the problem that is bothering Washington, is how to balance the budget. It is not fair for us to put it all up to the President and to Congress.

It is our problem as individuals because the government is our government. We should make a start right at home to see if we cannot get greater value for the taxes collected. In that way we will build a better community, a better country and make of ourselves better and more useful citizens.

Spiritual Awakening

But perhaps the greatest need of all today in this country is a genuine spiritual awakening; and I am particularly proud to have been given this opportunity to meet all of you in your church this morning because you are the ones who are taking an active part in the spiritual affairs of this community. Perhaps I can best illustrate the importance of the spiritual life in the field of action by an observation told to me shortly after the war.

Mr. Marcosson had visited all five fronts three times during the war and had lived at the headquarters of every general of all the Allied armies. I asked him if he had noticed any one outstanding characteristic common to all of the great leaders with whom he had lived. His

The greatest need of all is spiritual awakening.

reply was, "Yes. They were all spiritual men, read their Bibles regularly and said their prayers nightly." I did not come here to preach a sermon but I regard that point as highly significant.

It is perfectly true, of course, that in every community you will find men who are taking things lightly, but it has been my experience that the men who are doing big things and making real contributions to their country are the men who have a very real and deep-seated conviction and faith in matters which have to do with the spiritual life.

None of us can hope to get anywhere without character, moral courage and the spiritual strength to accept responsibility.

THE PRESIDENT AS SALESMAN IN CHIEF

Today, the word salesman is synonymous with money.

Mr. Watson, though, believed that being a salesman was an honorable trade. He desired IBM salesmen to be people of integrity, character and perseverance. They had a duty to bring to their customers any product that would make their businesses more efficient. Selling was a win-win relationship. Money was not the focus, but rather a reward for the proper focus.

Thomas J. Watson Sr. was the "Salesman in Chief." His priority was building a service organization. If a Chief Executive Officer built a successful business with high customer service then money, status and a long tenure were just rewards. A Chief Executive Officer accumulating personal wealth at the expense of service was walking a different path from Tom Watson. To him, such misplaced priorities contributed to the Great Depression.

Selling begins at the top of the business.

He spoke with passion that society, "we," as he said, needed to get a jolt, come back to earth, get back to fundamentals and have a spiritual awakening. Accomplish that and business would move forward again. In "Real Salesmanship," he discusses his belief in one of the root causes of the Depression: In 1929, nearly everyone had dollar signs in front of them. Everything, including social and religious standing, had become based on the dollar.

In "How to Get More Business in 1933," he emphasizes the need for anyone desiring to be president to learn how to supervise others. They must practice five steps in order to be successful: hire, train, supervise, promote and finally discharge men.

His constant theme of education and self-study reappears in "The Sales Promotion Factor." He states that a person must read, listen, discuss, observe and as always, THINK. Of course, this was all done to support the selling process.

We should all endeavor to think of our employees as salesmen and talk with them as salesmen.

Finally, in "The Need for Individual Action," every employee should be a salesman. As was so typical of The IBM culture, there were many positions within administration, marketing and research; but there was only one true vocation—that of salesman for "The IBM." It was an honorable profession calling for character, enthusiasm, self-education, leadership, determination, knowledge and wisdom; all the best qualities he admired.

Tom Watson Sr. embodied these characteristics.

At his death, he was called "The World's Greatest Salesman."

He would have been proud.

Selling begins at the top of the business.

Real Salesmanship

Principal Speaker
The Machinery Builders Society

Sky Top, Pennsylvania
May 4, 1932

It is a real pleasure for me to meet with you tonight, not only because it is a privilege to address you, but also because of what I know I am going to learn from association with you.

With reference to giving advice to you on how to sell your goods, I want you to know I am not going to attempt to do that because I do not know how. We are all given to feeling sometimes that the other fellow is sick and we are all right. I do not feel that way because I have a great many problems.

The problem of getting goods sold is the greatest of all in every business, and more particularly in times such as we have been going through. What your chairman said about the Depression and the frame of mind in which it has put us all, I fully endorse. We are certainly in the wrong frame of mind and taking the wrong attitude toward the situation just as, back in 1929, we were taking the wrong attitude toward everything we were doing at that time. We are too prone to compare everything now with what it was in 1929. Yet where would we be today if we continued at the pace of 1929? I am sure none of us could have stood up under the strain.

In 1929, nearly all of us had the dollar sign in front of us—that and nothing more. Everything was measured in terms of the dollar. A man's success, his social standing and, in a great many cases, even his religious standing were based on the dollar.

I am not going to preach a sermon, but I do think it was necessary for this nation of ours to get a good jolt, do a right-about-face, and get back to earth and more of the real fundamentals of life. What we need in this country is a real spiritual awakening. Then, when we have ceased to measure all things in terms of dollars, we will begin to move forward again.

As I look around me and at the people with whom I associate, I find more happiness now than in 1929, when everybody was under that terrible strain—when the radio was turned on only for stock quotations and the financial page of the newspaper was read before the editorial page. Those days are over and we are getting back to a good sound basis.

History Will Be Repeated

I am absolutely sure in my own mind, and I am sure you feel the same way, that we are going to get out of this depression. I will not give the date—I do not know—but every day we go at the rate we are going we are getting nearer to the turning point. History, I believe, will repeat itself. We are going to reach greater heights of prosperity than ever before because we are going to think along sounder and better lines.

In the last analysis you have to consider the law of supply and demand. The demand is bound to change, but I think we can do more than is being done to help the law get into action. I believe that now is the time for all of us to prepare for what the future is going to demand of us, because I am sure the future is going to demand more from all of us.

You men are engaged in building machinery. Other men are building other things. We are all trying to build things that will enable people to make better goods for the same money or more goods for less money. It is merely a question of giving better equipment to the people who use our products.

If you take your own line and look back twenty years and compare

We want our salesmen to cooperate with other salesmen in other businesses.

what you are giving now with what you gave then, you will get some little idea of what the next twenty years are going to demand of you. I have here a few points I want to emphasize:

We want our salesmen to cooperate not only with one another in our own business but with other salesmen in other businesses. Cooperation is a prime essential. We see it much more in evidence today than we did back in the dollar days of two or three years ago. We are giving considerably more thought to the other fellow.

Back in those days, a great many people did not really understand cooperation. At that time most men's idea of cooperation was, "You do everything you can to help me and I will do as I please about helping you." Cooperation must be in even balance.

Your chairman spoke about our THINK sign.

This has done more for my organization and me than any other word we have discovered. It is a continuous reminder that we must think about our product. You have been thinking about various problems; that is why you have met here—to discuss the things you have been thinking about. Doubtless all people do not "think right," but the main idea is to get them thinking. Individual thought is very important.

With our wonderful newspaper system, our magazines, the radio, etc., disseminating news every hour of the day, we are likely to get into a channel and all think about the same on every subject. It seems to me that what individual businesses of this country need is more individual thinking and action. The success of every business in working out of this depression and carrying on depends more on what we do as individuals than on anything else.

We hear constantly the cry for leadership. "We have no leadership," people say. I heard a man make a fine speech the other day. In the course of it, he said, "Oh, if we only had a George Washington today!" and I wondered what Washington would do with our problems if he were here.

After thinking about it I decided that, with all due respect to his great ability, he could not handle the situation at all. I do not think there is any one man anywhere who could lead us all to success. We waste too much time demanding leadership.

As a matter of fact, we have first-class leadership everywhere. The businesses represented in this room have first class leadership and you know it. Business as a whole, finance, transportation, manufacturing, wholesaling and retailing, public utilities, all are in the hands of capable people and will work out their own problems.

So when I hear people shouting for leadership, it does not impress me very much. We have gone beyond the point where we can depend on any one man to think for us or to lead us all to success. So let us make up our minds to spread the doctrine of individual leadership and individual thinking on the problems is the various industries. Let us start with individual action right now.

I think a little effort on the part of every man in every organization throughout the country would produce an accumulated flood of thought that would soon change what we call depression to what we understand as prosperity.

Research Pays Dividends

I would like to explain to you how we have been able to keep our own business going. It has not been due to any outstanding leadership or to any one group of men of unusual ability in our organization. We have just ordinary men doing their best to do a good job. Why we have been more fortunate than most businesses is because, for a number of years, we have been spending more time and effort in our research department.

Naturally, when the Depression hit us we had some new machines and ideas to give our salesmen. These not only broadened the scope of our regular salesmen's activities in the field, but also required the employment of more salesmen to call on more people, thus enabling us to keep our factories working. If we had had to depend on the line we had five years ago it might have been a different story.

I am a great believer in the research end of the business as the greatest aid to the salesman, and the salesman is the one we must think most about because the success of our business depends on how much we sell. A great deal will depend in the future on what we are doing now in improving our products and developing new machines to meet new needs.

Where Selling Begins

To sell his policies, the president must think and study to ensure his policies are sound and right.

You have been told that I am going to talk about selling. What I have been saying is all along selling lines, but I do not want to talk to you tonight from the standpoint of your salesmen and what they should do out in the field. We all know that selling begins at the top of the business, with the president. Regardless of whether he came up from the selling ranks or gained his experience otherwise, the president first of all must sell his policies and the company's policies to the vice president, general manager, sales manager, salesman, etc. That makes him think and study to make sure the policies are sound and right.

There are two people in a business that I place above everybody else in importance. One is the sales manager and the other is the factory foreman. They stand between the executive staff and the rest of the organization. I give a great deal of time and thought to these two positions because I can do more effective work here than anywhere else in the business.

If the sales manager knows and does his job, he has the hardest spot in the organization. His thought must be everywhere and he must try to be in as many places as possible. He must sell his ideas to his salesmen and keep posted as to whether they are carrying them out properly. His duties as we classify them in our business come under five heads: these are to employ his men; teach and train them; supervise them; promote them; and discharge them if they are not making good. The sales manager needs the support of all the people above him in carrying out these five functions.

If he gives proper attention to the first four, he will not have to give so much to the fifth, which is the most disagreeable but necessary if a man does not deserve his job.

Our greatest difficulty is to get our salesmen to put in the proper time with prospective customers.

Salesmen and Productive Time

I do not know how to pick out a salesman, to judge offhand whether he is a salesman. I would simply select a young man of good character and give him a try-out. I would soon learn whether he was a salesman. The greatest difficulty in our whole plan of distribution is to get our salesmen to put in the proper amount of time in the presence of their prospective customers. We spend a great deal of time watching the productive and non-productive time in our factories because we realize the importance of keeping the two in balance. So for several years I have been giving my attention to the non-productive time of salesmen.

We try to get the salesman to realize that what counts is not the time between when he leaves home and when he gets back, the time spent on the letters he writes or the plans he lays out, but only the amount of time he spends in front of his customer trying to get an order. I tell my men to keep track of this time themselves, and when they do they are ashamed of their records. They then realize how little time they are putting in on actual selling.

A great deal of attention is given by many businesses to the training of employees. Everybody knows the importance of this and each business represented here probably has a different plan for teaching salesmen. I would like to mention one thing that I believe has helped us more than any other in the teaching line.

Executive Schools

Who is teaching the teachers?

We have always had schools for salesmen, servicemen, foremen, clerks, etc., but about ten years ago we asked ourselves, "Who is teaching the teachers?"

Then we decided to establish an Executives' School, to see what we could learn from one another. The school is composed of the executives, sales managers, heads of departments and factory foremen, about a hundred people out of a total of approximately 7,000 employees. There is no prepared program. Someone is asked to start the meeting and the program develops extemporaneously. Once started, the chief difficulty is to get the meeting adjourned.

Every man knows something about the business that the others do not know, and the purpose of the school is to distribute this knowledge. It serves as a clearinghouse. Many good ideas are advanced by the factory foremen, particularly on how to reduce production costs. Notes are taken which form the basis of whatever may be decided to adopt as policies.

Our Executive School has no teacher, no one person who leads it. We simply get together, usually twice a year, but always once at least. Each one in the school is a teacher. At every one of the sessions we all learn some things about the business we never knew before.

That is the kind of school you are having here tonight—a meeting of executives from various businesses—though this school is on a very

184

much broader plane, with proportionately greater educational value than a meeting of the employees of a single business.

Exchange Ideas

I was much interested in some of the things your chairman mentioned. I found out years ago that because I gave so much time to my own business I was getting into a rut. So I decided to get out and see what other people were doing, to broaden my mind on business in general and see what I could bring back to apply to my own business.

I have some friends who would smile at a meeting of this kind—a waste of time, they would call it, because they do not understand. I cannot comprehend why anyone fails to appreciate the importance of an exchange of ideas among a number of different people. In addition to that the friendships that are made are valuable. It counts a great deal, this making of friendships with people in other lines of business and other parts of the country.

Sales Policies

Another point I want to make as an important policy to apply to the sales organization is the matter of entertainment. This is especially important at this time. Those of us who worked as salesmen years ago remember this evil and its gradual elimination. I am trying to guard against this in every way by keeping before our men the fact that what the customer wants is the right kind of goods at the right price with the right service, rather than entertainment. I think extensive entertainment is something that should be opposed by every sales manager, and it is up to us to see that he does it.

Within the organization, if the sales manager elects to entertain his salesmen, it should be after business hours and should be the right kind of entertainment—in keeping with the standards and policies of the company he represents. I think this very important because we all know the great value of influence, how far-reaching it is.

Another thing of great importance is the personality of the salesman. We try to teach our salesmen to get their personality behind the product instead of in front of it. Sometimes a salesman with a fine, outstanding personality fails because his personality is kept in front and the prospective customer's mind is on that instead of the product.

I do think we are going to need a few years from now more salesmen than we have. My idea on new salesmen is to select a young man, right out of school, and start him out as an assistant with an older salesman. This enables him to learn and enables the regular salesman to make more money with less effort.

We have been very successful with young men who are willing to start at a nominal salary in the belief that they are starting their careers. We have seldom failed to get a man who is not willing to give good service in comparison with the money he wants. At the same time, we are grooming those men for future sales work. We start these young men on salaries, but wherever it is practical we pay our regular men on a commission basis. We find this more satisfactory to the men and to the company. On a straight commission basis they can set their own standard of earnings.

Each man is given a quota of so many dollars a month based on the number of prospects in his territory. Where a man feels his quota is too high we show him just what it is based on. Our statistical department has been working on this for years and is held responsible for keeping records up to date, from daily reports of salesmen telling whom they have called on, any changes that may take place in their territories, etc.

If the salesman gets a hundred percent of his quota for twelve months, he becomes a member of our One Hundred Percent Club. We make a feature of this, keep the pot boiling all the year, and it helps a great deal. A salesman needs a great deal of encouragement to keep up his enthusiasm. He cannot work without it. No enthusiastic man is lazy. The executives should do all they can to keep up the enthusiasm of the men in the field. Many things discourage them when they are out in the field with things going badly and no one to talk to, but if they get some kind of encouragement from headquarters it is very helpful.

I hope I have dropped a thought here and there that some of you can profit by in some way. If there are any questions you would like to ask that you think I can answer, I will do my best.

The executives should do all they can
to keep up the enthusiasm of the men in the field.

186

How to Get More Business in 1933

Guest Speaker Opening Address
National Association of Direct Selling Companies

New York, N.Y.
January 27, 1933

It is always my desire to attend meetings of an educational nature, such as this is today, because I can really learn something from them. The basis of success is knowledge. In the atmosphere of a meeting of this type, finding myself in a group of men engaged in direct selling, I add to my knowledge and gain real inspiration. The subject of selling is close to my heart.

Although my title in the company with which I am associated is that of "President," I think of myself primarily as a sales manager. Of course, as head of the business I must know about finance, manufacturing and other angles of administration, but selling is the most important part of business. The head of a business can employ experts to perform the other types of work. What he cannot hire is his own sales knowledge.

Learn to Supervise Others

My advice to all who wish to become presidents and heads of their companies is that they continually add to their sales knowledge. In that direction they will find success; they will be able to supervise others who will sell for them. I have no new formula for successful selling. There is only one right way to get things sold and that depends wholly upon what the man at the head of a sales organization does.

It is very important, for example, that instead of calling your salesmen into your office you visit them periodically in their own territories. A visit to, let us say, your St. Louis branch where you can talk with the manager and his men and actually see his local territory gives you a better picture of that territory and produces better results. This statement is based upon my own personal experience.

Last September, in my company we decided during a conference that all the vice presidents, sales managers and other sales heads would go out into the field for the remaining months of the year. The only principal executives in the sales division who remained in the Home Office were our senior vice president O. E. Braitmayer, and myself.

We did all the absentees' work while they were away. That sounds like a big job, but it was not, for we called in the secretaries and assistants of the executives who were in the field.

We explained the situation to them in this way:

"As secretaries and assistants you have been handling the work of the executives now out in the field. Continue to do so. If a question arises, come to us and we will talk it over with you as your assistants. Do not think of us as 'bosses' but rather as assistants. If you can possibly do a job yourselves, do not call upon us."

Those young men handled that work and they never came to us in excess of twice a week. We called small meetings and gave them encouragement, asking what we could do for them. They told us there was nothing.

I am bringing this out to prove a point. The selling proposition is simple. We often swathe it in so much mystery that we make selling seem difficult.

What is the function of selling? Simply this: You have something to sell and you must find somebody who can use it. You must think of who is a likely user and then tell prospective purchasers of your product.

The Sales Manager Must Know Duties

SALESMAN   **MANAGER**

The successful sales manager must employ, train, supervise, promote and discharge men.

It is necessary for the sales manager to be able to perform the following five functions of successful sales management:

Employing men - Get the right type of man. A man may be fitted for my business, but be worthless for yours. At this point you have only started. The next point is a very important one.

Training men - It is constantly necessary to keep training men. Conditions change and post-graduate courses are needed.

Supervision - Unless you properly supervise a man, he will be a failure no matter how clever, alert and trained he may be. Constant supervision is essential. The commission salesman requires as much supervision as the salaried man. Remember that supervision does not

188

consist of pressure. Encouragement is a necessary part of supervision.

Promoting men - Every man is looking for something better. A man who is really interested in the business expects that there is advancement in store for him. There are many ways in which you can promote him. It is not necessary to advance him to a higher position with a title. You can give him more territory. If he can handle men, give him the chance to make money from other men's work. As men grow older in their business, they must have this incentive. One man is limited as to what he can do. There are few salesmen who cannot handle men. A good salesman should always have someone to help him in his territory. In doing so he is training an assistant, which is to the company's advantage.

If more attention were paid to hiring men, there would be no need to discharge them.

Discharging men - This last function is disagreeable. If more attention were paid to hiring men, there would be no need to discharge them. Before employing a man, weigh his qualifications carefully, for after you have spent money in training him it will be a costly proposition to discharge him when you find that he does not measure up to the necessary standards. Hiring and firing have a definite relationship.

Every day of your business lives you run the risk of making a mistake in the performance of these five functions of sales management. You must know your duties. If you ask some sales executives what their work is they make some vague answer about "correspondence," "orders," etc. The duties of a sales manager are simply those I have just explained.

Sees Bright Future

Now—regarding the future—it is my sincere belief that every business is going to experience great progress during the next five or ten years. We shall get out of the Depression, and the lessons we shall have learned will be a great benefit to us in our future conduct. We are going to enjoy still greater and better things in life.

Some people are saying in a spirit of pessimism that a new era is beginning, an era of lower prices, lower salaries and decreased comforts and conveniences in life. They are wrong. In 1929, people talked of a new era of lower percentage of return on one's money. They, too, were wrong. Listening to talk about a new era was one of the things that slowed us up and caused the Depression. It is my firm belief that workers in this country can look forward to higher wages and more of the comforts of life than ever before. The history of past depressions supports this statement.

During periods of depression, inventive genius always gets busy. Something new appears. This is happening today. I have seen more development work in these last three years than I have ever seen in business before. In our own company, we are contemplating paying $400,000 for better engineering facilities. We feel justified in considering this expenditure and in paying for development work because we are convinced that the future is going to demand more and more of our company. We shall bring in more in return as we measure up to our job. If you give something worthwhile, you will get it back.

The world has slowed down temporarily but it has learned a lesson.

How did we get into this depression? Try to decide that for yourself. Your own reasoning is as sound as that of anyone else. We have arrived where we are through ignorance and lack of education. If we had known the right things to do we would have been glad to do them. We did not realize that the war was not over. Some of us do not realize it yet. The war will not be over until our debts are paid.

We need greater cooperation nationally and internationally. We are so close to the rest of the world that I do not believe we could carry on without the cooperation of every nation.

There is an undoubted tendency toward adopting the brighter outlook. We turn from hesitancy to assurance and optimism as the result of a gradual change. It does not happen in a moment's time.

Encouragement is a necessary part of supervision.

The Sales Promotion Factor

The New York Advertising Club's Course
Alexander Hamilton Institute

New York, N.Y.
November 17, 1932

There is nothing I enjoy more than spending an evening with a group of men and women who are interested in studying and learning. I am particularly interested in this class, and I can say to you ladies and gentlemen that what you are doing and what you are going to do this year in this class will bring profit to every one of you. I have been dealing with business problems for a great many years and always have been very closely identified with sales and advertising—in fact, my whole life has been devoted to sales work.

I started as a salesman and they call me "President" now; but I call myself "salesman," and I will never let my thoughts get away from selling and from the conviction that my duty is selling. When any man in any business moves up from the selling to other positions and loses sight of the importance of selling, advertising and sales promotion generally, he is going the other way—he isn't going up; he is going down.

He may not know it but he will soon find out.

All Aids to Salesmen

If you are writing advertisements, you are selling goods or helping to sell goods. There is just one thing that we always must keep in mind. That is that the advertising language and the sales language must always be the same. No matter how good the ad is if it is not in the language that the salesman is going to use when he follows that ad into the prospect's place of business, your effort on your advertising is wasted.

I should like to impress that one point on all of you here tonight, because I know from experience that you must do that or your advertising and sales promotion work will not be effective. The advertising department and the sales promotion department in a business are simply the advance agents of the salesman.

You are supposed to pave the way and get the customer in a receptive mood so that he will receive the salesman and be interested in what he has to say.

If you use any kind of language other than that which he is going to use, you lose your case before you start. So just keep that one simple little thing in mind and when you write an ad write it just as a salesman would talk. When you do that, you boil down your advertising problem to a very simple proposition. To begin with, you are going to know all about the goods you are trying to advertise and trying to help to sell before you start writing the ad.

We teach salesmen that there are different ways of presenting a proposition. Bear in mind that your own personality, your own individuality, is 95 percent of your whole proposition. Don't ever try to present any proposition as I present it or as any other man or any other woman presents it. You must present it in your own way. Listen to everybody who talks sales and advertising, and read everything that you get an opportunity to read on the subject, but always keep in mind that you are listening and reading in order to stimulate your own thought and your own mind so that you will be prepared to determine the proper way of presenting your proposition.

If you will simply get into your system all the knowledge you can about whatever you are doing and then use your own personality, your own individuality when you present it, you will find you won't have any trouble in making a success in sales promotion, advertising or selling.

A Sale Is Just "Work in Process"

This is what we call in the factory "work in process." In making an article in a factory we start with raw material. Then we begin to work that up and we call it "work in process." When that goes through we assemble it into the finished product. That same process enters into the making of a sale. The sales promotion and the advertising departments taking it up, and the salesman calling and constantly re-calling on the man and talking to him—that is all work in process, and finally if it is handled properly all the way along the line, and is developed into the sale, it becomes the finished product.

There is no mystery about it. It all comes down to this: that people who are interested in a particular thing should keep studying it and know more about it.

Then another very important thing is for the sales promotion men to study the possibilities of the improvement of the product, because there isn't any product that is being sold today that will carry any concern right along, unless it is sugar or tea or coffee or something of that kind. In the things that we call "specialties," like the many mechanical devices and automobiles and things of that sort, if you cling to the same style and methods you are out of business before you know it, because the march of business is very rapid and it isn't going to stop.

Remember, people will not stand for the same thing all the time. They want something new. So I always like to have the people in the sales promotion and the advertising departments alert to the possibilities of improving the product. In your line of work you have the type of mind that is always alert; and then you read more than men in other lines.

You are constantly studying advertisements, so you are in a position to make suggestions to the heads of the business, to make this change or do this other thing.

Another thing—talk to your salesman about your business. Find out from the salesman what the customers want. Never let up on that particular thing, because we all must keep improving as we go along or we are not going to get anywhere. Find out from the salesmen what the customers want.

I want to tell you another thing that is interesting, I think. The future is going to deliver to us more than has ever been delivered to us in the past. We are not enjoying the kind of times that we would like to enjoy right now, ladies and gentlemen, but school isn't out. This is just a temporary vacation. The United States is not finished. The world is not finished. The big job of building civilization is only begun. I want to say to you, whether or not you feel you are doing as well now as you would like to do, you should look forward with confidence to the future.

Depression has always brought new things into the field. The people have had time to think and have thought out better ways of doing things and it has benefited everyone. The present depression has shown business and financial leaders the need for economic research—of better planning—to insure mutual benefit to stockholder, management and employee.

What are we all most interested in—everyone in this room?

We are all interested in the same thing here tonight, and that thing is success. We may have different ideas of success. Some people may feel that money is the only thing that means success, but there are a great many other things. It does not make any difference what our individual conception may be; we are all interested in that one thing, success. That being the fact, what are we going to do, what should we do to be successful?

There is no one in this room or any other room tonight who will say that he does not want to be a success, that he is not interested in it. There is one thing without which no one can be a success. That is work. When I tell you that, I have not given you any pioneer thought, because you have heard that all your life—that if you want to be a success you must work. Everybody knows that.

Why are we not more successful and why are not more people successful if we know that work brings success? It is because a man must have something to make him want to work. What is that?

Work comes from just one thing—the desire to work, enthusiasm. You never saw an enthusiastic person in your life who was lazy. If you are enthusiastic about your proposition, you want to go right out and go to work at it.

Well, now that we have gotten so far, why are we not enthusiastic? Because enthusiasm is something that one cannot hand out to you and that you cannot buy. There is only one way to get enthusiasm, and that is through knowledge. Knowledge creates enthusiasm, enthusiasm creates a desire to work and work brings success.

How are we going to get the knowledge?

Read, Listen, Discuss, Observe and Think

You are going to get the knowledge through just what you are devoting your time to here tonight—study. However, I would like to call your attention to this fact—which you will have to study in different ways. You will have to study through reading, listening, discussing, observing and thinking. Those are the five ways that we are going to study and gain this knowledge. We cannot afford to neglect any of them. We cannot depend upon any one or any two.

We must read and we must listen.

How many times we lose out in our pursuit of knowledge because we are not willing to listen to the other fellow. Any salesman could take you to places where he lost good orders because he was not willing to listen to the prospective customer. He wanted to tell the prospect all about it, you know. The prospect had something to say, but no, the salesman just had to tell his story. We must never forget that one of the greatest ways in the world to gain knowledge is through listening.

Discussion is another road to knowledge, but you must keep in mind that there is a great difference between a discussion and an argument. When you start on this proposition of discussing, do not ever drift into an argument. When we are discussing a proposition there are two of us and we are both searching for the truth, for the right answer; but if we get to arguing, then it resolves itself into a proposition where each one is trying to prove that he is right. So keep out of arguments when you discuss.

Then, observing! There is one of the simplest and most effective ways to study. If, as we go to and from our work, we will observe what is going on around us, we will learn something valuable every day.

Last, and most important of all, is to THINK. In our business we have that word framed and hung in everybody's office. It is in every department in our factory, it is in every branch office and we hope it is in everybody's mind all the time, because we cannot afford to stop thinking about the business that we are interested in.

I am not telling you what to think about. We do not include it in our motto.

If I can impress that one thing on you here tonight so strongly that you will determine from now on that every day you will do some thinking, that you will give your brain some real mental exercise, it will be of tremendous value to you.

I am not telling you what to think about and we do not include it in our motto. If you will get to thinking you will be surprised how many things you will think about that you learned in days gone by and have forgotten all about.

You are going to take up this subject from week to week; you are going to have the opportunity here to listen to some wonderful speakers. I have been looking over the list of thirty-one people who are coming here to talk to you. I know a great many of them personally and I know every one of them by reputation.

I want to congratulate you on what you are going to hear after this meeting tonight, from these other speakers. Every one of them knows his subject. They have gained all their knowledge and information through study and experience, and they are going to bring to you the result of it. Make notes as you go along.

Then, if you will think these things out when you get home, and build up your whole case based on what you pick up each night as you go along, until you have built it into your line of thought and your own language, you will have no trouble in making a success.

Above everything, look forward with hope, because better times are coming.

There are a great many people sitting back who are not willing to put forth the effort or spend a few dollars to improve themselves and to gain more knowledge, and they are not going to come into as good positions, they are not going to be able to command as good salaries, as you and many others who are taking courses of this kind, and who are willing to put in some time at night and deprive yourselves of a little temporary pleasure to study and add to your knowledge.

Last, and most important of all, is to THINK

The Need for Individual Action

Opening Convention Principal Speaker
The National Stationers Association

New York, N.Y.
June 7, 1932

To me personally it is a great pleasure to be invited here, because I have been very closely associated with the retail business all of my business life. I wish that I had a big message to give you about your line of business today. I am going to make one prediction, however, and that is that I believe within a reasonable time you are going to see a greatly increased use of black ink, and I know that is what we are all looking for.

The chairman referred to the business which I have the honor of heading, The International Business Machines Corporation. I wish to say just a few words in explanation of our record. There is nothing special about our business. We are thankful we have been able to do as well as we have. The reason for it is that as a result of our efforts along research lines, we were fortunate in having several new products to put on the market just

We have no supermen in our organization, and no great genius. We are just like you, trying to do our best.

about the time the Depression struck us, so that it broadened our field and gave us an opportunity to employ more salesmen and call on more people.

I wish to explain that, because if we had not had those new things to broaden our field, it would have been impossible for us to have accomplished what we have. We have no supermen in our organization, and no great genius. We are just like the rest of you, struggling along trying to do our best.

No Business More Important

The business that you represent is very closely allied with everything that I have been interested in, and there is nothing I know of that is of more importance in the business world than the things you handle. It is business equipment all the way through. It is the kind of business equipment that businessmen could not get along without. We all must have the things you are dealing in, for without them we could not keep records of any kind. So I congratulate you on being in an industry that you can count on as one of the most stable industries in the country.

Now as to your meeting here: I am a great believer in conventions and meetings of this kind. I think it is of the greatest possible benefit to everybody in an industry to meet and exchange ideas, hear about the other fellow's problems and air our own sometimes. When you get home from this meeting, try to apply to your own business the knowledge you gathered here—try to apply the ideas that you are sure will work in your business.

We drifted into accepting too many of the other man's ideas.

In other words, use individual thought and individual action. I believe that one of our greatest troubles in the last two and a half years was the fact that we got away from individual thought and individual action. We started mass thinking, because we were being given the same kind of news about everything at about the same time, and we drifted into accepting, I think, too many of the other man's ideas. Giving more serious thought to our own problems is the most important factor in reestablishing our individual prosperity and progress.

Who is there as well equipped to think out the correct answer and the correct solution to the problems about your individual store and your individual business as you yourself? I always like to feel that a man running a business can do more towards solving the problems of his business than anybody from the outside, although I do believe in procuring outside advice, analyzing it and using whatever can be applied safely and soundly to the business concerned.

I feel that in the affairs of our government and in all civic affairs, we see more individual interest, more individual thought, put into everything.

Brighter Outlook

I know there are many problems that you are going to discuss here, and I wish that I might have the privilege of attending all of your sessions because I know that I would gain much knowledge that I could use in connection with my own business.

I believe the matter of price-cutting is one of the things that will be discussed here; because that is being discussed everywhere. Of course that, to me, is the greatest problem we have to solve at the present time, because there is only one answer to price-cutting—particularly when we consider where prices are today—and that is disaster for many, if not for all.

Again, I wish I had the answer to that problem. Perhaps you in discussing it as applied to your business may be able to find some remedy that will meet with the requirements of the people in Washington, a remedy that will enable you to procure a satisfactory price for the goods that you are selling.

Not Clerks – Salesmen!

The matter of your employees, of course, is another very important subject, and one that has always been a hobby of mine. We often hear your employees spoken of in a general way as clerks, but I never liked to think of a man employed in any store as a clerk.

I always like to think of that person as a salesman, because that is what he really is—a salesman or a saleswoman. And I think that in these times we should all endeavor to think of our employees as salesmen, talk with them as salesmen and try to teach them to sell more goods.

We should think of our employees as salesman.

I know that you in the stationery business have always had the reputation as a whole of having as high a type of organization as can be found in any branch of retail trade, and that is one of the reasons why the stationery business has always had such a high standing among retail businesses. The percentage of failures has always been far below the average for business in general, and that is due to the type of people in the business and to the sound and constructive thought and effort that they put into it.

The things that have happened to all of us in the past two and a half years, I believe, have taught us many lessons which we will be able to capitalize as time goes on and when business becomes what we think of as normal in the United States.

Note of Optimism

It is my personal opinion that we are going to recover from this depression and establish on a sounder and better basis, and we are going to reach greater heights of prosperity than ever before in this country. Now, that is just my personal opinion, but it is based on history because that is what has happened following every depression. As we read the history of the various depressions, we find that the people all felt about them just as we do about this one.

One of the reasons we go ahead rapidly after coming out of a depression is that inventive genius and business talents have been put to a

Go into the field and call on the customers.

test, and they have always devised new and better ways to do things.

Following every depression that we have had in this country, we have come out of it and found that we have all had more things to work with, and I know that that is going to apply to your industry. That is what I am banking on as one of the things to help us when we get started again.

Better Machines Build Industry

As we look back over the developments of the past quarter of a century, we think of the automobile, which has created the largest manufacturing industry in the country. Practically that whole development has come to us in the last twenty-five years, due to improvements effected and the ability of that industry to make better machines for less money. Now I think that applies pretty well all the way down the line.

That is the whole American idea.

Another thing, in the United States we have one great asset that always gives me a little comfort because no other country has it anywhere near the extent that we do. That asset is the desire on the part of everybody in the United States, rich and poor, to have something better than he now possesses.

We all have been held back, and when the time does come for business to move, we are going to go out and satisfy that desire in many ways. Because we have everything in this country, all that is needed to put us right back into the midst of prosperity is confidence.

200

Encouraging News

I think in spite of the criticisms which most of us indulge in from time to time in regard to what is going on in Washington, we are getting some very encouraging news from down there—news of action that will help to reestablish the confidence of the people, so that we will be willing to go out and spend an extra dollar. If we can reestablish confidence in the minds and hearts of the approximately 40 million people who are gainfully employed in this country, they will spend enough money to increase production to the extent where we can absorb the approximately 8 million who are now out of employment. That is our great problem in the United States today.

I believe that confidence is coming gradually. I see signs of it in every direction. Just as soon as confidence is restored and the buying public starts out, we will soon absorb those who are out of employment.

We are going on to real success in the United States, and I am never going to let myself feel for one moment that we are going backward. We are going ever forward in this country.

We have no supermen in our organization and no great genius.

Executives Must Be Sales Minded

The Sales Executives Club of New York

September 15, 1932

I want to thank your chairman and your committee for extending me the privilege of meeting with you today. There is nothing I enjoy as much as meeting with a group of sales executives. There is no place I go where I get the inspiration and the help for my own business that I get through an exchange of ideas with a group of sales managers in other lines of business.

Your chairman told you I was once a sales manager. I was for a great many years and I still am. I will not let myself get away from the thought that I am really the sales manager. I feel it is the duty of every executive in every business to continue to think along the lines of a sales manager even after he has moved up to some other position, because that is the most important, the most vital office in any business.

Sales Manager Important

It does not make any difference what type of president a company has. He may be the most brilliant man in the world and he may be surrounded by twenty-seven vice presidents who also are brilliant and able men, but if there is not a first class, intelligent, sales-minded sales manager on the job, no business can possibly succeed.

You men who are in sales work have a perfect right to feel you are important to the business. You stand between the executives and stockholders, and the men out in the field who have to bring in the orders. You have a double task to perform. You frequently have to sell the management—and usually those are the hardest sales the sales manager has to make—and then you have to sell your salesmen on your policy.

Everybody in the business, from the president down, must be sold on the sales policies, including the controller, the advertising manager and everybody else.

The whole organization must back up the sales manager.

It is the duty of every executive in every business to think along the lines of a sales manager.

202

Product Must Have Value

It goes without saying that there is no excuse, no legitimate reason, for any sales manager trying to build a sales organization to sell something that is not of some real value to the people who buy it. Every sales organization must have certain fundamental rules and principles every salesman must follow.

There is no legitimate reason to build an organization to sell something that is not of real value.

Of course, the salesmen must use their own personalities in their own ways, but they must follow the company's policy if there is to be a smooth-operating sales organization.

Sales Manager Has Five Duties

The most important thing for a sales manager to do is to realize fully what his own duties are before he undertakes anything else. We believe and teach that there are just five duties of a sales manager:

- First, he must employ salesmen.
- Second, he must teach those salesmen.
- Third, he must supervise them.
- Fourth, he must promote them.
- Fifth, he must discharge them.

If you think that over, you will realize that those are the five essential duties of a sales executive. You cannot drop any one of them and I do not know of anything else you can add to that list.

It is hardly necessary for me to tell such a gathering as this that a most important thing is the type of men you select. I do not want you gentlemen to feel I know something about selling or sales management that you do not know. That is not a fact. New methods for selling goods cannot be manufactured; you cannot discover new ways every few minutes for a sales manager to operate.

There are sound, fundamental principles to follow year in and year out, and following these principles you know what kind of man you need for your business. Be sure you give proper thought and attention to getting the right type of man because the man who is qualified for one particular line of business might not do at all in another.

Must Have Right Men

While I feel that I have had a great deal of experience in employing men, I think I know less about picking the right man for a sales job today than I ever did. There was a time when I thought I could look a man over and decide from his appearance, personality and conversation whether he would be a success or a failure. That theory was exploded years ago. Something inside of you may help you to determine who the right man is. You do not always get the right one, but you know what to do with him when you do not.

A great many men, good men, fail in sales work because they are not properly taught. You do not have to teach a man what to say to the prospect when he approaches him. Anybody can figure that out.

The big thing to get into a man's system is belief in his line. He must believe 100% percent all the time that the article or line of goods he is selling has real merit and he must know all about its value and what it will do for the man who buys it.

The big thing to get into a salesman's system is belief in his line.

Then he must be taught about the various kinds of business that he is going to call on. He must be able to talk intelligently with the purchasing agents and others with whom he comes in contact. That is very important. Too much cannot be said in regard to the teaching of salesmen.

Close Supervision Vital

After you have taught your salesmen, you have to supervise them. That is where we sales executives are likely to fail. Because we have a good group of salesmen, know they are honest and energetic, know they are ambitious, we oftentimes get a little slack in our supervision.

The closer your supervision of your men, the more money they will make and the more money the concern will make. The best method for supervising salesmen is to keep close track of their records, not only of the orders they send in, but of what they are doing with their time. I think that every man who sells goods should make out a daily report of his activities.

In supervising salesmen, a sales manager has to use good judgment. You cannot crowd your men, urge them and drive them all the time and get anywhere. Nor can you praise them all the time because some of them do not always deserve praise. We have to give praise where it is due and something else where it is due.

I urge upon every sales manager if he has not every possible check on the time of his men, to try to get such a check at once. A salesman's time is his stock in trade and it is your stock in trade. Every hour the salesmen waste during the working day is that much time wasted out of their lives and out of the profits of your business.

You cannot crowd your men, urge them and drive them all the time and get anywhere.

Promotions Stimulate Salesmen

After you have done all those things, the next thing to watch for are opportunities to promote men. That is the way to build large organizations—through promoting men. I do not know of any method that is as satisfactory as promoting men from the sales end of the business into its other branches.

It is true we do get some of our very best men right from the factory bench and the office and we have some in our business who have grown up in it, educated themselves and gone right up the line. As a rule, however, you will get from your sales organization a higher percentage of men who will grasp the big problem of how to run the business than from any other division of your organization. I like to hold that prospect out to the salesman from the day he starts working. If he is ambitious and has it in him, he knows he has something to work for. He knows he will get somewhere if he works.

I lay very great importance on the matter of promoting men. Every time I see in our house organ the picture of a young man who has been promoted, I feel our business is just that much stronger. That man is going to bring something to it he has learned from other people. Just think of the opportunity a salesman has to learn and gather knowledge about business in general and about what is going on in the world as compared to a man working on the inside.

There are many salesmen who do not realize their great opportunity or they would put forth a greater effort. There is an opportunity for every salesman in every organization to gain promotion if he will apply himself.

The last thing, which of course is the most disagreeable for a sales manager or anybody else, is to discharge men. Unfortunately, we have to do it. Of course, there is only one reason for discharging a man, and that is for cause and he should be told that reason at the very beginning. Then the separation is made pleasantly and you get someone else in his place and go on.

Sometimes, we let down in our sales efforts. I think during the "dance of the millions" a few years back when everyone had money and everyone wanted to buy something whether he needed it or not, in many cases we, as salesmen, slowed up a little. I think in many cases we began using the kid glove method of selling goods, simply greeting the man pleasantly and letting him buy something from us.

Gentlemen, this is not salesmanship—this is order taking.

That kind of selling is successful only in boom times. Now we are in a period when we have to take off our coats and go out and really sell. You sometimes hear people criticize various sales methods. They

 object to the so-called strong-arm method of selling or to what they call high-pressure salesmanship. Do not listen to that. What they really mean is that you have a group of salesmen who hang on to their prospects until they get the order and bring it home.

That is what you employ them for.

Promoting men is the way to build large organizations.

If they are selling an article of merit, it is their duty, as salesmen, to use every conceivable argument they can that is honest to convince the prospect that he ought to sign the order. That is the only way your business can run.

I have noticed a great deal more of that kind of selling going on in the past few months than I observed in the last two or three years; and it gives me great cheer for the future.

I know that that kind of selling means a little harder work, staying a little longer with the man, walking a little farther every day to find the man who will say yes. But it gets results. That is what we have to do, gentlemen; that is what is going to help every one of us in this room to build our businesses bigger and better. It is going to enable us to have more promotions for the young men I have been speaking about.

Getting results means working a little harder, staying a little longer and walking a little farther each day.

We cannot get results if we sit around with our kid gloves on and wait for someone to hand things to us.

The whole organization must back up the sales manager.

WE ARE ALL ASSISTANTS

Watson's greatest respect was reserved for his first-line managers—factory foremen and sales managers—who he described as "carrying water on both shoulders." The sales managers had on one shoulder the IBM sales representative trying to close deals. On the other shoulder, they had the IBM executives trying to run a profitable business. Like the maxim about "oil and water," the two rarely went well together, but together they had to go or his business could not succeed. It was for this reason that Watson invested so much time, money, education and personal effort into his first-line managers.

I would feel this spirit still alive in 1980 when I was a first-line manager for The IBM. The Watsons designed a system to empower, inspire, train, educate and support that person carrying water on both shoulders. Serving as an administration operations manager, a first-line manager in a sales office, I felt that pressure.

You stand between the management at the top and your men in the field.

Yet it was the most exciting and powerful position I have ever had in my life. "Powerful" in The IBM though, meant being an "assistant to men." To Tom Watson, the more powerful you were, the more you were to be a servant and assistant to those around you. In Watson's IBM, you were to be pushed up from below not pulled up from above.

Executives Must be Assistants

In September 1932, Watson sent all his executives into the field to assist the sales force. They were not to return home until two weeks before Christmas. The Home Office was emptied of all its executives. Watson called the executives' secretaries, left behind to run the business, into a meeting.

He told them they were about to enter "a practical business school"—a school for which there was no match in any business or educational institution of the time. He was their educator and assistant until the executives returned from the field.

209

Watson was taking personal responsibility for the education of a room full of Home Office executive secretaries. This flowed with his nature. He desired to extract the best each man was capable of giving. Whether it was the best salesman, the best engineer, the best foreman or the best executive, he believed they all needed continual education, training and self-study to reach their fullest potential. As each person reached their singular pinnacle and maintained it, both the individual and The IBM won.

Constant Study

The best way to teach a man how to do something is to assist him in doing it.

Throughout these speeches and editorials Watson consistently says, "There is no saturation point to education." But to him, education in the classroom was only beneficial in its application in the real world—this was the training the individual needed to exercise his or her capacities to the fullest extent.

Tom Watson was one of the first business leaders in the modern era to establish technical schools, sales schools and management and executive schools. He needed every individual within his business constantly striving to keep up with the pace of change. To him, education was the only means of accomplishing this and he was determined that The IBM was going to lead the world in quality, educated men.

He constantly reinforced this message at every level within The IBM. In this chapter, he discusses his views in a meeting with his major executives. Then he covers the topic with employees studying at a night Owl School. Finally, the topic was broadcast in an editorial in *Business Machines* to all of The IBM.

Assume responsibility for the elimination not of men, but of practices, policies and everything that hinders this business.

We Are All Assistants

Editorial Appearing in Business Machines
The Company Newsletter

September 29, 1932

We are extending this week the practical application of our policy that there should be no bosses in business—that every manager, assistant manager, department head, foreman, etc., of an organization must be instead a good assistant to and leader for somebody else. Accordingly, all the managers, assistant managers and heads of the various divisions of our sales department have gone out into the field where they will work as assistants to the men under their supervision.

The best way to teach a man how to do something is to assist him in doing it and that is what our executives are doing.

While these executives are in the field, their duties at the home office will be taken over by their secretaries to whom I will act as assistant. This program will help our salesmen to do more for themselves and for the company; it will give the young men in the home office an opportunity to show what they can do in an executive capacity, and it will enable the executive to learn more about the problems of the salesmen and also of our customers.

The development and progress of our business depend entirely upon our ability to work together, to assist one another in every way possible, and, in doing so, to prepare ourselves individually to assume the greater responsibilities that the growth of IBM will entail. Responsibility is a mark of leadership, and the men who measure up to the greater responsibilities with which they are now entrusted will be assured of leadership in the future.

The development and progress of our business depend entirely upon our ability to work together.

I am confident, therefore, that every member of our organization will be benefited by the extended application of our "assistant's policy" and that the business itself will reap the rewards in bigger sales and bigger earnings.

The best way to teach a man is to assist him.

211

A Practical Business School

Meeting of the Home Office Sales Secretaries

Mr. Watson's Office at 270 Broadway
September 30, 1932

We have called this meeting in the absence of your chiefs, who, as you know, are out in the field helping our salesmen to get orders. They are not just telling them what they should do to get orders, but they are out in territories working alongside them.

You men, being in the sales department, know that the securing of orders is the most important thing in this business. Our engineers and factories can produce the most wonderful machines that could be devised, but they are of no value unless we can convince businessmen that they need them. From now until the end of the year, you young men have an unusual opportunity to do executive work, to take on your shoulders certain of the responsibilities that have hitherto been borne by the men with whom you work. Do not be afraid to take these responsibilities! Seize every chance to learn more about our business and prepare yourselves for better jobs.

Executives Really Assistants

Your chiefs have gone out to help the salesmen—not merely to act in a supervisory capacity, but to really assist them. That is something I have always held, that executives should really be assistants. And I want you men to look upon Mr. Braitmayer and me as assistants. We will be glad to help you whenever you feel that you need our aid.

Take these responsibilities! Seize every chance to learn and prepare yourselves for better jobs.

The experience you gain during the next three months will be the equivalent of training that you would receive in an executives' school or school of business administration, except that it will be more practical. You will actually be doing the work and not just learning theories.

Just as self-supervision is the best kind of supervision, self-teaching is the most important kind of education!

One of the important duties of a secretary is to take care of correspondence. You men, who handle the great flow of communications that we receive here at headquarters, must recognize the fact that there is too much letter writing in business today. Too many letters are written, and most of them are too lengthy. Busy executives will not wade through two or three pages of a letter to get information that could be given in a few short paragraphs. Do not let letter writing become a mania.

Simplify your work and eliminate all unnecessary letter writing.

You secretaries are in a position to learn this business in a shorter time and with less effort than men in any other department. You have the opportunity to learn our business from the ground up and you learn phases of the business that you could learn in no other job.

I want to see every one of you young men advance to a higher position in this company, and it is within your power to do so.

Self-teaching is the most important kind of education.

Success Depends on Selling

Semimonthly Meeting
The New York Sales Managers' Club

New York, N.Y.
October 7, 1932

I am embarrassed when it comes to standing before a group of sales managers to talk to them about selling. You have the whole picture, and that makes it hard for a man in my position to know just where to start. I want to tell you at the outset, however, that I am one of those sales managers who believes that the old-fashioned, common-sense, every-day duties of employing, training, supervising, promoting and discharging salesmen is the same today as it always was and always will be.

I am mindful of the fact that you are all successful men in your various lines of business and that you understand how to handle those propositions. The best that I can hope to do tonight is to give you a few of my ideas and, perhaps, start a discussion that will get all of you talking. Then I can learn something to take back to my business, and I will appreciate that because I always feel the need for more knowledge. The more experience I have in business, the more I feel the need of studying and learning more about how to do things.

Speaking of lack of knowledge, this point comes to mind: After rolling along, enjoying good times, for several years we have found ourselves in an economic state that we had not anticipated. Some of us thought that this period would be of very short duration but it has lasted for a long time. During all this time, I have not been able to get together in any meeting five men who could agree on what caused the present state of things—and that is exactly why we are where we are. Now that we are in the present state we cannot get five men who can agree on how we can get out of it.

There is always an argument and I claim that is proof of our lack of knowledge. That proves, to me at least, that we reached our present economic state because of lack of education. We all want to do the right thing, and had we all known the right thing to do during the "dance of the millions" we would have done it and we never would have landed where we are.

Furthermore, if we had been able to learn enough since this depression set in, we would have known before this how to get out of it. So it seems to me that the one thing for each of us to do now is to determine that we are going to learn more about our own jobs. When we do that we sales managers are going to get together more often to exchange ideas, and we are going to build up a sales curricula that will carry us further and along more successful lines than we have ever traveled before. There is nothing else that will do it. No one man can give you the curricula; it must be developed by good hard work on the part of all of us.

Must Stick to Fundamentals

What we must do first is to go back to the beginning of our sales experience and think over the things we have done that proved successful, things we used to do but have discarded. Understand, gentlemen, I am not depreciating the value of new ideas; those are what we need. But I do not want to overlook the good old fundamental principles and laws of marketing.

Do not overlook the fundamental principles and laws of marketing.

Then we must add to that and expand our knowledge, just as our ideas, our country and our businesses are expanded. We are always going to need more knowledge in marketing. There is going to be more marketing to do in the future than there ever was in the past.

I say, notwithstanding all that you read and hear in some quarters to the effect that we are going to go along a different line, that this depression has marked a new era in business, that it has brought us to the realization that we cannot have all the things we have become accustomed to and that we are going to get down to a lower level. I do not believe that at all. We have merely had a temporary slow up. In other words, we have had a little vacation; but school is not out for good. We are going to start up again and we are going to go ahead faster than ever before.

Success Depends on Selling

The very largest percentage of the future success and development depends on the people who are interested in selling. I am not overlooking the importance of the research department. They are of the greatest importance, as are also good factories, able executives, presidents, vice presidents and so forth. All these have a place in the scheme of business, but, after all, when you have all these things, what good are they if somebody does not get the goods sold?

You stand between management and your men. You have to carry water on both shoulders.

I regard the sales manager's position as the most important in any business, and I am not saying that simply because I am talking to salesmen. I have said it before, recently in talking to a group of controllers and on other occasions. You all know it is true.

High in importance in the successful business I put the factory foreman, because he is in the same position in the factory that you are in the marketing end. You stand between the management at the top and your men out in the field, and you have to carry water on both shoulders. You have to do what you know is absolutely fair to the stockholders in the business on one side, and you have to do what is absolutely fair to the man out in the field. You have to take a much broader view of every problem that confronts you than anyone else in the business.

Factory Foremen Important

The factory foreman stands in a similar position—between the management on one side and the workmen on the other—and I enjoy talking to factory foremen as I do to sales heads because when I talk to a group of factory foremen and am associated with them, I have the same sales feeling that I have when I am with sales managers. I think one of the things that make it hard for the sales manager is the fact that some of the people higher up in some of our businesses do not place a fair estimate on the importance of the sales manager.

If there is any one message that I would like to get over tonight—it isn't to you men at all, but it is to the men who are occupying higher positions in the business with which you are identified—it is this: The sales manager is the most important man in any company. And the reason I would like to get that message across is that I feel if I can do anything to make any man give more consideration and more help to his sales manager, I have made a contribution to that particular business.

216

The work of a sales manager never has been an easy task and it never will be. It just isn't in the wood. I have been a salesman. I was a salesman on the street for a good many years, and I am going to be perfectly frank with you gentlemen and admit that when I was a salesman, I needed supervision. When I did not get supervision, I did not put in my time to the best advantage, and every sales manager in this room who ever sold goods has had the same experience. It does not make any difference with the salesman whether he is working on commission or on salary. Someone has got to supervise him in order to keep him going.

His problem is different from that of the man in the office or in the factory. These men have a specific job to do each day. But the salesman is "out on his own." One of the things that a sales manager has to keep in mind first, last and always is the fact that he must supervise his men constantly; supervise them daily, in order to get the best results. The only way I know of to supervise men is simply to insist on their telling what they do every day.

The salesman is out on his own. Find out what kind of service he is giving to his customers.

Keep track of them in that way, follow their daily reports and analyze their records to see where they get their business. Find out whether they are following up their customers and what kind of service they are giving to their customers. I will not go into that in detail because you men understand all that, but I say this because I feel it is always wise to keep that point in mind. We get to know our salesmen. Every sales manager in the world loves his salesmen. His heart is with them; and it is sometimes hard to criticize and find fault the way we should with a group of men we really love and respect. But it sometimes is necessary to do it and we are doing our salesmen a real service when we do it.

A few years ago when everything seemed to be just about the way we would like to have it, we didn't realize just what was going to happen to us later. Everybody was pretty happy. It was not hard to get business. Most of us—I know it applied in my own business—fell into what I call the "kid glove" method of selling. Now, however, things have changed. The "kid glove" method will not do today.

Time to Get Busy

I feel that now is the time for all of us who are interested in selling to brace up and go after this selling job. We all are talked out about the Depression. We have talked about it from every angle and there is nothing more to be said about it.

BE AN OPTIMIST

We must be optimistic, yet tempered with good sound sales judgment.

I am not trying to spread any wild optimism. I believe that we in selling work must be optimistic if we are going to get anywhere, but our optimism must be tempered with good sound sales judgment, or we can do more harm than good.

I am not going to tell you gentlemen that if you just talk louder you will get more business. But I believe that a great many men have gotten out of the habit of buying. Many of them have the money to buy something and really need that something, but they have formed the habit of saying, "No." It is going to require some of the good, old-fashioned sales work to jar them loose, and get them to place the orders. They are the people we must go after first.

Some people condemn high-powered salesmanship. They sometimes call it the strong-arm method of selling and speak of it in other such terms. Now just what does that mean? The high-powered sales force?

That simply means that you have a crowd of salesmen who are hard workers.

Of course, we are all engaged in legitimate lines of business. We are selling things that people actually need. When a man is selling a useful article, he has a legitimate right and it is his duty to use every honest means at his disposal to get the order.

That may be called "high-power selling," or "strong-arm methods" or whatever some people wish to call it; but it is the salesman's duty as a salesman to pound and hang on until the order is signed, provided he is selling something that the prospect should have.

I find in my own business that we do not hang on and stay with the prospect as long as we should. Now we are trying hard to get back into that method.

Sales Executives in Field

I do not want to be personal, but just at present the first vice president of our company and myself are the only executives you can find at headquarters; and we are there merely working as assistants to the secretaries to our sales heads who have gone into the field to mingle and work with the salesmen, to get in and learn present field conditions first-hand so that they will know exactly what every salesman in our business has to contend with in his daily work.

This is merely one phase of the practical application of our policy of making every member of our organization, regardless of rank or title, an assistant to somebody else. They left two weeks ago to be gone until Christmas. They divided up the country and each executive took a certain territory. They are not to hold conventions or preach sermons. They are to go right out with the salesmen.

Many of the men who have been on the inside during this depression, getting all of the discouraging letters that come in, are the ones who have gotten into a rut, and it is going to be a wonderful thing for those men to be out in the field once more. I know they are going to do a wonderful amount of good to the men already out in the field. We like to have our men in the field feel, believe and know that the people who are trying to supervise them are really their assistants rather than their bosses. That is one thing that we lay a great deal of stress upon, because every man likes to have somebody assist him, somebody who will help him.

I think that one of the things that held us back when things first went bad in 1929 and 1930 was the fact that bankers began to make speeches and give out their views. They said business must do this and business must do that. Then we businessmen began to think about what the banks ought to do. We told the banks they ought to loan more money, be more liberal.

Our sales heads have gone into the field to know exactly what every salesman has to contend with.

The bankers criticized us, we criticized the bankers and then the bankers and the businessmen jointly criticized the government for doing this or not doing that. The result was that there were a great many of us who did not put enough time into our own businesses.

I have noticed recently that we are not getting so much outside advice. We are getting down more to the good, common sense practice of tending to our own business and solving our own problems within our own organizations, with the assistance in some cases of people from the outside who are making a constant study and who have real contributions to make.

Should Simplify Advertising

There is only one object in advertising—sell goods.

I would like to say just a word about advertising. Advertising and selling go hand in hand. The advertisement is the advance agent of the salesman. I think that some of the advertising done today could be improved upon. It could be simplified.

I feel that one of the chief duties of a sales manager is to keep in close touch with the advertising department. In fact, I believe that the advertising department should be supervised almost entirely by the sales department, by the sales manager.

There is only one object in advertising, and that is to sell goods. That is the only object in spending money on advertising. If a sales manager is sold on advertising and knows the kind of advertising that he wants, he is in a position to go to the president and the controller of his company and get the proper appropriation for the advertising department.

Reward for Investors

I am not here to sell securities, but I say that because I know that the United States and the world are going on and I know that the very best minds in this country, regardless of political parties and political affiliations, have all been working together along constructive lines. It has been noticeable not only here, but also all over the world. Everybody is interested. Every thinking man and every thinking woman is deeply interested in helping work out this problem of adjustment.

That is all it is. No calamity has happened to this country, to this world. We are simply out of step. We are out of adjustment, out of tune if you like.

We are going to get back into adjustment and get into tune. We are going ahead and we are all going to have, in my judgment, a greater opportunity in the future than we have ever had in the past.

I do not want to take up any more of your time, but I would like to hear you men discuss this problem—or proposition, as I call it, because it isn't a problem—I would like to get your ideas and your criticism of everything that I have said that you don't agree with. Let us see if we cannot have an open forum here, because I want to get something from you to take back to my business.

Our optimism must be tempered with good sound sales judgment.

A Proper Regard for Education

Meeting of Major Executives

New York, N.Y.
September 25, 1933

Mr. Hastings and Mr. Nichol know that when I started in this business I did not know everything about it. There were men in the three divisions who knew all about their own divisions, but none who had studied all the divisions.

I started trying to work out a plan for building up the business. This had to be a one-man job in the beginning because I had to develop the plan I thought would be for the best interest of everybody concerned. I tried at all times to take into consideration all the elements that would affect the different branches of the business and the different people in it.

Must Develop Ideas

I have just a few thoughts along that line to pass out to you today.

Now, when we reach the point where every man in this business has developed his ideas and his knowledge so that he can think in terms

Instead of our individual divisions, we must think of every person, machine, branch and country.

of every branch of the business, every type of machine and every country in the world instead of his own division, there is not any business in any country that has a greater opportunity for development, on a percentage basis, than has this business of ours. I will challenge anybody in this room to contradict that statement or to take away from it. It is a fact.

I have decided that The IBM is going to move forward from now on faster than it has, faster than any of us can visualize today. I have been thinking over this whole proposition in the United States and the world and it is absurd for anyone to try to make it seem that the future is not going to be wonderful.

It may not be wonderful for us as individuals but that is up to ourselves.

Think About Future

Let every man think about his own future and how he is going to make it better—whether or not his opportunity for a better future is with this company. Think about it from every angle, and if anyone wants to ask me for help, come along. I would like the opportunity to help.

The important thing is that from now on I want you to assume the responsibility of elimination not of men, but of practices, policies and everything that may be hindering the progress of this business.

When you find out that it may affect you temporarily, you are going to correct it because it is the best thing for the business. After all, whatever is the best thing for the business is the best thing for the

Eliminate not men, but practices, policies and everything that hinders the progress of this business.

men in it. Let us keep that in mind—what is the best thing for this business is the best thing for everybody in it.

Any policy that helps any set of workmen or one class of employees and does not help them all is not sound business policy. This task of keeping the policy clean and sound, keeping the organization trained, keeping the organization built up with new men, rests upon the men individually.

We must all believe in the future more than we have ever believed in it before, because of the great opportunities for everybody. I am going to expect more constructive recommendations—not "half boiled," but completely cooked and ready to serve. I realize that it is good to get suggestions, but it is even better to get recommendations for workable plans.

I am going to expect more in the way of recommendations, and that means I also expect you men to pass what I have said along to the other people in our company. We wish to have all our people know that they share the responsibility for whatever success we make.

Assume the responsibility of elimination not of men, but of practices, policies and everything that hinders this business.

223

Education Makes Young Men More Valuable

The IBM Owl School for Home Office Employees

270 Broadway, New York, N.Y.
October 20, 1932

It is always a great pleasure for me to meet with a group of young IBM men. Before coming here today, I attended a meeting in connection with the Share the Work Plan. Hearing some of the things that were said there made me feel very grateful that our company has been able to keep our people employed, and I want to thank all the people here for the part they have played in helping to carry on The IBM program which has enabled the workers in our factories to have steady employment.

The men who are handling the records, the correspondence and the other necessary work between the home office and the factory and the field are playing a very important part in this business.

While here at the home office and in the factories the men have all put forth their best efforts to carry on, there would have been nothing for any of us to do had not the men in the field put forth extraordinary efforts to send in orders to keep the factory wheels turning. I want you to get that fixed in your minds. You have an obligation to the men in the field. It is a very great obligation.

Importance of Education

There is one thought I have in regard to this Owl School: The longer I am in business, the more importance I place upon business education and education in general. I take some interest in education in a general way, but my real thought and my real effort along educational lines is centered in IBM education.

IBM education enables young men to make real contributions to future progress in the shortest time.

I am trying to make it possible for the young men who come into The IBM to receive the proper education in the shortest space of time, to enable them to make real contributions to the future progress of our business. Why are we employing so many young men in this business every year? It is because we know that we are going to need them later on to do more important work.

Some of our friends outside The IBM are very complimentary in telling us that we have done a wonderful job, but we on the inside who have been studying this problem, who have been broadening our vision and looking into the future, cannot make ourselves believe that we have done a big job. We are grateful for what we have achieved, but if we had had the proper knowledge, if we had been doing enough along educational lines twenty years ago, we would have done a much bigger job than we have done.

Along with the building of the engineering laboratory, we are building at Endicott a schoolhouse—a real schoolhouse. In order to make sure that it would be a real schoolhouse and have none of the earmarks of a business institution, we employed a school architect to draw the plans.

We want to surround our educational program with all the atmosphere that we can. That is why we have Professor Brown of Harvard, who has been with us so many years, and Mr. Limper, who has had years of experience in teaching, and other men whom we are going to bring in from time to time to help our educators and develop The IBM educational program in proportion to our vision of the future of this company.

Education is the way to become more valuable to the company and yourself.

We are willing to spend any reasonable amount of money on education in our organization, because we have a group of men and women in our business who are constantly seeking knowledge, knowing that is the way to make themselves more valuable to the company and, automatically, more valuable to themselves.

Plans Broader Program

We are working out a plan that is going to take in everybody in the organization. We are going to have post graduate schools for our men in the field, and postgraduate schools for our executives—and many of them, because the executives of this company need to study more than the men in any other department of the business. This is particularly true of any business that has grown as our business has in the past and as it will grow in the future.

No Trick to IBM

There is no trick to our business. Its record is not due to any particular genius on the part of the management. It is due to what we believe and what we know is a sound business policy—a policy of never relaxing our efforts—and a belief that the public is going to demand more of us every year. Throughout the history of our business, the demand for our products has been growing constantly greater and if we are not ready to meet that demand the orders will go to somebody else. Therefore, we propose to put forth every effort and to spend any reasonable amount of money to keep always ahead of the times and to be ready to supply the requirements of the business of the future as well as that of the present.

We want every young man to bear in mind that his position with this company calls for more than just filling the particular job that he is doing today. We want you all to feel that you are in this business because it is going to grow and be many times larger than it is today. We want you to feel that it is more than an ordinary business, that it is a worldwide institution that is going to go on forever, that you are going to make it your life work and that you are going to bring your sons into it in the future. That is the kind of a business you are engaged in, gentlemen.

The only things we need are knowledge, faith, determination and the will to make up our minds that, regardless of how small a position we now hold in this company, before twelve months roll around, we are going to think out something, that we are going to make some suggestion that will add to the growth and development of this business.

The only things we need are knowledge,
faith, determination and the will.

Science, Business, Education

Business Machines *Editorial*

December 15, 1932

Most significant in the onward march of business today is the increasing recognition by industrial leaders of the value and necessity of education. Research is the advance guard of business progress, and no research is possible unless it is engaged in by those who have been educated for it. Industry is leaning more and more on the great universities of the world, not only for the men it graduates and fits for positions of business responsibility, but also for the research that is so generally carried on within university walls for the direct benefit of business.

The importance of education and research has been recognized in our own company to a marked degree, a fact that has contributed tremendously to the progress we have made. All plans for the future of IBM revolve around a continuation and an extension of the policy of searching for the best way to do things and of finding the best way to impart the knowledge that has been accumulated to those who are entrusted with the task of carrying on this great organization.

Our research and engineering department may be properly called the heart of IBM. From this live and pulsating center of our circulatory system come all the splendid machines, which nourish the sales department and which, at frequent intervals, revitalize it by the perfection of newer and finer devices to help business.

We must impart knowledge to those who are entrusted with carrying on this great organization.

Our sales department shows steady gains in technique and in enthusiasm because it is kept abreast through the various company schools with the progress of the research and engineering department. Nowhere better than in the sales department can one find the exemplification of the truism that Knowledge is Power; power to master the details not only of the operation of our devices but also of their application; power to tell the story to other business men for whose benefit they have been placed on the market.

It has been said before, but it cannot be too often repeated, that there is no saturation point in education. No man ever goes so far that he can afford to say, or even afford to think, that his education is completed. No young man starting in business can afford to ignore the necessity of increasing his knowledge. The wisdom of the truly educated man is made up of the accretions of day-by-day observation, study and discussion of the world about him, and particularly of that part of the world that most closely affects his own life.

Our research and engineering department may be properly called the heart of IBM.

The basic principle of The IBM program of education is that it enables the men in the organization to keep abreast of their times. Conditions in business change constantly, and rapidly, and only by keeping in step with these changes can a man in the modern world of business win the success that is the goal of every one. That is why IBM sales schools are carried on and expanded; why meetings are held at frequent intervals throughout the sales field forces; why conventions are called—so that all that is known about this business may be made available to every man in it who will take advantage of the opportunities that are placed before him to learn.

Education fits men for life. The wise policy of the heads of the businesses, who are determined that no opportunity to educate himself shall be denied to any man in it, is fitting more men for better life, enabling them to serve their companies and their customers better than they have ever been served before and above all else enabling them to make the most out of their own lives.

Research is the advance guard of progress.

228

THE BUSINESSMAN'S GREATEST OBLIGATION

"Research," Watson said, "is finding out what we are going to do when we can't keep on doing what we are doing now."

It was September 1932, the third anniversary of a series of stock market panics starting in March and continuing through October 29, 1929. Industrial production was in a continuous free fall for over three years. Perhaps he was feeling that it was time for everyone in business and government to perform more research—do something different.

In this chapter, he answers two questions: "What is a successful businessman?" and, "What is the businessman's greatest obligation?"

In the first, standing before a Freshman Business School Convocation, Watson was asked to speak on the earmarks of a businessman. Instead, he stressed success throughout his presentation, starting with a favorite topic—that of democracy in business. A businessman may be "tall or short, corpulent or slight of build; he may be old or young; handsome or homely . . . almost anything as far as externals are concerned." No matter the physical specifications of the businessman, personal appearance, to Tom Watson, was a top consideration. He told them, "You cannot afford to disregard the necessity of looking like a successful man."

You cannot afford to disregard the necessity of looking like a successful man.

He then dispelled any notion in these youngsters that success in business is determined by mere possession of wealth. A businessman, on the exterior, may need to look the part, but success resides in an individual's heart. To Watson, success in business was bound inexorably in emotion-filled words such as character, moral courage, vision and personality. Success was trademarked by decisions made with certainty yet balanced with enough humility to ask for opinions and advice when needed. Ultimately, a successful businessman accepts full responsibility for his decision.

As he finished, he told the students to base their actions on independence of thought. He believed that, from their youthful midst, the leaders of tomorrow would emerge. He hoped his presence, words and encouragement would reach that future leader somewhere in that audience that day.

Government cannot do all that ought to be done without the cooperation and backing of businessmen.

From New York, he traveled to Dayton, Ohio, where his audience transitioned from a room of smiling, eager students to a convention center of 300 desperate industrial, business and civic leaders—the Great Depression was in full swing. This audience was there to hear his suggestions, insights and solutions to solve their desperate plight. The payroll in Dayton had dropped a staggering $60 million—families had seen their incomes shrink, in total, to just $36 million from $96 million. His speech, entitled "The Obligations of a Businessman," was a bold topic to such an audience at such a desperate time—his message even bolder.

He believed it was the responsibility of business to drive payrolls. Businessmen must regain their composure, restore confidence and cooperate with each other and their government counterparts. They must learn from each other, yet think as individuals, avoiding mass thinking. They must focus on driving improvements in their individual areas of expertise. They must affect change in their own environments.

He closed by looking at the room full of business, industrial and civic leaders and saying in essence, "I am talking to you." He does not mince words.

> The greatest responsibility of the businessman, as I see it, is to take a real, genuine interest in the political situation. We must wake up and stop finding fault with whoever happens to be in power. Those men [government leaders] alone cannot hope to do all of the things that ought to be done unless they have the cooperation and the backing of the businessmen. I consider this one of our greatest obligations.

Business and government must cooperate.

The Earmarks of a Business Man

Freshman Convocation of the New York University
School of Commerce, Accounts and Finance

September 21, 1932

There was a time, not so long ago, when for a businessman to have addressed a gathering of this kind would have been a rarity.

The fact that education and scientific research are contributing substantially to advancing industrial efficiency in this country, and that the two are going forward hand in hand, contributes to the feeling which your invitation inspires, that a businessman is in a business atmosphere in these classic halls.

Naturally, there are a number of different schools of thought as to the best method by which young recruits for business should be trained. But there is no difference of opinion as to the vitally important part which education in general, and higher education in particular, must play in the training of future business executives.

Nor is there any difference of opinion among enlightened businessmen as to the

Wealth is not a reliable criterion by which to judge the measure of a man's success in business.

benefits that have come to industry through the progressive development of education and of scientific knowledge.

For years we have heard of the college man in business, and lately we have been hearing more of the businessman in college.

Education and Business

The situation in American industry today demanding executives who are thoroughly educated, trained and intelligently resourceful, is itself a result of education.

It is education, scientific research and invention to which the United States owes its industrial leadership of the world. To make this point clear to you, let me point out that, though this is a new country as compared with those of the Old World; more attention is paid in the United States to elementary and to secondary schools and to institutions of higher learning than in all the rest of the world combined.

231

Also, the enrollment in our colleges and universities exceeds the combined enrollment in similar institutions in all other countries. To my way of thinking, our material and cultural progress has been made possible through the broad view that the United States has taken of education and especially of higher education.

The subject upon which I have been asked to speak to you men tonight, "The Earmarks of a Businessman," is an interesting and important one—especially to you young men who are about to lay the foundation for successful careers in the world of business.

Can we definitely state that to be successful in business, a man should come within certain specific physical dimensions? No, we cannot!

He may be tall or short, corpulent or slight of build; he may be old or young; handsome or homely. In short, he may be almost anything so far as externals are concerned. Therefore, in order to ascertain what constitutes the successful businessman, we must take him apart and find out what "makes him tick."

Personal Appearance Important

Personal appearance is of prime importance. You must dress like a businessman and act like a businessman, because you are judged by your personal appearance; and you know from your own personal reactions how lasting are first impressions. You are judged by your

You are judged by your personal appearance. First impressions are lasting.

personal appearance. You cannot afford to disregard the necessity of looking like a successful man as well as being one. They go together—the man who wishes to be a success in business must dress the part.

We might, I believe, dismiss the matter of appearance with the thought that the businessman must at all times keep himself well groomed, in a dignified fashion and appear properly garbed on all occasions.

Having covered what the successful businessman looks like, let us get under the surface and see who he is. Let us discuss him in his substance—the outstanding characteristics, the abilities and the traits that make for success in the field of business.

The popular conception of a successful businessman is often bound up with the idea of wealth and power. However, mere possession of wealth is not a reliable criterion by which to judge the measure of a man's success in business any more than it is a criterion to judge a student's success in his college work.

Whether a man be in business or following a profession, or whatever his pursuit, we distinguish certain essential qualities of which he must be possessed in order that he may succeed.

Character Most Important

Of these, undoubtedly the most important of all is character. Character should never be confused with reputation. It is not a matter of externals. It is a thing of moral fiber—of moral strength or weakness—it is what you are. No man can ever hope to be a great leader if he does not develop a strong character.

Moral courage impels a man to do the right thing when it should be done.

Closely allied to character we find courage. I do not refer to physical courage, but to that finer quality—moral courage. This attribute, without which a man cannot get very far in life, impels him to do the right thing, when it should be done, no matter how hard it may be or how much his physical being shrinks from the task.

Another important quality is personality. True personality is largely inherent, but in a measure it can be acquired and developed. In business, a pleasing personality is a wonderful asset.

To be successful in business you must develop the ability to make decisions. When you are called upon to make a decision, you should, without delay, obtain all the available facts and pertinent data. You should examine these in the light of any special or general knowledge you may have. When you have done this, you should be ready to make your decision.

Do Not Shift Responsibility

Perhaps, in certain cases, it may be necessary for you to consult one or more of your associates to assist you; but, in any event, never try to shift your responsibilities to the shoulders of another.

Another quality we find in the make-up of the successful businessman is ability to organize. Before you can hope to organize people or things, you will have to learn to organize yourselves.

Never shift your responsibilities to the shoulders of another.

If we are to get ahead in business, we cannot afford to grope blindly along. We must plan ahead. To do this, vision is necessary—vision which pierces the future. No one, it is true, can look ahead and foretell with unfailing accuracy what the future will bring, but that is not necessary, for just as historians judge the past in the light of the present, we can envision the future out of our knowledge of what has taken place in the past and what is going on about us now.

This quality of vision is one that you men should start developing now. You should prepare yourselves now so that when you are ready to go into the business world you will have the qualifications necessary to insure your success.

Should Be Cultured

You must prepare yourselves through the education you will receive here so that you may enter business not only as educated men, but also as men of culture and refinement. You must so train yourselves that you may prove yourselves real gentlemen under all conditions.

You young men who are enrolled in the New York University School of Commerce, Accounts and Finance have a real opportunity to prepare yourselves for careers as business men; and not only to appear as business men but to qualify as such. It is really not as difficult as you might think. In fact, it is simple, if you only realize that the faculty of this school understands thoroughly the requirements of businessmen and that your curriculum is designed to meet those requirements. It is not only essential that you have this realization, but you must act accordingly.

If you young men will simply learn the lessons that are being taught in this institution, you will have nothing to fear when you go out into the business world after graduation. There is no mystery about it. The same qualities that will enable you to get along in college will help you to forge ahead in business.

234

Must Continue Studying

When you go out into the business world—if you are intent on a successful business career—you cannot afford to stop studying. As long as you desire to make progress, you will have to continue to study and learn.

Remember, also, you cannot skip grades in business any more than you can in school, for you must qualify in every phase of the business you enter and must know each phase thoroughly before advancing to the one above.

You took a most important step toward insuring successful careers in business when you enrolled as a member of the New York University School of Commerce, Accounts and Finance, and I congratulate you on the initiative and good judgment which caused you to do so. Here, in this school, you will receive a background of training for business, and that is more important than many of you realize today.

You cannot skip grades in business. You must quality and know each phase before advancing.

Go downtown and attend any of the meetings of the NYU Men in Finance Club and note the caliber of the men you will find there. Check up the big part these men are playing in the financial and business activity of the city, and then you will have some idea of the great asset you will have as a graduate of this institution.

All they can do for you here is to teach you. You will have to do the learning. Your success will not depend on how much is taught, but on how much you learn.

Remember, when you go out into the business world, you have more of a responsibility than just that of your personal success. You will be known as a graduate of New York University and this institution will be judged by your conduct and achievements. So always carry with you the thought of the responsibility you have to your school, and take pride in carrying that responsibility.

Importance of Education

Of the acquired qualifications of the successful businessman, I would place first, education. The successful business executive of today must not only know his own business thoroughly, but he must also know a great deal about many other businesses, and he must be quick to sense and to understand changing conditions.

He cannot afford ever to stop studying his own and other businesses, and he must be a close student of current social and economic trends. Only in this way is he enabled to keep abreast of the times. When he fails in this changing world to keep abreast of the times, he is lost.

Nothing is more fatal to progress than self-satisfaction. We must never admit, even to ourselves, that we are successes. We should recognize the fact that we are succeeding, yes!—but until we are ready to retire, we must not make the mistake of basking in the sunlight of our past accomplishments.

Knowledge without wisdom is just so much excess baggage. Wisdom is the ability to apply knowledge to some useful purpose. If you lack the ability to apply your knowledge, it is of no use, either to you or to anyone else. It is of the utmost importance, therefore, that in the process of acquiring knowledge, you also acquire the ability to put that knowledge to its proper use.

Knowledge without wisdom is just so much excess baggage.

It is a matter of common knowledge today that the age of the rule-of-thumb businessman is past. The successful business executive of today is a scientifically trained business administrator. But just as all the knowledge in the world is of little value without wisdom, so the training in scientific business administration is of little value if you do not think—think straight and think constructively.

My company has a universal motto for everyone in it, the single word, "THINK."

The visitor to any of our factories or offices anywhere in the world will find this word, "THINK," or its equivalent in another language, prominently displayed as a framed wall motto—a constant reminder of the prime necessity of exercising mental faculties, of avoiding acting on impulse, without reflection, or through habit.

No man ever attained greatness who did not think for himself.

Business Men Must Think

I consider the finest lesson that you men can learn during your course of training here at New York University is summed up in that one word, "THINK."

The man who bases his actions on independent thought, who reflects and considers before doing anything and whose judgments are arrived at through logic, is the man who will go farthest today.

What we do with our leisure time has considerable bearing on what we accomplish during our working hours, and very largely determines the degree of our success. Young men who, like

The finest lesson you can learn here at New York University is to "THINK."

yourselves, devote a predetermined amount of their leisure hours to study and to serious thinking, are the men who are going to progress far and fast.

The business leaders of tomorrow will be the young men of today—men like you who are preparing now for the great future which lies ahead. You may view the future with confidence, knowing that from the youth of today will emerge the leaders of tomorrow.

The business leaders of tomorrow will be the young men of today.

The Obligations of the Business Man

Three Hundred Business, Industrial and Civic Leaders

Dayton, Ohio
December 3, 1932

Not long ago a magazine representative asked me to tell him about the best sale I ever made. I told him I could not do it. He asked me why, and I told him. It was because the best sale I ever made was in Dayton, Ohio, when I sold Miss Kittredge on the idea of marrying me.

Another thing that has always kept my heart warm toward this city is the fact that until I left here a little less than nineteen years ago to take up my present business, I had put in most of my business career with a Dayton company—the National Cash Register Company.

The Business Man's Obligation

The obligation of the businessman is to take more interest in education. The expansion of our curriculum of education has not kept pace with the expansion of production in all lines of industry, and it is up to the businessman to see that it does.

The obligation of the businessman is to take more interest in education.

I am not in favor of doing away with anything in our system of education; I am in favor of expanding it. That brings me to Dr. Kettering's definition of research. Research, he says, is finding out what we are going to do when we can't keep on doing what we are doing now. Is there anyone who wants to keep on doing what he is doing now? What is going to get us out of this depression?

The payroll! That is the only thing I know of that will do it. You can talk for a long time about that. Take the payroll right here in the city of Dayton, for example. Your payroll has dropped from $96 million to $36 million, a fall of $60 million. You must get back this money and you are going to get it back.

A few years ago we did think we were very smart.

When I say we, I mean the financial and industrial leaders. The financial and industrial leaders were the people who were charting the course and steering the ship of finance and industry, but we just did

238

not know how to do it. Now we must find out how. How are we going to do it? By holding meetings and saying this cannot be done and that cannot be done?

Why, ladies and gentlemen, if we do not find the right answer—and we must find a complete and correct answer—our leadership will be challenged and justly so, because we then must admit defeat.

Must Increase Payrolls

There are out of employment in our country today more than 11 million men and women who are willing and able to work. What are we doing about it? We talk about how hard we work in collecting money for the unemployed. That kind of help is not what they need or want.

To increase the payroll is our obligation as businessmen.

We are sharing the work, which is a sound and helpful proposition, but is only a temporary and partial remedy and should not be carried to the point where it will work a hardship on those who are employed. We must get money back into the pay envelopes—get people back into gainful employment—and we are going to do it.

We realize the seriousness of our obligation as businessmen—our obligation not only to the 11 million who are out of employment, but to the 40 million who are employed and working on short time. That is an obligation to which we must give every consideration.

What is our chief trouble and what is the worst thing that can happen to anyone?

Our greatest trouble is lack of confidence. We have everything in this country that we had in 1928 and 1929. We have the same amount of money, all our natural resources—in fact, we have a surplus of everything that you can name—and yet here we are, in this state of depression. It is due, principally, to lack of confidence.

Some people have lost confidence in our financial structure, in our businesses, in our educational system, even in themselves. Losing confidence in oneself is the worst thing that can happen. We must reestablish this confidence; we must make up our minds that school is not out—that we are just having a little vacation.

This Is Man Age

We hear a great deal of talk about this machine age.

I claim it is not a machine age, but a Man Age, and that these machines that most people know very little about are simply tools that men have designed to help them do a better job. We have much more to do along the line of research and of improved machinery.

United States statistics of labor, which have been compiled every ten years since 1870, or thereabouts, show each time a higher percentage of our population gainfully employed. That is due to the engineers.

Take the automobile, for example. Twenty-five years ago it was a luxury; today it has become the servant of all. I might say, even, that it has become a family necessity. We are going further in the same direction not only here, but also in other countries. We have gone on and we have made it possible for our people continually to get better things in life. We must continue to do that. We must make this country of ours a better place for the masses.

We must make this country of ours a better place for the masses.

The people who are building things and who are consuming the goods in this country are the people who demand our immediate attention and they must have it, because we cannot carry on unless they are in a position to buy our goods, and they cannot do it with the small payroll of today.

To increase that payroll is our obligation as businessmen.

We have built up our per capita consumption in this country to a point where it is three times as great as that of the rest of the world, and we are going to continue to increase it.

One thing I have noticed in my business trips through Europe is an improvement in the standards of living abroad. You may ask what that has to do with it. If we handle our international affairs properly and we give proper attention to our foreign trade it is going to mean a great deal to us. They are going to need and want in various countries many things that we produce here—produce to better advantage than they can.

240

Must Help One Another

I think that, as we go on, we are going to hear less talk about America standing alone. We are going to hear more talk about the interdependence of nations; we are going to be more charitable toward our home institutions; we are going to believe more in the fact that, as Marcus Aurelius said, "Men are created one for another; either then teach them or bear with." And we are going to extend greater cooperation to one another.

If we get the right spirit of cooperation it will pay us in dollars and cents throughout the world.

What do we mean by cooperation? In some people's opinion it boils down to, "I am all right and the other fellow is all wrong." In effecting greater cooperation we must think beyond merely the help we can give one another; we must think further than our country. We must think not only of cooperation with our leaders in all walks of life, but of cooperation with other countries.

If we get the right spirit of cooperation it will pay us in dollars and cents to extend real cooperation throughout the world.

Individual Thought

Just a few years ago we got into the habit of mass thinking. We took up mass production and then got into mass thinking. What we need in this country today is more individual thought and action.

We need it not only on the part of the so-called leaders, but also on the part of the men down the line, particularly the young men, because they are the ones who are going to enjoy the great prosperity that this country is going to see. It would be fine if every man lower down in our organizations would tell us what is on his mind and what he believes would help us out.

I always look for young help. I get from 100 to 150 young men out of schools and colleges every year. I know that they are trained to think. That is what we must have—more thought and more new ideas from fresh minds. When I say that, I am not discrediting the older minds, which work along progressive lines. We have no right to think in any terms except those of progress. We cannot overcome our difficulties otherwise.

Cooperation is Most Important

The greatest responsibility of the businessman, as I see it, is to take a real, genuine interest in the political situation. Our local, state and national affairs are costing us too much for what we get. We must wake up and stop finding fault with whoever happens to be in power. We are crying for leadership; we hear on every hand the cry, "If we only had a leader." We need more than one leader, because the job is too big for any one person.

The political job is not a one-man proposition. It requires the coopera- tion and backing of the businessmen.

Your political job is not a one-man proposition; nor is your state or national organization and, in all due respect to the hundreds and thousands of honest, intelligent men who are contributing their best toward the running of our government, those men alone cannot hope to do all of the things that ought to be done unless they have the cooperation and the backing of the business men. I consider this one of our greatest obligations.

I could talk to you a long time along these lines, but I am just saying things that we all know. We know what we ought to do, and I have great confidence in American businessmen to do it. I have associated with them all my life and my experience with them has been most satisfactory. I have always received from them the best cooperation.

I thank you all very kindly for your attention. It has been a great pleasure and privilege for me to come back to the old hometown and meet with you again.

*We have no right to think in any terms
except those of progress.*

THE CONTROLLER'S DUTY

Tom Watson Sr. performed research within IBM. His research reached into the office of the controller. An IBM controller was to help grow and expand the business, not just control expenses. Speaking before a gathering of controllers, he instructed them, as he did his own controller, to "Forget your title. Forget that your position is merely to control expenditures."

Tom Watson never believed in isolated departments within The IBM, and this philosophy applied to the office of the controller, too. During the Depression, every corporation needed its controller to be successful. And the key to a controller's success, in his opinion, was to have his "presence, advice and instructions gracefully and thankfully received." Watson expected the controller to earn the respect of the business. He expected him to acquire such a deep knowledge and competence in running the business that he could even replace a sales manager. This required a person of great tact, noticeable flexibility and an extensive knowledge of the corporation's inner workings.

Forget your title. Forget the position you fill is merely to control expenditure of cash.

Watson exercised these beliefs by requiring The IBM's controller to spend his first year getting fully acquainted and thoroughly familiar with all that was The IBM. He needed to intimately understand the business—especially the sales manager's perspective.

He distinguished between the controller's *responsibility* and *duty*. He believed everyone in the audience understood their fiscal responsibility. He focused on their corporate duty: recommending ways to spend money and expand the business.

The greatest service a controller can provide is to spend money to expand the business and bring in more orders.

The Controller's Responsibility

Opening Session Principal Speaker
Controller's Institute of America

New York, N.Y.
September 19, 1932

Mr. Chairman and gentlemen, it is a great privilege for me to meet with you today and to say a few things in regard to the responsibilities of a controller, because there is a great deal of difference of opinion as to what those responsibilities really are.

A controller must study every branch of the business.

To me, the responsibilities of the controller come second only to those of the sales heads of the business. I believe that, if you can get a good sales organization, headed by a good sales manager and then a good finance department, headed by a good controller, the problems of your business will be very simple to work out.

I would rather talk to you about the duties of the controller than the responsibilities, because you all know what your responsibilities are.

It seems to me that the first duty of a controller is to forget his title, forget that the position he fills is merely to control the expenditures of cash.

The Controller Must Know the Business

That is important, but there is something more important: a controller must study every branch of the business; he must know and understand all about the cost of manufacturing and of selling. It is not a very hard problem for a controller to learn these things. Your main problem is to get all the people in the business to understand that it is important for you to know about their work, because sometimes men in other departments feel it is not necessary to tell the controller all about how goods are made or sold or what they are used for after they are sold.

A controller must know all these things, and his biggest job is to educate all his associates up to the point where they are part of the controller's department.

244

You will meet with a little resentment at times in doing this, but you have to convince all the other people that it is important to them as individuals to help you. The controller is an individual and he cannot possibly hope to have perfect control of everything that is going on in a large business unless he has the whole-hearted cooperation and support of the heads of all divisions and departments of the business—and unless those people feel that it is their duty to help him.

A controller is an engineer, a purchasing agent, a credit man, a salesman and a manufacturer as well as a financier.

The controller has to be an engineer, a purchasing agent, a credit man, a salesman and a manufacturer as well as a financier.

It is not necessary for anybody to talk about the importance of the controller in a business during the present economic state of affairs, because the controller is the man who has had to come to the front in recent years and take part in every branch of the business and help effect savings in all of them.

The gentleman on my left is controller in our company, and when he came with us I told him I would like him to spend his first year without taking up the duties of controller, that I would like him instead to spend the year visiting our factories, getting fully acquainted and thoroughly familiar with all that was going on in our factories and in our home office. Then we made it convenient for him to visit all our principal sales offices and to spend a great deal of time getting acquainted with the sales end of the business.

We also put him down to make a talk at every sales convention it was possible for him to attend, our field sales conventions and our annual convention, and we feel that we have made him a part of every division and department of our business. We know he has a thorough knowledge of every division of our business.

We feel that, in the absence of a sales manager, he could go out into the field and intelligently discuss with our representatives all the affairs of the sales end of this business and that his presence, his advice and his instructions would be gracefully and thankfully received.

I think that is the position that every controller should be put in by his company if they expect him to give them best results.

We all know, of course, that in some organizations this takes a little time and a controller has to keep certain things in mind. He cannot step in quickly and participate in all these things without first making his way and educating his people.

The Controller Must Spend Money

Another thing that I consider of great importance for the controller is to find ways to spend money.

I know that some people expect their controller to do only one thing, and that is preventing the expenditure of money. I always want our controller to find ways for us to spend more money. We believe and we know that a controller naturally measures everything by the dollar sign and when he says, "I recommend that you spend money for this, that or the other," you can feel pretty certain that such expenditure is going to bring returns to the company.

If the controller can find more ways to spend more money where it will expand the business, where it will bring in more orders to the factory, that will be the greatest service he can perform for the business with which he is connected. Everything we can do in the way of spending money that will bring good returns will help. I am opposed to spending any money, either in these times or in boom times that will not bring good returns.

I am opposed to spending any money that will not bring good returns.

You cannot always be sure of this, but in every case you must have a proposition that will convince the people who are interested that it is a good proposition, that it is a good investment to make because you believe it is going to pay dividends.

We now know we are nearer the time when things are going to be entirely different from what they have been for the past three and a half years. Personally, I believe we are nearer that point than any of us realizes. We have been holding back so long that there is a tremendous pent-up buying power in this country. There is a desire on the part of every American for something better than he now has.

That is the American idea and the American spirit. We are always looking forward, always hoping that someday we will have something better than we now have, and that is the way everybody should feel. That is the one great asset we have developed in this country to a far greater extent than you will find it developed in any other country.

Everybody here, regardless of his position in life, always looks forward with the hope that someday he is going to be in a better position and is going to have more than he now has. We are going to get back into our stride and the controllers of the various businesses in this country are to be congratulated and thanked for the very wonderful job which they have done during the past three and a half years. There is no man in the business who has had more to contend with, who has had more demands made upon him, than the controller.

You have been asked to cut and cut and cut; you have been asked to reduce everybody and reduce everything; your job has been a very unpleasant one. But gentlemen, I trust and I believe that we are on the verge of an era which will give you an opportunity to take a long breath, to get on the other side and have the pleasure of expanding rather than contracting, of spending more money rather than demanding the expenditure of less money.

I thank you for this opportunity to talk to you and wish you all good luck during your convention and in the future.

*The controller has to be an engineer,
a purchasing agent, a credit man, a salesman,
a manufacturer and a financier.*

THE DARKEST HOUR BEFORE THE DAWN

Tom Watson Sr. loved maxims—sayings that summarized to him a basic and fundamental truth. His maxims were legend in The IBM.

These "one-liners" would express an idea, a concept or a truth for him to grab hold of and then elaborate and expand on; but most of all they served as a focal point to educate and communicate his thoughts. These maxims, sometimes written on pieces of cardboard, were strategically placed around the room for all to see. He used these earliest of sales aids to develop, strengthen and embolden the delivery of his message.

Unknown to him, as he stood in front of his salesmen in January 1933—the trough—the very bottom of the Great Depression was only a month away. The maxim to best capture this moment in time would have been, "The darkest of all hours is the hour before the dawn." From his perspective, looking into the eyes of his salesmen and factory foremen at the 1932 One Hundred Percent club, there was nothing before him but a cliff falling away into a dark abyss. There was no "light at the end of the tunnel" or any other maxim that could have been used because there was desperately little good news to support such optimism—except his belief in his people.

The darkest of all hours is the hour before the dawn.

Going into early 1933, the Great Depression was now entering the start of its fourth year. All anyone could see before them was more downward motion, more agony and pain. During these times, dividends were in many cases life-sustaining for those who owned them. Stocks that paid consistent dividends had become known as "widow-and-orphan" stocks because widows and orphans could least afford the vagaries and whims of a volatile market.

They depended on that dividend check to put their daily bread on the table, care for their children and avoid homelessness. Dividends during the Great Depression meant survival. The core value of such a stock was not money—for many it was life.

The IBM stock was now in that category.

No one at the time seemed aware of how bad it was for The IBM except those at headquarters—the executives at the home office. Mr. Watson's closest advisors felt that for the first time The IBM would either reduce or miss issuing its dividend.

Widows and orphans, could least afford the vagaries and whims of a volatile stock market.

Tom Watson personalized this responsibility. He was probably one of the few executives of his time who, presumably through his own mechanical devices, tracked exactly who owned The IBM stock. He knew it wasn't the J.P. Morgans or the extremely wealthy, but women and small investors who during the depth of the Depression trusted in The IBM to reliably deliver that income to them. For any Chief Executive Officer who personalized these facts, it must have been a great burden.

Watson, at his own admission, felt he had failed during the recession of 1921 to increase The IBM's profits because he lost faith in his people. He was not going to let history repeat itself. He rallied himself and his team. He felt, this time, that The IBM's character, responsibility, knowledge, wisdom but most of all its spirit was going to carry it through.

In more than nine speeches, all of them at the One Hundred Percent Club, he was once again depending on his sales team to close deals and his foremen to improve product quality. He would continue to speak with confidence to this team but with a renewed sense of urgency. He would speak before this team over three days, on at least eight separate occasions, with more than 10,000 captured words—probably more that weren't captured.

He would welcome them as the most "outstanding Hundred Percenters in the entire history of the Club," encourage those salesmen who had fallen short that we are "doing our utmost to help the man with a low record" and confirm that the path to success was to "give the best possible service you can to your customers."

He would encourage those that made the One Hundred Percent Club to keep doing what they were doing. He encouraged them to share their knowledge with those who had not made the club that year.

To those that did not, he would speak directly and say, "Do something different." He would speak of getting back to the basics of good salesmanship that had taken him through his personal storms in life and hope it would carry his company through this, the greatest test it was about to face in 1933.

He spoke during this three-day event about determination, experimenting to find new ways, sailing turbulent seas and yet he closed this session talking about how he foresaw a "century of progress."

How any leader could have looked past the current situation and set a vision of a future of wealth and progress is hard to understand. Yet somehow, here was a man who always found the balance in his presentations; that equilibrium of demanding more, yet balancing it out with honest communication that "we are all in this together."

No one person stood alone in The IBM. "We" stood together.

This was a time when Tom Watson needed his team to deliver. Watson found that balance in his tone, demeanor and words. He showed his true character.

He achieved it during these, the darkest hours of the Depression.

Such is great leadership.

Work your way out even if you have to do a lot of experimenting.

It is during the storms when the seas are running high and the going is rough that you develop your sailors—and that is how you develop men.

The Triumphs of High Position Are Yours

Message of Welcome
1932 One Hundred Percent Club

January 23, 1933

Once more it becomes my pleasant duty to extend a welcome, on behalf of the stockholders, directors, executives and all other members of the International Business Machines Corporation, to those men from the sales force who have won the distinction of membership in an IBM Hundred Percent Club. Never before, in all the years that this famous club of leaders has assembled, has there been more reason to congratulate the men who have won their victory over an entire year's quota.

Membership in any IBM Hundred Percent Club is a mark of distinction, but the men who won this honor during the year 1932 may justly consider themselves the outstanding Hundred Percenters in the entire history of the Club. More than in any other year they are entitled to the appreciation of the company and the plaudits of their comrades.

The triumphs of high position are yours, and we accord them to you gratefully, appreciating to the full how manfully each of you has fought to earn them. The responsibilities of leadership are yours, and we know you will discharge them with credit both to yourselves and your company. No word of welcome would be complete without an expression of the appreciation of your efforts that is felt by every person in the business. In the offices, in the research and engineering laboratories, in all our factories, there is general recognition of the sales force as the most important branch of IBM.

All of us in the supporting organization behind this line pledge to you once more our own 100% cooperation to make the attainment of your 1933 objectives easier and more certain.

Membership in any IBM Hundred Percent Club
is a mark of distinction.

252

Men of Character and Courtesy

Factory Foremen
1932 One Hundred Percent Club

New York, N.Y.
January 23–25, 1933

The real object of these conventions is to stimulate the sales organization to get more orders for you men to handle in the factory. Thus, my time has been entirely taken up with the salesmen who are here at this meeting.

This is the fourth session that I have been in this morning, and there isn't much that I can say to you men except to express my appreciation for the work you are doing as individuals and in the direction of the men under you and to offer you a word of encouragement for the future. There is no question about the future of this business demanding more of you men than the past ever has. There is absolutely no question as to the future growth and development of The IBM business. That is an assured fact, as I have said to you many times.

It ceased long ago to be a business in our eyes. It is a great world institution and it is going to go right on forever. We are in a business that gives service to other people; and it is going to go right straight on along with the other great institutions in this civilization just as education and the church are going on forever. There are certain kinds of industries that are going on forever, and ours is one of them.

That gives us something to think about. We cannot afford to think about this business in terms of today, tomorrow, this year or next year or even in terms of our lifetime. We have to think of this business in terms of an institution that is going to go on forever. That is a pretty serious business for a man to be engaged in, because it means so much.

There are so many things for us to do—that we want to do—while we are here. And one of the most important things to do is to train the men under us so that they can do their job better. You men have a lot of trouble, particularly you foremen, because you stand between the executive end of the business, so-called, and the workmen who are making the machine.

You foremen have to look beyond to the sales force. Keep in mind your duty to those men out there.

Sometimes a foreman looks upon that as his whole duty. But it is not. You foremen have to look beyond the executive end of the business and beyond the workmen who are underneath. You have to look out to the sales force, and you have to keep in mind that your duty is to those men out there. You have to keep that in mind all the time. If you do not, you are not fully measuring up to your jobs as foremen.

If you will stop to think about that, gentlemen, you will realize the importance of it. The one object of this whole organization is to get more goods sold. Just as soon as the salesmen stop selling goods, then what happens? Something happens in the factory and in the office.

Now, how can you men as foremen do the most for the salesmen?

First, you can do this by giving careful attention to the quality of men you bring into your department. If you need a man in your department tomorrow morning, do not take the first man who John Barton sends over, because he is not responsible as an individual for your department; and he has not the time to go into every angle of the qualification of that man. Make sure yourself that he is suitable for your particular department. It is up to you to say "yes" or "no."

If you are not absolutely sure that he is the right type of man, the kind of man who will extend cooperation to you and to his fellow workmen and if he isn't backed up with the proper kind of experience, or if he hasn't got the right kind of character—and put that first—then do not take him into your department. I think every foreman in our business and every foreman in every other business, has been making a lot of mistakes in that direction.

If you need a man, hire him, but hire the right kind of a man. Dr. Nicholas Murray Butler said there were only two things in connection with education that were of real importance, and without which you could not educate anybody or do anything with him. Those two things, he said, were character and good manners. And he said a great many of our educational institutions were falling down on both those points.

I have thought about that a lot. You men never had a successful experience in your life with a workman who did not have good manners. The fellow that is always rough and doesn't show you the consideration and the courtesy to which, as foreman, you are entitled is not the kind of man you want in your department. You need the kind of men who are gentlemanly and courteous, and whose manners are backed up with good clean character. I want us to keep those two things in mind right through every branch and every department of our business. If we have anybody in any department—sales, factory or office—who we discover is a man of real character but does not display good manners, we must get rid of him and give the job to somebody who does possess those qualities. Then we will have a real organization.

Of course, we must always set the right kind of example all the way along the line as to character and good manners. Then you can teach the men anything, because they are with you, they will listen to you. They are not trying to show off or be smart. They get right down to business.

I was just talking to some salesmen and I made the confession that there was a time when I used to give a great many sales talks. But it should not be necessary. It is so easy to sell things if you just know what you are going to sell. Get enough knowledge about what you are going to sell, and then be willing to put in a little walking time and talking time and you will bring back the orders.

That same thing applies to your division of the business. It is not hard for anybody to learn how to make our goods if they are interested. Whenever an experienced man neglects anything that he is doing in his work, get rid of him. If he is a new man and you are breaking him in, teach him how to do it. But if he knows how to do it right and does not, you cannot afford to keep him. We cannot afford to have anything wrong with our machines. What I want you to do is build a real organization. Train your men how to do your business properly today and you will have no trouble with them in the future.

I wonder if you men noticed Monday morning when I was introducing the officers of the One Hundred Percent Club that with the exception of Mr. Brown from Chicago and Mr. Brown from Portland, Oregon, all of those men have come into this business since 1929. There was not one of these comparatively new men who have been in this business three years. That is something to think about. They came into this business and found that they had to get out and hustle. They had to do things right. They had to be on the job.

Fair Weather Sailors

The reason they were up there on the platform instead of some of the older men is that many of the older men came into the business in boom times, when it was just a question of going around and taking orders. They did not have to get down and figure a plan and prove their cases. That is why they are not Hundred Percenters today.

Sailors are developed
when the seas are rough.

They learned to sail the boat in smooth water. They have never sailed it in a rough sea. When the storm came they did not know how to set their sails; they did not know how to fix the sheets. They did not know anything about it.

As I said to one of the divisions this morning, there never was a good sailor developed in fair weather. It is during the storms when the seas are running high and the going is rough that you develop your sailors. And that is how you develop men.

You have to test men just as you test metal. And, by Jove, men are getting the test today, and I am mighty proud of our organization as a whole for the way it has stood the test in the last three years. I am glad that we have had vision enough during that time to keep bringing these young men in. Otherwise, this One Hundred Percent Club would have been a sad affair. What does it mean to see boys come into our business during the Depression and make such a showing? To me, gentlemen, it means simply this: it means that I had no vision as to the future of this business.

You men have heard me boast about the future—if you want to call it boasting—and make predictions that many of you thought were overly optimistic; yet, as you know, I have always been wrong. You have always done better than I predicted. Though I got to a point where I thought I had some real vision.

But two years ago, you could not have made me believe that this year, only two years later, all of the officers except two would be men who

256

weren't in a territory at that time. Some of these men were still studying in our schools. This is a state of affairs I would not have believed two years ago would exist today. But that is what has happened.

Employing More People

Now, gentlemen, you know we have devoted a lot of thought to giving men employment. We are employing more people today than we employed in 1929, and I am mighty thankful that this is so. We have let out some people, but we have put more on. And I am sure that you men have not let out anybody that was deserving of his job. As long as you run on that basis, whether it is good times or bad times, you are running on the right basis.

Today no man is entitled to a job who does not appreciate it enough to give you the best that is in him. I do not care whether he is in the factory or in the executive end of the business. It would be awfully hard for any of us to go out and get what we have now from any other company. After we fully realize this as it applies to ourselves, let us get that message into the hearts, not into the heads but into the hearts, of all of the other men in the organization. I want to tell you, your jobs as foremen then would be a real pleasure.

When your men get it in their hearts that they have something they could not go around the corner and get, that they have a company back of them that has some heart and wants to help them, and a foreman who is ready to work overtime to help them, your troubles are over, and a great deal of our service troubles are over. And that is one of the important problems in this business.

I am thinking about the amount of money involved in the service end of our business, correcting mistakes, most of which never should be made. Now let's stop that right at headquarters.

You have to test men just as you test metal.

257

More Thought, Effort and Determination

Tabulating Machine Division
1932 One Hundred Percent Club

New York, N.Y.
January 23–25, 1933

I do not want any Hundred Percenter to pay any attention to what I am saying. We do not want you to experiment. Your present methods are successful and therefore should not be altered. In fact, if you can get other salesmen to adopt your methods, do it, because you will be doing both them and the company a favor.

You Non-Hundred Percenters do something different.

Every once in a while, here at headquarters, we run up against a brick wall and we do not know which way to turn. After trying and trying and trying to do something, we find that it will not work. We say, "Well, let us do something different. We are wrong now and we will not be any worse off if we try something else."

Every once in a while at headquarters we run up against a brick wall. Do something different.

Whenever you find you are wrong, gentlemen, turn around and try something different. Work your way out even if you have to do a lot of experimenting, because no one man can stand on this platform or anywhere tell you exactly what to do and how to do it in order to achieve success. That is an individual proposition with each man.

Did it ever occur to you Non-Hundred Percenters that you are the men we work for all the time? We have not done anything for the leaders except tell them to work harder. When a man gets 150 percent of his quota we send him a telegram and tell him we expect him to get 200 percent. Why? Because we know we can depend upon the men in the lead—they always respond. All of us who are not actually out in territories are doing our utmost to help the man with a low record. Gentlemen, jump in and help us and we will help you. Let us work this thing out together! I am not here to criticize you. I merely want to see those of you who are not Hundred Percenters come up to the front and put yourself in position where we can pay you more money than we are now paying you.

What we need and always will need, in this business, is greater intimacy and simple honesty between us. That is what I am trying to get over to you this morning—the plain, honest fact that you are in this business for the purpose of making some money for the stockholders of the company and you know, and you will all agree, that the company is willing and anxious to divide that profit with you men on a fair, honest and reasonable basis.

What we need and always will need, in this business, is greater intimacy and simple honesty between us.

We cannot afford to carry men who do not operate their territories on a profitable basis. It makes no difference whether you are working on commission, salary, or salary and commission. We have to figure everything on a straight commission basis. When a man runs a territory at a loss he reduces the profit on the territories that are operating successfully. There never has been a time in the history of industry when business people have had as great a need for our products as they have today. It is harder to sell today, of course, but the business is there. There are fair-weather sailors and rough-weather sailors and it has been mostly rough sailing lately. It requires more thought and more effort and more determination in rough weather, but it can be done.

That does not mean that a man has to be a slave to this business. All we want is an honest day's work. You are the ones to decide how much that is. We cannot walk around with you and check you up. You must supervise yourselves. It is an honor system, and we know that every man in this room can do a little better this year than he did last year. We are not telling you that you must double your record this year over last, but we do expect every man to show improvement. If every man in the organization shows just a little improvement, the accumulative effect will be a very satisfactory result at the end of the year.

Success is an individual proposition.

Pride in the Past – Faith in the Future

Concluding Banquet Opening Message
1932 One Hundred Percent Club

New York, N.Y.
January 25, 1933

To look over this body of men in this room and realize that we have throughout the civilized world more than 6,000 of the same type of people that we have with us here tonight, all putting forth their efforts in the interests of serving the world's business through the distribution of IBM products, must make everybody here realize and appreciate that the future of this business is far beyond the vision of any of us.

We are always happy to greet the Hundred Percenters. We are also happy tonight to greet those members of our organization present who this year are not Hundred Percenters, because we have confidence in your ability, in your ambition, to become Hundred Percenters. And I want to say to you gentlemen if we didn't have that confidence in you we wouldn't have invited you here. So we want you to feel right at home here in this One Hundred Percent Convention.

The business part of the convention is over and tonight we are not to celebrate but to give thanks for the accomplishments of last year. We

FACTORY EMPLOYEES

We should give thanks as we have been able to keep our people in our factories and offices employed.

should all give thanks, because we have been able to keep our people employed in our factories and our offices. We have not contributed to the army of the unemployed, as we hear it called. We have more people on our payroll today than we had in the boom period of 1929, and I am more thankful for that one fact than for anything else that has ever come before me since I have been connected with this business.

Most of us have had something to do with trying to assist the work of taking care of the unemployed, and we have had an opportunity to realize what it means to have a great number of people out of employment. To have the knowledge back of you that your company is giving out more pay envelopes than ever before in the history of the

260

business is something that you can be thankful for and perhaps a little bit proud of. How have we been able to do this?

There are two main reasons. First, our engineering department has always measured up to our expectations, and when the Depression came along, our engineering department was just ready to begin to give us improvements, which meant encouragement, in addition to broadening our field. Then our sales organization was ready to step out, increase its forces, increase its effort and bring in orders to keep the factory wheels turning.

The greatest satisfaction to me is the fact that never once during the past three and a half years has any man or any group of men come to my office to discuss the Depression. They always come to discuss something that will improve our business. Everybody's mind is centered on that one thing. Gentlemen, during these times, the increased effort and the never-failing confidence of the sales organization are what have put us where we are today. And it is that same policy, those same reasons that are going to carry us on to greater success in the future than we have ever dreamed of in the past. The future of this business is far beyond the vision of any of us.

Men come, not to discuss the Depression, but to discuss something that will improve the business.

First Winner of the Watson International Trophy

(Editor's note: The presentation ceremony was interrupted by the reading of a cablegram from Rio de Janeiro. It announced the election of Mr. Boucas as the first 1933 Hundred Percenter.)

Of course the members of the sales organization realize that the record represented by this cable, which was just read by Mr. Boucas, makes Mr. Boucas the first member of the 1933 One Hundred Percent Club. As he is already in, we might just as well keep him here until next year.

I wish to explain to all of you in this convention that at the time we gave Mr. Boucas the title of manager of our company in Brazil, there was really no opportunity existing there. When we give a man a territory in the United States or any other country where our business is established, and where we have customers and friends and organization, we call that giving a man an opportunity.

But when we merely give a man the privilege of representing us in a country where our goods are unknown, where they are not used by anyone and where the laws of the country impose a 300 percent duty, I would like to have anybody explain to me wherein lies the opportunity.

Mr. Boucas created the opportunity. That is why we appreciate him. And when we hear that a man could do that for us in a country where we were unknown and where he had to change the laws before he could even go out and attempt to do business, it should inspire every one of us in the United States, and in the European countries as well, to look our records squarely in the face and say to ourselves that we haven't yet begun to realize our opportunities or to take advantage of them.

**I am an American citizen.
In The IBM I am a world citizen.**

We owe you a great deal, Mr. Boucas, and we welcome you now to the 1933 Hundred Percent Club. Your cablegram tonight bespeaks perfect organization, looking ahead, having men who will carry out orders. Your record of 400 percent, putting your country in the lead for 1932, also is a wonderful record. I wish to remind all present here that in 1930, your country also was the leader of all countries in the world. In 1926, Mr. Boucas, you also put Brazil in the front rank as the leader of the world.

I leave it to you gentlemen of The IBM to think this over! With the start that he has, what may Mr. Boucas do to you in this year's race!

A World Citizen

I happen to have been born in the United States. I am an American Citizen. But in The IBM I am a world citizen, because we do business in seventy-eight countries and they all look alike to me, every one of them.

I want to claim that I am a part of the country that produces the leader. So I am still with Mr. Boucas, and I am going to stay with him right straight through and claim that I am a part of Brazil and part of Mr. Boucas—until some of you fellows can beat his record.

Mr. Boucas was a pioneer in our business in Brazil. It was his pioneer work and his great vision and ability to organize and manage men that was instrumental in establishing our business throughout South America. Furthermore, Mr. Boucas's friendship, his knowledge of the business and his vision of the future have helped us in building our sales in all of the countries of the world. All the people in our business know what the motto, "THINK," means to us and how important it is in our work. Mr. Boucas represents the finest type of thought that could possibly be represented by any man in our organization or in any other organization.

A High Compliment

Ladies and gentlemen, my tribute tonight is paid to Mr. Boucas first as a businessman. He represents the highest type of businessman; he stands for the highest standards of business. He trains his men along those same lines. He stands before you tonight as the highest type of business executive that we have in our whole organization.

I wish to also pay tribute to Mr. Boucas tonight as a citizen, because he is always thinking and putting forth effort along the lines of doing something to benefit his country. That is never out of his mind.

He cooperates with the officials of the country, regardless of party affiliation. They can all call upon him. He represents citizenship of the highest order. When you say a man is a good citizen and represents the highest type of citizenship, it is my judgment that you are paying him the highest tribute that one man can pay another.

I also wish to pay tribute to Mr. Boucas as a friend and in what I have to say along that line, I will take the liberty of saying that I am speaking for all of his friends, both inside and outside of The IBM organization. It affords me great pleasure and satisfaction tonight to be able to pay this tribute to you, Mr. Boucas.

All the people in our business know
what the motto, "THINK," means to us.

Foreseeing a Century of IBM Progress

Closing Address
1932 One Hundred Percent Club

New York, N.Y.
January 25, 1933

The Century of Progress to be held in Chicago is going to be a very wonderful affair. I hope that as many of you as possibly can, will attend it. It will have a great deal of educational value. But it deals entirely with the past. They are talking about the progress they have made in the past hundred years; it is going to be a very great picture and a great lesson.

If we measure up to our job, we shall get more in return in the future than we ever did in the past.

My mind went out into the next century, and the progress that IBM is going to make in the next century.

Some of you people may be thinking that I am looking a long way ahead. But as I said in one of the divisional meetings this week, it is our duty; we have no right to think about our institution in terms of today or tomorrow or this year or next year. We are in a business manufacturing machines that are business necessities today. We are taking our part in the progress of the world, in the development of this civilization, and we must think ahead. Tonight marks the beginning of our thoughts along the lines of the "Century of Progress," the century that is to come, and we must lay our plans accordingly.

Prosperity Coming

We do not know when we are going to be back to better times than we had in 1929; but we are going to get back, and we are going to enjoy greater prosperity in the future than we have ever enjoyed in the past. The future is going to demand more of us than the past has demanded, and it is going to give us more in return.

If we measure up to our job, if we give to this world everything that is in us, we shall get more in return in the future than we ever did in the past. I want you to think about that in terms of our business. School is not out. This world is not through. There are very definite signs of improvement in many parts of the world and in many lines

264

of business. We see it. It has been demonstrated; it has been proven to us tonight by the announcements of a great number of men who have told us about their January business, which represent some of the greatest January records that have ever been made. I cannot recall any similar records that measure up to the January records that were mentioned here tonight. That is all very encouraging.

More Manpower

The additional men who have been brought into executive work tonight by these promotions mean more manpower at home, and that manpower is going to develop more manpower out in the field. Our proposition is one of building and selling machines. We might call it a machine business, but it is not. It is a man business, a man-power business.

Notwithstanding all that you hear and read in the papers about the "Machine Age," I just cannot see it. I cannot subscribe to that at all. I look upon this age in which we are living as a Man Age, the greatest Man Age in which mankind has ever lived. The machines that we hear and talk about are simply small tools that men have devised to help them do a better job.

What have machines done for us in the past—our machines and all other machines? They have made men dear and their products cheap. That is the purpose of improved machinery. What else have they done? They have shortened the working day and removed the drudgery from all kinds of work in factories, offices and homes.

I have enjoyed this convention because I have learned more than I have ever learned in any other convention that I have ever attended. I need to learn more, because there is so much more to do. I know that the demands of this coming year are going to be greater than they were during the last year. This has been a wonderful convention. It has been the kind of convention about which we can say that, as the curtain rolls down tonight, the good that we have done here will roll on forever.

Give the best possible service you can to your customers.

CONFIDENCE IN THE NEW ADMINISTRATION

After putting every ounce of strength that he had into getting his sales force knowledgeable and excited in February 1933, Watson found a partner in what many at the time considered an unlikely place for a businessman: a Democrat—the president of the United States of America.

Tom Watson was looking for leadership in his government—a style of leadership that would match his own. He wanted someone to cooperate with, build excitement with and together move his company and his country down the path to recovery.

The greatest research engineer the world has ever known.

He was known for often quoting the definition of research as "simply discovering what you are going to do when you can't keep on doing what you are doing now." In this respect, he calls Franklin Delano Roosevelt (FDR) "the greatest research engineer that the world has ever known." I can only imagine the sense of empowerment, energy and enthusiasm he felt when FDR said those famous inaugural day words, "The only thing we have to fear is fear itself—nameless, unreasoning, unjustified terror which paralyzes needed efforts to convert retreat into advance."

Watson wanted to advance, not retreat. He knew there was no standing still. You were either moving forward or backward.

This one line captured the essence of what he had been saying since November 1929. He knew that during the greatest depression man had ever known, a new direction needed to be taken. To him the New Deal was research—an experiment in bringing back the economy. Right or wrong, he would not let the New Deal fail because of his lack of cooperation.

FDR was the pioneer in government. Tom Watson, the pioneer in business, needed his help to conquer the fear, anxiety and caution holding back his people, his company and his country.

To that end, a renewed energy, sense of drive and purpose entered into his speeches and writings. On March 9, five days after FDR's first inaugural speech, Tom Watson expressed his unequivocal belief in the new administration by publishing a supportive editorial in *Business Machines*.

He then, through the end of 1933, reiterated his focus on the men in the field: the salesmen—the ones on the front lines. He sent his executives, staff and any non-essential Home Office personnel to be assistants to his salesmen, "not a supervisor or a director." In a rare moment of superlative for him he added, "I mean just that!"

It is apparent that Watson was roaring down this path and committing his company along with him. He sensed hope on the horizon. He was sailing forward and not looking back.

When this plan has been worked out
we will find ourselves in a better world.

Courage! Confidence!

Business Machines *Editorial*

March 9, 1933

America, under new leadership and with a new national unity that has for the time wiped out party lines and partisanship, enters a new era based on courage and confidence.

These were the dominant notes of the Roosevelt inaugural address. They were the dominant notes of the president's proclamation the day following his inauguration, declaring a national bank holiday until Congress could be assembled for the first forward step toward the New Deal.

America was pioneered by a race of men who had courage and confidence. This heritage they have handed down and our generation needs only a reawakening of these qualities to go ahead to an even greater destiny than it has yet achieved. These are days when we must all pull together. We have a new administration at Washington, pledged to a constructive program. To get this program started there is a unity in Congress that puts country over party, common welfare over sectional advantage.

America is still the world's richest nation. Its credit is good. There is more money than ever before. These are the bulwarks behind which America is starting to rebuild on a firmer foundation than the past has known.

Our new administration is pledged to better methods of distribution, better control of credit, better use of the national revenues—to better understanding of the problems of government. What will this mean to IBM, to the men whose lives are woven into this great corporation, whose confidence and courage have been buttressed by the way in which IBM has weathered the storms of the past?

Now is the time for all of us to look forward with renewed courage and renewed confidence.

It will mean better times than they have ever had before. It will mean more demand for their products. It means that business in every line will go forward at an accelerated pace, which will create greater demand for all IBM products. And

269

this will not be confined to America, for as this country progresses and prospers the rest of the world will progress and prosper with us—so that our worldwide organization will benefit.

Now is the time for all of us to look forward with renewed courage, renewed confidence, to meet the demands of the future, which will be greater than any we have known in the past. With this courage and confidence we will reap greater rewards than we have ever known.

America was pioneered by a race of men who had courage and confidence.

Salesmanship, the Greatest Need of Our Country

Executives, Department Heads and Secretaries
Launching the Field Work Campaign

New York, N.Y.
April 17, 1933

In order to bring about the increase in business that we expect to realize during the period between now and July 1, we must get the field viewpoint. I want every man in this room to realize, more seriously than ever before, our duty to the men in the field. We must give them more help, and we must help them in the right way. We must realize, more and more, the importance of each one of us being a real assistant.

When I say, "Every executive must be an assistant to the man under him, rather than a supervisor or director," I mean just that!

When I say, "Every executive must be an assistant to the man under him," I mean just that!

What little success we have met with in this business up to the present has been due to the policy of assisting one another. Here at headquarters we know what is going on, what we are planning to do to help the men in the field—the work we are doing in developing new machines and the many other things we are planning and working out to help increase our business—but the man in the field does not always know what we are doing, and if conditions in his territory appear unfavorable he is apt to become discouraged.

I am not worried about the return of prosperity. I know our country will come back stronger than ever. I know the world will do likewise. I know we are going to do a greater business than ever before in the history of our company. I confidently expect that our organization will show an increase in business this year over last. We have a better opportunity to do it.

What is needed most in this country today, in our business and in every other business, is better salesmanship. We have to do a better job of selling.

So far as our own business is concerned, I believe that we can show a big increase in our business during the next two and a half months over that done in the last two and a half, and that is what we must do. That is why the executives are going out into the field—to help the salesmen do a better selling job. This plan of having the men from headquarters go into field territories to actually help men to make more sales embraces all of the sales executives, department heads, special representatives and every other man who can be spared from headquarters.

We want every man at the Home Office who has the ability to help a salesman to go out into a territory not as a supervisor or instructor—because our men in the field are well instructed—but as a salesman's assistant, and really help our field representatives to get more orders. We want to show a substantial increase in our business between now and the beginning of July, and we are depending on you to go out and work as hard as you can to help the men in the field accomplish this.

Focus on the Salesman

We owe it to our salesmen to do everything in our power to aid and assist them, because the success of our business depends upon the results they accomplish in selling our products.

Don't make calls, make sales. Calls of themselves do not pay commissions.

It is due to them that we are able to keep our people at work in our factories, in our laboratories and in our offices, and we must not forget that! You must put in all of your time on the sales end of the business and I know we are going to get results. One thing I want to say to the men in the field, "Don't merely make calls; make SALES!"

In other words, calls which do not result in sales or in developing a prospect for future business are non-productive and a waste of time. It is not the number of calls a man makes, it is the number of sales he makes that counts. Calls of themselves do not pay commissions. Sales are what put the commission check in the salesman's pocket. Let us remember that, and make every call count. It is necessary to get prospects, but prospects are of no use unless they become users.

What we have to do is to add new customers. There are plenty of opportunities. All we have to do is find the people who need our machines. We also must help our customers to get more service out of their equipment. We must see that they use our machines in every possible way that is to their advantage. We are equipped to render a service to all businesses that will be more valuable and more economical than any other service they can get.

We must not think merely in terms of today and tomorrow—we must think ahead! It has been our policy to focus our attention on each coming five years; and, in a broader way, we can look much further ahead.

Let us keep on planning ahead and be ready for every opportunity that comes along.

Don't merely make calls, make SALES!

America Is Coming Back

Business Machines *Editorial*

April 20, 1933

We believe that the new administration at Washington is paving the way for the resumption of the country's march toward progress and prosperity. We believe that business this year is going to be better than it was last year. We believe, further, that the future of American business will be far greater than the past. We believe that America is coming back! There are signs of this at every turn.

World trade relations are steadily assuming more favorable aspects; our banking structure has proved its stability by successfully coping with one of the most serious emergencies in history; the problems of agriculture are being gradually ironed out; recent upturns in the basic industries are being maintained; employment is increasing; retail sales are improving—confidence is returning.

We believe that the thing now most needed, in our business and every other business, is salesmanship. We believe that the return of better times, the re-employment of all our workers and the reestablishment of our higher standards of living depend upon the resumption of just plain, good old-fashioned selling. And to this end we have rededicated our efforts.

Every executive and every other member of our organization who is fitted to assist our salesmen is going out into the field. From now on they are going to work side by side with the men on the "firing line." They are going to throw the full force of their energies into the task of helping the salesman in every way possible to improve his record, increase his earnings and become a bigger asset to himself and his company.

We are throwing the full force of our energies into helping the salesman in every way possible.

They also are going to work with our customers and our prospective customers. They are going to add still more to the service that this company extends. They are going to help IBM users get more service from our equipment. They are going to show other businesses how the use of our machines will simplify and improve their operations.

And they are going to find out how, if possible, we can broaden even more the service we are now rendering.

We believe that through this plan of mutual helpfulness, of everyone assisting someone else, we can greatly hasten the return of prosperity, not only to this company and this country, but also to the world at large.

We believe that every company that will adopt an aggressive campaign of salesmanship accompanied by a more liberal buying policy will be contributing importantly to the return of American prosperity.

What this country needs most is salesmanship.

Endorsing a New Deal

President Watson's telegram to the
Chief Executive following his radio address

July 24, 1933

—

INTERNATIONAL BUSINESS MACHINES CORPORATION
ENDORSES YOUR PROGRAM AND HAS TAKEN STEPS TO
PUT IT INTO EFFECT. CONGRATULATIONS ON YOUR
SPLENDID ADDRESS.

—

In this inspiring address by our president, I find another evidence of the truth, which is being realized, more and more by every thinking man who has studied the "New Deal."

It affects everybody favorably.

The Recovery Plan, in support of which the Roosevelt Administration is enlisting every business in the country, is especially meritorious and workable because it is not limited to any single class or size of business. It includes them all, large and small.

**IBM endorses your program and
is putting it into effect.**

When the president said that the United States would pull out of the crisis if it wanted to, I was struck by another angle of the same thought, which is that those businesses that do not pull out will be the ones who do not want to.

Everyone with courage and ability is going to pull out and be better off than ever before. When this plan has been worked out to its logical conclusion, with the cooperation of all of us, we will find ourselves living in a better world than mankind ever before has known.

When this plan has been worked out
we will find ourselves in a better world.

The New Deal

Entire IBM Organization
National Recovery Act (NRA) Pledge Card Meeting

New York, N.Y.
September 7, 1933

I am very happy to be here this morning and hear from Mr. Nichol and Mr. Holt the plans for the NRA parade in New York next Wednesday. I hope that we shall all be in that parade, representing our company and furnishing inspiration for others. Mr. Nichol referred to the prompt and full support we have given NRA. There were two very definite and important reasons why I felt it was necessary for me to send a telegram to President Roosevelt just as soon as he finished his radio address in regard to the NRA.

First, I have been interested all through this depression in keeping our people employed—in our offices, at our factories and in the field—not only in this country, but also in various other parts of the world. We were reaching a point in the affairs of this nation where something different had to be done.

We could not continue to go on as we had been going.

Stockholders Protected

The second reason that I had in mind, one that is of very great importance to all of us, was the protection of our stockholders—the people who have money invested in The IBM. The National Recovery Act, to me, is one of the fairest and squarest propositions that have ever been presented, because it not only takes care of employees, but it also looks after stockholders. If we do not take care of the financial structure, there is not going to be any chance for any of us as employees for a very long period of time.

That is the thing that I like about the Act—and I want to bring that out this morning. In the NRA, they are looking after every element in the entire situation.

There are a few people who are skeptical as to what is going to happen under the NRA. I have had several discussions recently, but I have not found anyone who can suggest another remedy. I should like to leave this thought with all of you this morning: when you hear anyone criticizing, or displaying any signs of fear as to what is going to happen, ask him what he will suggest if this does not work. That is what I have done, and I have not received any suggestions.

All Leaders Must Share

George Bernard Shaw once said, "We must all share in the evils of the world or move to another planet." I say that the leaders of industry and finance in this country have to share in the evils of today, because we have all been here during the Depression, and, if we knew the answer, why did we not prevent it?

None of us knew the answer, and the reason was that none of us was thinking along new lines. We were all thinking along the lines of old business and political policies. We did not have enough vision to get outside of those boundaries. We just ploughed along and tried and retried all of the old methods and remedies, and none of them worked, because the situation was different.

This went on until March 4, when President Roosevelt took the oath of office. When he delivered his inaugural address, which was heard all over the world, people realized that they were listening to a man who had a new idea, and a man who was not afraid to stand before them and say, "This is the truth as I see it," regardless of precedent—because precedent had proved itself to be wrong.

That is what happened on March 4, and we all began to feel better. We got some new thoughts when our president said, "This is the beginning of a New Deal."

It was about time for a new deal or we were gone.

What New Deal Means

Now, what is this New Deal? What is it going to mean?

To me, the New Deal is going to mean better things for the majority of the people in this country. There is no question in my mind but that the New Deal will mean certain restrictions in regard to some methods that have been employed by certain people and corporations, whereby they, perhaps, will not be able to profit as much for the benefit of the few.

In our own business, I am looking forward to an era, under the New Deal, in which we shall be able to pay everybody more money—and I am looking for that in every industry. I believe it is coming. But we have to build up to it.

As I said in the beginning, we also have to protect the capital structure as well as to get people back to work, and that is what the NRA is doing in a very fair way. As individuals, all of us must do our part. I am thinking about the NRA and the New Deal as a research laboratory, with President Roosevelt, the greatest research engineer that the world has ever known, at the head of it.

In this connection, I want to repeat a definition that Dr. Charles Kettering, head of the General Motors Research Corporation, gives of research—a definition that is understandable. Research to many people is something mysterious. They think that to know anything about research you must be a great scientist, or you have to dream great dreams. Dr. Kettering says, "Research is simply to find out what you are going to do when you can't keep on doing what you are doing now."

Everyone Is a Researcher

The more you think of that the more you realize that everyone must consider himself in the light of a research engineer, because no one wants to say, "I am always going to keep on doing what I am doing now." That is what President Roosevelt had to consider. He realized, before he took the oath of office, that we could not keep on doing what we were then doing; so he had to figure out some way of finding out what should be done to change things.

He established, under the New Deal, a great research laboratory. He surrounded himself with people who are not saying, "Well, we tried that last year and it won't do," or, "There is no use in trying this, because it is new." He selected people who were willing to experiment, and we are experimenting.

The success of the New Deal must not be left entirely to the president and his associates. We have been making the mistake of talking about the things that have been done in Washington of which we did not approve, and we have talked about what we thought should be done, but what do we do? It is very easy to criticize what someone else is doing. The success of the New Deal depends on individual effort.

The success of IBM does not, never has and never will depend upon me or my immediate associates. The success of IBM depends upon the spirit, the thought and the effort of each individual in the business.

Individuals Make Success

It is because of the spirit, the thought and the effort of IBM people that we have been moving forward and having a little success. It is because the individual IBM employee has the spirit and is willing to make individual contributions, rather than wait for the head of the business or the chief executives to tell him what to do about his work.

I wish to extend to you my hearty thanks for the individual thought and individual action you put into this business. Let us decide that as individuals, and then let us do what we can to help make that kind of future—because that is all there is to it; under our form of government, we must share in the evils and we must help remedy them, or else we are not entitled to any consideration. I know that we have an organization here that can spread the right kind of information and the right kind of thought.

We have a big job to do in helping President Roosevelt and his associates make known to the people their individual duties. Too many people are wondering what is going to happen down in Washington. What is going to happen at home? What are we going to do in our own business? Everybody has to take his own business first and do everything he can to make his own business measure up to the standards set by NRA.

Let us look around us and see the great extra effort—the untiring effort—that is being put forth by the president and his cabinet, the NRA officers and all the other people working in the government.

The success of the New Deal depends on individual effort.
The success of IBM does not, never has and never will depend upon me or my immediate associates.

The National Research Association

Guest of Honor and Speaker
American Chamber of Commerce

London, England
October 24, 1933

I consider it a privilege to be invited to lunch with you today and to say a few words regarding present day conditions.

It is true that all countries are having political difficulties, but in spite of the fact, I find that business conditions are better in all the countries I have visited, and they are very much better at home. If the businessmen of the various countries can continue to show improvement in business, we can make it much easier for the political parties, which have such a tremendous responsibility, in working out their problems.

I feel very much encouraged with regard to both the present and the future. I remember well that when I spoke to you three or four years ago—as your chairman said, under very different conditions, particularly in the United States—I expressed my belief that the industrial progress of the world was still in its early stages and that it would continue to develop.

Confident of Future

In spite of all the troubles in the world today, I wish again to express my faith in the future of the world, in the future progress of industry in this country, in my own country and in all other countries, because, as we look around us, we find there is a great deal of unfinished business. The world is not yet finished.

We made a good start. We made a lot of mistakes; then we had a check. Now we are correcting, or trying to correct, and

It is our duty to put our shoulders to the wheel and help eliminate evils rather than complain.

will correct in my own country, many of the mistakes which have brought losses and sorrows, and, in some cases, suffering to our people. We can learn, it seems, only through trial and practice. We are experiencing conditions now that we never experienced before.

We are going to meet them, and we are going to solve the problems involved.

When I arrived in England last Saturday morning I looked at a paper, and the first thing my eye rested on was this headline: "America revolts against President Roosevelt." That did not alarm me at all—not the least bit. America has not revolted against President Roosevelt. America is not going to revolt against President Roosevelt because America appreciates President Roosevelt. America appreciates what he is trying to do and what we know he is going to do for us.

It would be unreasonable to expect President Roosevelt to solve all the difficulties of the United States in the few months he has been in office. Some of our problems, as you know, extend way beyond the borders of the United States. He has a big job and has made a good start. The people in the United States are back of him and are going to remain back of him. There will never be any revolution in the United States.

We express ourselves every four years at the polls. If we are not satisfied with what is going on we go to the polls and vote for something different. That is the only kind of revolution that you are ever going to hear of in the United States regardless of scare headlines in papers in foreign countries and sometimes in our own.

I am glad to have an opportunity to speak about that headline, because to people who do not understand what is happening in the United States that is rather a startling thing to see in the paper.

I am looking forward to an era in which we shall be able to pay everybody more money.

George Bernard Shaw once said, "We must all share in the evils of the world or move to another planet." It is very easy to sit around and blame the leaders of the different countries and the leaders of our industrial organizations and financial institutions for the various things that have happened. If we stop and think logically about the matter we shall realize that we are all a part of all of the evils that exist in this world today, and that it is our duty, as individuals, to put our shoulders to the wheel and help eliminate them rather than sit back and complain about the people who are doing their best to solve the problems of the world. That applies, in my judgment, to every country.

Need Individual Thinking

We acquired the habit of mass thinking, due to the great number of publications and to the news that comes to us over the radio. We started on mass production in our factories and then instituted mass thinking. We were all thinking just about the same things all the time.

That is what, in my country at least, threw us off balance. What our country needs— and, in my judgment, what the world needs—is to get back to individual thinking and individual action. Each country must get down to thinking about its individual problems and about means for solving them, always keeping in mind the need to cooperate with other countries. We must give more good sound advice to ourselves and less to the other fellow.

We must give more good sound advice to ourselves and less to the other fellow.

In the United States, the Depression finally reached a point where it seemed that none of us knew what to do about it. In fact, none of us did know what to do because if we had known we should have done it and conditions would have been better. I am an optimist when you give me something real to base my optimism on; I like to be optimistic, but I do not like to be optimistic without a reason.

On March 4, when President Roosevelt was inaugurated and by radio gave us some of his ideas and told us what he thought would be good for us, we realized that there was a man who was not afraid to step out in front and say, "This is the truth, as I see it, regardless of precedent." Precedent had failed us. From that day the psychology of the people changed, conditions began to improve and have continued to improve ever since.

There has been some dropping back and always will be, but we have made real progress. We have 4 million more people employed than we had six months ago. That is our problem, to get the unemployed back to work and earning money. The NRA was brought into being to that end. Sometimes I hear in this country, "I do not think your NRA will work." I have had people say that to me at home.

Definition of "Research"

What is the NRA? The National Recovery Administration. President Roosevelt decided that something different must be done and the NRA was the outcome. I often refer to it as the "National Research Association." Research is finding out what you are going to do when you cannot keep on doing what you are doing now. That is the only real definition of research that I have ever heard. As we think it over, we decide that each one of us must consider himself a research engineer because no one will admit that he is always going to do what he is doing now.

Labor Conditions

President Roosevelt realized that we could not continue to do what we were doing at that time. The NRA was therefore brought into being, and it has accomplished a great deal. We found—particularly in the large cities, and in some of the smaller ones in the South, in the cotton mill districts—that people were being underpaid.

We found in New York City, in some of the sweatshops, that young women were earning less than $3 a week. Such wages not only worked a hardship on those employees, but also enabled unscrupulous employers to undersell employers who were paying a living wage and dragged the whole price level down to a point where nobody could make any money. One of the principal things achieved by the NRA was a correction of that condition.

Another abuse that all of us always resented was the employment of child labor. The NRA has corrected that evil. So when you hear people say that the NRA is not going to work, do not believe them. It is working.

I am not going to tell you that the NRA in everything that it has done has been perfect, has satisfied everybody. It has not. If we find that a code is working a hardship, it is up to us to correct it, to present, argue and prove our case. Changes will then be made. In our own particular industry we asked for a change, after we had signed the blanket code; we gave our reasons, and it was granted to us without any argument. We are very grateful to the NRA and to President Roosevelt for giving us the opportunity to correct a lot of things in our industry that were handicapping us. So it goes all down through the various industries of the United States.

Must Be Better than Average

We are in times that require real effort, that require extra effort. The average will not do today. We have to develop into better than the average in order to bring ourselves up to where we want to be. I know it is going to be done, not only in America, but also in every country. As we look back over several years we find that some countries were very prosperous and others were experiencing great difficulties.

Then it came to a point where every country had just about the same troubles and problems. It was then we all got busy and began to think individually about them; that is why we are moving forward.

I have found business in France improved; I have found business in Germany very much improved; and everybody I talked with in both those countries was very hopeful in regard to the future. It is not necessary for me to tell you that I find business very greatly improved in England. Business is very, very much better in the United States.

Some people say that security prices have no bearing on business; but they do have a great bearing. The average price of our bonds on the New York Stock Exchange since last spring has gone up, I believe, thirteen and one-half percent. The average increase in stock prices, which, in some cases, had gone down to almost zero, has been over sixty percent. Think for a moment what that means to our country.

That does not just mean increasing the value of the individual's assets: it also means saving a lot of banks who were carrying those securities as collateral; it got down to a point where some of them could not be considered as collateral any longer.

The efforts of President Roosevelt and his organizations, the NRA and other movements that he is backing, have brought about an improved condition in the United States that has helped our whole situation; for underlying this whole proposition is the need to take good care of our financial structure if we want to go very far.

Our financial structure has very greatly improved and is going to continue to improve because of certain measures that have been adopted. While a few of them are not perfect, according to some of us, they are being improved and worked out on a basis which makes us believe that we are heading in the right direction.

Employer-Employee Relationship

Another thing I should like to say is that the relation between the employer and the employee is, on the whole, very satisfactory. Even though you may read headlines about strikes—and we have had a few—it is nothing serious. Our laboring people are interested—we are all interested in trying to solve this problem, and I am sure we are going to solve it in a way that will be satisfactory to our country, and, we believe, in a way that will help other countries.

In closing, I should like to say that we ought to believe in the philosophy of Marcus Aurelius that, "Men are created one for another; either then teach them better or bear with."

Each one of us must consider himself
a research engineer.

THE IBM ARRIVES

In January 1933, Tom Watson gazed out onto The IBM's horizon and saw his potential failure to meet his core obligation, his greatest responsibility to his stockholders. For him, there was no worse failure. This responsibility was personal.

He saw the IBM stockholders as individuals—a woman with a dependent child who had made a personal decision to invest her few precious Depression-era dollars in his company, in his leadership and in him. Utility stocks became known during the Depression as widow-and-orphan stocks. These were purchased for their steady dividend checks. The IBM stock had become such a stock. He was not going to lose this stockholder's trust and confidence.

NEVER BE
SATISFIED TO
BE AMONG
THE AVERAGE

No man deserves any special credit for being an average man.

At the 1930 Hundred Percent Club, he made this responsibility clear to his sales force, saying, "Gentlemen the fact is that more women than men are stockholders in our business. . . . Most of our stockholders are small stockholders—so that is our great responsibility."

Even as he spoke positively that January at the 1932 Hundred Percent Club, the tension could be felt in his presentations captured in a previous chapter *The Darkest Hour Before the Dawn.*

Some chief executive officers would have looked at the situation and not been concerned. They could have easily explained away a bad year in an annual report; after all, this was the Great Depression. An average CEO would have done just that. The Great Depression affected every person, every business and every country in the world. If ever there was a common, average explanation for not paying dividends, this was the time and excuse.

Such an average explanation would have been acceptable to many an average Chief Executive Officer.

Tom Watson, though, held his team and himself to a different standard. As he explained to his men in 1930 at the outset of the Depression, "No man deserves any special credit for being an average man. It is the men who are striving to be above the average who are the men who build business—they are the men who build nations." This belief applied to every person, including himself as the person holding the title of the CEO, because a policy was "a policy for the entire organization; not for just one man." The average, in his eyes, was "the average" because the "above average" carried the rest. He was determined to be one of the great CEOs who would carry the rest.

In these last two articles, in the closing days of 1933—a few days before Christmas—he learns that a dividend will be paid. He closes the year with two positive and uplifting messages to The IBM Caretakers.

In "We Are Progressing," he finally sees the corner on the Great Depression. It is a corner he has been actively seeking and forecasting would come since November of 1929. He joins FDR's positive spirit, telling his team, "In the twelve months just closing, we have seen fear conquered by confidence. We have seen unemployment greatly lessened. We have seen industry rise from virtual prostration and start forward again."

In "Keep Faith in the Future," he acknowledges that he has made decisions that not everyone agrees with but offers a unique view on the kind of cooperation he looked for as CEO of The IBM. He tells his team that their cooperation is "what has built this business of ours." Cooperation built his business—always "ours" in his eyes.

Cooperation is what has built this business of ours.

Watson kept his finger constantly on the economic pulse of the United States. He felt the change in the business environment writing, "The upswing in business that started last March continues with increasing force." He was a scholar, involved and intimate with this economy that was affecting so many.

Although the climb out of the Depression would take years, economists today set the trough, or the beginning of the end of the

Great Depression, in March 1933. Watson called the bottom in December of that same year without all of today's financial statistics, economic wisdom and computers.

In these articles, not once does Watson refer to our company as merely "IBM." The Great Depression was behind them. He wanted his team to know that they had proven themselves in the worst of economic storms—they had proven themselves capable.

Character, idealism and hope had been preserved through the worst economic storm in the history of mankind.

He was now at the helm of **The IBM.**

You can cooperate with a man without believing in everything he says and does.

We Are Progressing!

The IBM Organization in Business Machines

December 21, 1933

Cooperation will ensure not only our own prosperity, but the welfare of all our fellow citizens.

The approach of the New Year 1934 is an occasion for true rejoicing. In the twelve months just closing we have seen fear conquered by confidence. We have seen unemployment greatly lessened. We have seen industry rise from virtual prostration and start forward again. The upswing in business that started last March continues with increasing force. In 1933, we have experienced a rebirth of courage and we can face the immediate future with a confidence that is built on solid foundations. We have seen industry line up under the National Recovery Act (NRA) codes that have insured fair competition and sounded the death knell of cutthroat price-cutting.

In less than a year, we have seen 4 million workers return to permanent employment, with 4 million more engaged in public works in all parts of the United States. We have seen, in the third quarter of this year, a report of $162 million in net profits by 205 corporations that in the corresponding quarter of 1932 reported net losses of $25 million. We have seen the inauguration of President Roosevelt with the promise of a New Deal, and we have seen the New Deal in only a few brief months bring about all the blessings enumerated above, and many, many others.

Every member of The IBM organization will recognize that the strides we have taken in the past nine months, great as they are, are really small by comparison with the progress we are going to make in 1934 and the years to follow. Each one of us, I am sure, will rededicate himself on this coming New Year's Day to the task of perpetuating our new prosperity by giving to the utmost of his individual thought and effort and determination. Such cooperation will insure not only our own prosperity, but also the welfare of all our fellow citizens.

The New Year is an occasion for true rejoicing.

Keep Faith in the Future

A Gathering of Employees
270 Broadway

New York, N.Y.
December 22, 1933

I feel that we of The IBM have a great deal to be thankful for, and that I have more to be thankful for than anybody else in the business, because at the beginning of this year things did not look as bright as they might have. I had to give thought to meeting the dividends for The IBM stockholders. We all saw, on every hand, dividends being reduced and in many cases being eliminated entirely.

It has only been through the cooperation, extra effort and genuine ability of The IBM organization, both at home and in all of the seventy-nine countries of the world where we do business, that we have been able to continue to pay our 6,000 stockholders their regular dividends this year. That is why I should be more thankful than anybody else in the business. Naturally, the stockholders look to me for the proper return on the money they have entrusted to us.

I cannot say enough in praise of the fine work that has been done by the organization in the home office. There has been a great deal of extra work, but I have never heard of anyone complaining. I have never seen anyone in the organization, anywhere, who looked downhearted or discouraged at any time, and that applies to the sales organization, those at the factory and everyone else.

I have more to be thankful for than anybody else in the business.

The IBM, due to the ability of our organization to stand up and work hard when the going was very bad, happened to be more fortunate than any other concern. However, we must give the most credit where it is really due and that is to our engineering staff.

It is not only what our engineers did for us during the last two or three years but what they started doing twenty years ago that saved the day for us. The thought and effort they put into their work, day and night, have enabled us to give people better machines and to do a better job. If these men had not worked so faithfully, so intelligently throughout a period of many years, we would have a different story to tell.

As for the next year you have received the December 21 issue of *Business Machines*. The figures given in the editorial under my name on the back page of that issue should give added courage to everybody in this organization. When we look over the published earnings reports for the third quarter of this year and see 205 companies with a net profit of $162 million, as compared with a net loss of $25 million for the corresponding period of last year, we have concrete evidence that business is better.

Benefits under NRA (National Recovery Act)

When we know that under the NRA there have been 4 million people taken from the ranks of the unemployed and put in permanent positions, and 4 million more men put to work on public improvements—a total of 8 million out of the 15 million unemployed put into gainful employment—we know that we are progressing.

I am thinking of the great many other improvements that President Roosevelt and his associates have effected since March 4. Anybody who has owned corporation shares will find that stocks have increased about 60 percent and bonds 13½ percent in value since last year. That means that not only were the holders of these securities saved from disaster but that the banks that were holding such securities as collateral were saved from failure.

Need for Cooperation

Cooperate in the things you believe in, others will cooperate in the things they believe in.

I bring up this subject because it means so much to the man who is carrying great responsibility to have the wholehearted cooperation of everybody. You know, you can cooperate with a man without believing in everything he says and does. If you do not agree with everything he does, cooperate with him in the things you do believe in. Others will cooperate with him in the things they believe in. That is what has built this business of ours.

I know very well that all of you have not always all been in agreement with all my policies and ideas. I do not expect you to be. You have ideas of your own. I have never undertaken any job in The IBM without having the support of a majority of my associates.

That is what I want to bring to your attention today, what I believe to be the kind of cooperation the president of the United States and his cabinet are entitled to from the hands and minds of all of us who are depending upon them to bring us out of the unhappy economic state into which we got ourselves.

Let us have constructive suggestions and remember that everything we do that helps the cause of our government reflects right back to our company and into our own pockets. That is the only way success can be assured.

Upon entering the New Year, let us look forward with hope and conviction. Let us be thankful for everything we have received in our country and for the great improvement that has been made since last March.

Let us push on!

Let us be progressive!

Everything we do that helps the cause of our government reflects right back to our company and into our own pockets.

We must always set the right kind of

example all the way along the line

as to character and good manners.

Then you can teach the men anything,

because they are with you,

they will listen to you.

They are not trying to show off or be smart.

They get right down to business.

"Men of Character and Courtesy"

Thomas J. Watson Sr.

January 23–25, 1933

AN IBM CARETAKER'S CONCLUSION

The Captain and Crew

The captain knew immediately that this was a storm the likes of which he and his crew had never faced before.

When the storm came they did not know to set their sails.

He was a strict disciplinarian who believed in education, in drills and in practice. What set him apart from all other captains was his expectation to find men of good character. Some ridiculed him for searching for such a nature in a sailor; some called him archaic and behind the times—but not his men. And after this storm, none would call him archaic. They would imitate him. It would be his and his sailors' combined character that would carry them through. He knew character couldn't calm the storm raging outside but it could control a man's raging fears inside.

He expected each crew member to have trust and confidence in those around them: the man below deck, sweating and heaving coal in the boiler room had to trust the man freezing above deck, being pounded with wave upon crushing wave. Most of all he focused on the trust and confidence between crew and captain. He constantly worked on solidifying that mutual trust. He knew that any seam or crack between them could, under the pressure of a storm, result in leakage that would make their jobs harder or result in the loss of life.

The captain strained to look out from the wheelhouse. He saw ships that were larger, stronger and newer than his, slowing and listing as they took on water. He saw the keels of great ships rise high above the water against the dark clouds—like gigantic breaching whales— but these were the blackened hulls of once mighty ships exhaling one last mighty gasp before sliding beneath the ocean's waves. He imagined many such ships descending slowly in perfect formation into the cold, dark graveyard beneath his feet.

These ships had been surprised by the storm's ferocity. It had come out of nowhere—many were caught unprepared. The weather had been calm and serene for so long that some captains and some crews thought there would never be another storm. Some thought there would always be blue skies. They had lost their memory of how bad it could get. They had lost their work ethic—even their common sense.

He felt deep anguish over the suffering that was playing out in front of him and his crew. He turned back to face the storm, and a moment of doubt flashed across his face as the storm's greatness, its depth and breadth of power, reflected in his eyes. He felt the weight of the responsibility he was carrying. He had set the course. He must now follow it to its end. There was no turning back. There was no way to outrun the destruction. He must depend on his crew. He had collected the best men he could find, and he knew that together they could survive this storm.

He looked out with determination and thought to himself, "Not my ship, not my crew, not my passengers." He was a man of emotion, with a quick temper; but when times were the most critical and the most desperate it was his calm, determined demeanor that inspired confidence in those around him.

As he observed the storm, he felt the rhythm of its movements and began to sense its nature. He felt his determination grow. Now, so

Each crew member understood and respected each other.

his crew could hear his determination, he said aloud, "Not my ship... not my passengers." His men, once fixated on the drama unfolding around them, awoke. They realized they were fighting for their lives. The captain they respected and trusted was at the helm.

He had just called them to their stations.

This captain and crew had not been caught unaware. They had been here before, and because of it they survived the storm's initial fury. He thought back, and remembered with shame his performance during that initial test of his captaincy. No other captain at the time would have been ashamed, having performed as any ordinary captain would have; but he still felt it. He had failed to meet his own high expectations—he had lost his trust and confidence in his crew's knowledge, understanding and abilities. He was always proud of his crew but under pressure he had almost failed them.

Fortunately, it had been a small squall—a preparatory test for what was before them now. Lives had not been at risk but the experience had exposed a weakness in him. He was determined to grow past the shame. He grew to understand himself and his crew and what they needed.

After the squall, he focused on education—every man would know his position inside and out. He expanded their knowledge so they would learn, understand and respect every other man's position and responsibility in keeping this ship of theirs afloat. He led by example; he never stopped studying.

He challenged the old and the new on his crew. He demanded that his most talented step up to lead the ship with him. Sometimes that was the oldest and saltiest of his crew; sometimes it was the new man with new ideas, the latest education and an enthusiasm only youth can provide. He worked constantly to meld old and new; he made them communicate and respect each other. He moved about the ship so frequently that his presence was greeted not with fear of inspection but with a reassuring comfort. The crew, growing to know his heart, believed he had their best interest in every decision. He modeled a standard of excellence, a striving for perfection, but always as a team. He replaced the weakness, the seam between him and crew, with a solid weld.

They were ready when the storm came.

A Sailing Analogy

Watson used a sailing analogy when the darkest hours of the Depression were before him and his men. He wanted to inspire the best in The IBM. The IBM was always alive with such stories. There were stories about Watson's wild ducks—men and women who refused to be tamed. There were stories about sales opportunities won and lost—and the learning from the mistake. There were stories about IBM Caretaker inspiration and courage. These stories reinforced The IBM culture; they relayed the culture to the new and reminded the old of what they might have forgotten or were taking for granted.

Would a captain ever leave the helm in the midst of one of the longest and worst storms in history? He would if he had personally trained the men at the helm. He would if he had personally studied their character, their personalities, their teamwork and had trust and confidence in their individual leadership. He would if he knew the storm was to be eternal.

This was not going to be a brief gale. It was going to wear away at this crew for years. Each of them had to learn to live with the constant pressure. The captain would place his life in their hands as theirs were in his. He would journey below deck to check the ship's structural integrity and boost his men's morale—and his own. Tom Watson knew the businesses failing around him. He knew intimately the industries he was dependent on for growth. Some had great captains and others had great crews. To survive it took a great team—crew and captain achieving together a greatness beyond their individual capabilities.

He will train himself to do a better job on everything new that he undertakes.

He and his son built a culture of trust and confidence. Instead of a "hierarchy of authority" with every person looking up for approval, they built a "web of trust." This allowed decentralized decision making. Each person was expected to think and make decisions based on their knowledge, their team's combined wisdom and their unique circumstances—without glancing up for approval. They believed The IBM was having a "little success" because the individual IBM employee had the desire and drive to make individual contributions, "rather than wait for the head of the business or the chief executives to tell him what to do."

Certainly the person in the engine room had to trust the captain to steer a path that kept the ship afloat but sheltered the critical engines from burning up under constant stress. In the years of the Depression, Watson knew the engines of prosperity were his salesmen. When he asked for maximum power, he knew these powerful engines of The IBM would respond.

Mistakes would not be met with recriminations, finger pointing or backbiting; just a renewed sense of determination to power through it. They all made mistakes.

That included him.

The IBM was a powerful ship. It was set on a course of greatness by a great leader; but the crew powered it forward. They didn't just survive the Great Depression; they emerged from it under full steam. The Depression, rather than exhausting The IBM, fortified and emboldened it. Watson, understanding his men's character, his men's desire to belong to something greater, gambled that he could build a team of interlocking trust and confidence—a culture of respect.

He succeeded.

IBM Basic Beliefs

The IBM has stood for almost a century on Watson's principles. He understood change better than any leader of his or our time. He believed that "Life is never static. The only thing we can be sure of is perpetual change. It is the part of business leaders to determine the needs of the future."

The principles of this business are fixed. They are lasting principles.

He believed, though, that he had founded The IBM on "fixed principles of business—lasting principles." His son, Thomas J. Watson Jr., would later codify and summarize these lasting principles in seven maxims that became the IBM Basic Beliefs:

- Respect for the Individual

- Service to the Customer

- Excellence Must Be a Way of Life

- Managers Must Lead Effectively

- Obligations to Stockholders

- Fair Deal for the Supplier

- IBM Should be a Good Corporate Citizen

These beliefs were our heritage.

Thos. J. Watson Sr. believed that, "You have to put your heart in the business and the business in your heart." [3] No one put more heart into The IBM than Thos. J. Watson Sr. He believed that the possession of a great heritage placed the owner under the obligation to preserve and increase that heritage. He believed we must be forever vigilant; asking of ourselves, "Are we preserving and increasing it?"

You will bring into this business new thoughts, new ideas and new principles that have never been heard of before.

The success of The IBM always depended upon the thought, effort and spirit of every individual in the business. Mr. Watson constructed a corporation founded on trust and confidence between employer and employee. As both a business pioneer and researcher, he mastered this relationship.

He understood The IBM Caretaker.

Great salesmen speak to the spirit in us.

Thomas J. Watson Sr. was the World's Greatest Salesman.

You are not coming into an organization

that has been built.

We are just building it.

You are not coming into a business

that has succeeded.

We are merely succeeding a little

more each year.

"Advice to Young Men Entering Business"

Thomas J. Watson Sr.

October 29, 1930

We all know that the welfare of the enterprises that we are directing is closely bound up with the welfare of our workers, but in attempting to counsel or advise those whom we employ, we must not adopt a paternal attitude.

In these times, when independent thought and action should be the order of the day, employees resent an attitude of paternalism.

It is a well-known fact, however, that an employee's efficiency suffers if his mind is ill at ease, and that worry over financial troubles is one of the most powerful sources for the destruction of mental peace.

"New York Savings Bank's Luncheon"

Thomas J. Watson Sr.

February 16, 1933

WHAT'S NEXT FOR THE IBM: A PREVIEW

IBM has changed. It is no longer the IBM many of us joined in the '80s. As I have shared this first book with my peers many have commented, "I wish this was today's IBM." Some have asked quite bluntly, "What IBM did you work for?"

Tom Watson Sr., an advocate of change, would have never wanted his company to stand still. As you have read, he believed: "Life is never static. The only thing we can be sure of is perpetual change." Yet he also believed that "The principles of this business are fixed. They are lasting principles." His son, Thomas J. Watson Jr., merged these concepts together in 1963, writing, "If an organization is to meet the challenges of a changing world, it must be prepared to change everything about itself except those [basic] beliefs as it moves through corporate life." IBMers have always understood the necessity for change, adaptation and evolution; but IBMers have always held, almost religiously, onto our Basic Beliefs. Anticipate perpetual change, yet hold fast to the lasting principles—these were concepts consistent with our heritage and our culture.

Today, a simple discussion about IBM's new path can quickly become tense. It can turn belligerent if it touches on the topic of IBM's Basic Beliefs—beliefs that had stood for the better part of a century before being discarded. People take sides along the boundary lines of age, service dates or positions held within the company. Lou Gerstner, from his position as Chief Executive Officer, expressed his perspective in *Who Says Elephants Can't Dance?*

These discussions have needed, first, a historical viewpoint provided by this book; then a new light, from an IBM Caretaker's perspective can illuminate IBM's current path. With that in mind, I have provided a preview of my next book, *A View from Beneath the Dancing Elephant*.

Pete

A Resilient Forest

There is no more majestic tree in all of North America than the coast redwood. It may reach heights in excess of 367 feet, soaring fifteen stories above the main dome of the Taj Mahal or seven stories over the torch of the Statue of Liberty. At maturity, it can scale to one-third the height of the Eiffel Tower or two-thirds the height of the Washington Monument. Unlike the Washington Monument, which has a foundation that burrows almost 37 feet deep, the coast redwood's root system is wholly contained within the first 4 to 6 feet of the soil's surface—barely the height of an average man. The mass of this support structure is just one-tenth of the trunk and limbs. It is the most top-heavy of giants. For all the redwoods' majesty, nature would quickly humble a solitary tree.

For redwoods, resiliency is in community. Theirs is a design of unity not individuality, and width not depth. Each tree scatters roots in all directions. They intertwine. They graft. They strengthen and stabilize each other. Together they withstand great winds, reduce the effects of erosion and increase the odds of survival. As a forest they withstand nature's relentless, repetitive assaults.

As each new season brings great storms, devastating winds sweep in from the ocean to pummel the land. Lesser trees collapse into mounds of debris, but the redwoods will not be dislodged. Summer brings relentless drying heat. The rubble and underbrush become dry tinder awaiting a spark. Lightning strikes, but the resulting fire laps harmlessly against the redwoods' foot-thick bark. Where it flares the hottest and longest, the bark transforms into a charred, blackened, almost impenetrable shield. The fire gains no foothold as the redwoods contain only trace amounts of flammable resins but immense quantities of stored water—the equivalent of a backyard pool. Nature, though, is undeterred. The blaze consumes the surrounding vegetation, breaking the bond between soil and hillside; torrential rains flush the valleys of the debris. Landslides of ever-rising soil engulf and suffocate the forest. Most trees die, but not the redwoods. In response to each season's surge of choking earth and rubble, the redwoods send out new, ever higher, interlocking horizontal roots. Finally, in the midst of all this devastation, a weaker tree's greatest enemy finds opportunity. Insects burrow deep into any open wound. They reproduce and devastate whole sections of forest.

They transform once green hillsides into nothing more than sparse, spindly, gray spectacles. But again, the uniqueness of the redwood—a tree steeped in tannin and benefiting from a unique genetic complexity of six chromosomes rather than two—prevents these predators from taking grip.[4] To the redwoods, insects are nothing more than incidental nuisances.

These desperate times give advantage to the redwood forest as they proliferate quickly through cloning. New sprouts arise from seemingly devastated stumps; fallen giants, along their formidable length, push upward-facing branches skyward; heavily damaged trees, previously holding saplings in check, now unleash them from the underlying root system. These cloned saplings will stand fifteen times taller in their first five years than their seeded competition.

The true resiliency of the redwood forest lies not in how it thrives during temperate times but how in the most desperate of times, it becomes stronger. Individual trees have survived for more than two millennia. Today's mightiest redwoods sprang up from the ground as the Great Wall extended across China. They ascended above the hilltops with the construction of the Roman Coliseum. They ruled the forest before the completion of the minarets of the Blue Mosque. They were present when we set foot on the moon and will still be present when man strides across another planet. We wonder at the majesty of the lone tree, but we should stand in awe of the resiliency, longevity and strength provided by its forest.

The Redwood Forest of Corporate America

The IBM was the redwood forest of corporate America. The Watsons, as true leaders, ensured success beyond themselves. They buried deep in the heart of their company a belief system that transcended their limited time in power.

They studied mankind. They understood mankind. They understood the dreams, hopes, aspirations and the very real desire of an individual to be part of something greater—to be part of a dynamic team. Where others would foresee employees moving fluidly, dynamically and uncaringly between corporations, the Watsons' vision for their business was always different. They stood together for six decades driving their corporation to be more. It was always intended to be our corporation.

IBM's corporate architecture was designed to a singularly Watson blueprint. It has ensured a century of resiliency through a loyal, dedicated and enthusiastic team. They desired their corporation to evolve, but only within the context of a preeminant, interlocking belief system that would reach across decades—and across leaders. This unifying culture was framed in the Recession of 1921, stressed during the Great Depression and proven through thirteen ensuing recessions.

Thos. J. Watson Sr. lived his belief system. He communicated it through maxims, modeled it for his executives and established it as the foundation for the future. He demanded adherence from his entire management team and from anyone who wanted to carry the title of "IBMer."

Thomas J. Watson Jr. captured his father's maxims, writing them down, reinforcing them, modernizing and proselytizing them. He carried them into every cubicle, manufacturing shop and business relationship. He used these beliefs to defeat the competition.

Summarizing the power of this belief system quite succinctly Tom Watson Jr. said:

> Consider any great organization—one that has lasted over the years—and I think you will find that it owes its resiliency not to its form of organization or administrative skills, but to the power of what we call beliefs and the appeal these beliefs have for its people. This, then, is my thesis: I firmly believe that any organization, in order to survive and achieve success, must have a sound set of beliefs on which it premises all its policies and actions.

> Next, I believe that the most important single factor in corporate success is faithful adherence to those beliefs. And finally, I believe that if an organization is to meet the challenges of a changing world, it must be prepared to change everything about itself except those beliefs as it moves through corporate life.[5]

Chief Executive Officers, immediately following the Watsons, relied on this belief system during difficult times. In 1971, in the midst of one of the thirteen U.S. recessions after the Great Depression, T.

Vincent Learson, IBM Chief Executive Officer at the time, wrote to his management team:

> You know as well as I that these are difficult times for IBM. The fact that this is a temporary situation—although when it will end we do not know—hardly eases the apprehension of employees who see things happening that they have not experienced before. They are being asked to work harder at a time when budgets are tight and promotion opportunities are fewer. Many are being inconvenienced by being asked to take different jobs or relocate.
>
> All of these things are necessary. How well they are accomplished depends almost totally on you. These times demand extraordinary efforts and ingenuity, extraordinary patience and sensitivity in working with people.
>
> The success of IBM always has been and will be based on its people. They have amply demonstrated their willingness to devote all their talents and skills to their company. You and I owe them skilled, understanding leadership for this is a proud, hard-hitting team—the best in the world—and we must keep it that way.[6]

The IBM concealed its resiliency in the benefits extracted from this unwavering belief system. Kevin Maney disclosed the power of this belief system in *The Maverick and his Machine*, writing, "The core of IBM—its ultimate economic engine—was not information machines; rather, it was its culture."

This culture was established on a rock-solid foundation that was immovable, unbendable and unbreakable. Just as the DNA of the mighty redwoods has preserved their resiliency between generations; the IBM Basic Beliefs defined and connected us as The IBM.

I personally experienced The IBM expecting individual growth during adverse, economically difficult times. In the recession of the '80s, administrators were fast becoming obsolete. It was time to adapt or leave, as personal computers replaced word processing centers, and automated order entry systems replaced old jobs, and with them my management position. We were encouraged to move into customer support roles. These roles provided higher value to The IBM's customers. The transition was arduous with high expectations. It was technically and personally difficult. I spent months away from my wife and children, but my IBM family was always there to provide support and encouragement; my training was adapted around the birth of a son.

Over my thirty-year career, I would over and over again be challenged to send out new lateral roots. It was always up to me to accept the challenge.

A Forest in Decline

In the late '90s, the Watsons' original spirit, vision and passion faded. I would only find it in isolated teams led by individually strong leaders. Gradually, outside of these insulated teams, "The IBM" became "IBM." Individuals were removed from the forest and are now isolated in home offices. For survival, they put down the deepest of roots. Many work to pad their resumes; they have become mobile, transient employees on their way to somewhere else. International teams have become dysfunctional, as there are endless ways to communicate but fewer ways to reach understanding, agreement and consensus.

The very foundation of The IBM forest is under attack. The company is moving from a living, breathing organism composed of IBMers to a company of IBM employees. We, the caretakers of The IBM, continue to feel the impact of individual trees falling all around us. Our incredible, intertwining roots are being ripped from the soil; the once solid earth uprooted and scattered skyward.

Much of this is being done in the name of remaining competitive, of being more nimble and adapting to changing market conditions. Some executives interpret being faster, quicker or implementing change as abandoning old tenets—discarding what seem, to them, archaic beliefs.

But the Watsons, forever the champions of change, were willing to change everything **except** their most fundamental and basic principles. I believe, from everything recorded about Thos. J. Watson Sr. and his son, they would be most reflective on the new IBM. They would not admire just black ink on the white pages of a balance sheet, pluses on profit statements or the sheer size of their corporation. These would be important—they set expectations beyond those of any corporation in existence today—but only attainable, maintainable and optimized as long as their belief system knitted the corporation together.

Through the eyes of executive and employee alike, The IBM was once unequaled amongst the world's corporations; but no longer. No axiom summarizes the last two decades better than, "This is not your father's IBM." This new path brought with it a new culture and attitude.

Mr. Lou Gerstner, to his credit as the Chief Executive Officer of the '90s, managed the financial recovery that brought IBM back from the edge of disaster; Sam Palmisano, as the current Chief Executive Officer, has shown great skill in continuing this financial execution into the twenty-first century. But as Mr. Gerstner acknowledges in his book, *Who Says Elephants Can't Dance?*, The IBM, or any great corporation, is more than just a financial entity. He foresaw, perhaps with apprehension, a herculean effort to change IBM's culture:

> Frankly, if I could have chosen not to tackle the IBM culture head-on, I probably wouldn't have. For one thing, my bias coming in was toward strategy, analysis, and measurement. I'd already been successful with those, and like anyone, I was inclined to stick with what had worked for me earlier in my career. Once I found a handful of smart people, I knew we could take a fresh look at the business and make good strategic calls or invest in new businesses or get the cost structure in shape.
>
> In comparison, changing the attitude and behavior of hundreds of thousands of people is very, very hard to accomplish. Business schools don't teach you how to do it. [7]

Louis V. Gerstner Jr. could have considered himself in what Tom Watson Sr. called in 1932 "a practical business school." The company that defined the term "corporate culture" surrounded Mr. Gerstner. The IBM had an eighty-year history with a strong, defining belief system that inspired a positive employee attitude and expected disciplined behavior.

If Lou Gerstner had dug deeper, studied further and persevered longer the answers were there. Every CEO before him, including the Watsons, understood the need for constant course corrections.

The IBM culture had drifted but it was not broken.

Mr. Gerstner's book and similar articles that examine IBM all culminate in 1999; it is as if with IBM's financial recovery, the story ended. It did not. The story had just begun for most IBM employees. History needs more perspectives before it closes the book on IBM's centennial celebration. History should demand the telling of the employee perspective.

IBMers continue to endure the effects of what many consider the **watershed event** of Lou Gerstner's tenure. On July 1, 1999, IBM eliminated its pension and health care plans.

In the 90 days following the announcement, IBM's U.S. employees inundated a Yahoo! website with almost 1.7 million views. [8] Congressional leaders called hearings. In September, the Treasury Department issued a moratorium on conversions from defined benefit plans to cash balance plans. Finally, because of the outcry, IBM modified its original plans—extending its defined benefit pension plans to employees over forty years of age with more than ten years of service.

Yet, even after this modification, the changes affected more than fifty percent of the IBM U.S. population. These employees, even twelve years later, shake their heads and remark of this one event, "I awaken each and every day reminded of what I and my family have lost. We will never forget who is to blame."

Lou Gerstner wrote of this change, "It created a great furor among a small group of IBM employees." [9] It was, rather, a great furor among a *great* number of IBM employees. And IBM continues down this same financial path. Employees and their families continue to fund IBM's on-going record earnings. There is no win-win relationship. The furor continues worldwide.

Thos. J. Watson Sr. had warned of one path that, if taken, would lead to potential failure:

> When we start thinking of men as automatons, clicking their respective ways through the processes of life with mechanical exactness, that day we lose our own identity and become automatons ourselves.

> When we cease to realize the interdependence of men we are on the brink of failure. [10]

Has this interdependence been broken? Are IBM's record earnings optimized and maintainable or below par, temporary and fleeting? The foundation for a century of resiliency was built on the interdependence, the intertwining loyalty, dedication and enthusiasm of every person within The IBM—executive and employee alike. It was in our DNA.

A View from Beneath the Dancing Elephant will use the basic beliefs of IBM's first eighty years to examine the changes of the last twenty. It will provide a common ground to discuss change, evaluate and challenge its effects. It will help a new generation of IBM employees understand what was lost and help retired IBMers to understand what IBM has become.

In 1914, Thos. J. Watson Sr., faced his watershed moment. He told the Board of Directors, "If you want me to come in here and operate this business for the benefit of the business, I'll do it, but I will not have anything to do with the operation of it from a stock standpoint." [11] That moment set the foundation for the first centennial celebration.

Has a new watershed moment put IBM's bicentennial celebration at risk? We shall see.

About the Author

Peter E. Greulich worked at IBM for thirty years. He achieved a wide variety of perspectives over that time as he became a shining example of the Watson mobility built into "The IBM." He will be forever grateful for their elegant design that enabled him to keep "The IBM" a challenging, cooperative and inspiring environment.

Thos. J. Watson Sr. desired enthusiasm. Pete was enthusiastic from the day he was hired until the day he retired in March, 2011. His enthusiasm for "The IBM" continues with the publishing of this book and a future work entitled *A View from Beneath the Dancing Elephant: An IBM Caretaker's Perspective: Looking Up.*

Pete started in the '80s in administration with "The IBM." He became an assistant to his team as a first-line administration manager. He then moved in and out of sales and technical roles for the balance of his IBM career. His job responsibilities included:

- Worldwide Brand Manager for OS/2 Warp Server
- Worldwide Sales Evangelist for OS/2
- WebSphere Direct Sales Representative
- Worldwide Marketing Manager for Tivoli Configuration Manager (TCM)
- Worldwide Tivoli Sales Evangelist for TCM
- Worldwide Tivoli Sales Evangelist for IBM Tivoli Monitoring
- Worldwide Tivoli Top Gun presenter
- Worldwide Product Manager for IBM Tivoli Netcool

Notes

1   Kevin Maney, *The Maverick and his Machine: Thomas Watson Sr. and the Making of IBM,* (Hoboken, NJ: John Wiley & Sons, 2003), 144

2   Thomas Graham Belden and Marva Robins Belden, *The Lengthening Shadow: The Life of Thomas J. Watson,* (Boston: Little, Brown, 1962), 94

3   Ed Grimm, "Think," 55, no. 5, (September 1989), 14

4   M.R. Ahuja and David B. Neale, Save-the-Redwoods League, and the Institute of Forest Genetics, "Coast Redwood May be the Descendent of Two, Origins of Polyploidy in Coast Redwood" 2002 (http://www.savetheredwoods.org/research/grant_detail.php?id=13)

5   Thomas J. Watson Jr., *A Business and its Beliefs: The Ideas that Helped Build IBM,* (New York: McGraw-Hill, 1963), 5

6   Thomas J. Watson Jr., T. Vincent Learson, Frank T. Cary, John R. Opel, and John F. Akers, *Thirty Years of Management Briefings, 1958 to 1988,* (New York: IBM Corporate Communications, 1988), 155

7   Louis Gerstner Jr., *Who Says Elephants Can't Dance? Leading a Great Enterprise Through Dramatic Change,* (New York: HarperBusiness, 2002), 187

8   Ellen E. Schultz, Jon G. Auerbach and Glenn Burkins, "Pension-Plan Controversy Escalates As IBM Gives In to Employee Anger," The Wall Street Journal, (September 20, 1999, p. A1)

9   Louis Gerstner Jr., *Who Says Elephants Can't Dance? Leading a Great Enterprise Through Dramatic Change,* (New York: HarperBusiness, 2002), 102

10 Thos. J. Watson, *Men-Minutes-Money,* (n.p.: IBM Corporation, 1934), 90

11 Thomas Graham Belden and Marva Robins Belden, *The Lengthening Shadow, The Life of Thomas J. Watson,* (Boston: Little, Brown, 1962), 100

Made in the USA
Lexington, KY
25 May 2014